DISCORDANT HARMONIES

A New Ecology for the

NEW YORK · OXFORD

Discordant Harmonies

Twenty-first Century

DANIEL B. BOTKIN

OXFORD UNIVERSITY PRESS · 1990

Oxford University Press

Oxford   New York   Toronto
Delhi   Bombay   Calcutta   Madras   Karachi
Petaling Jaya   Singapore   Hong Kong   Tokyo
Nairobi   Dar es Salaam   Cape Town
Melbourne   Auckland

and associated companies
Berlin   Ibadan

Copyright © 1990 by Oxford University Press, Inc.

Published by Oxford University Press, Inc.,
200 Madison Avenue, New York, New York 10016

Oxford is a registered trademark of Oxford University Press

Library of Congress Cataloging-in-Publication Data
Botkin, Daniel B.
Discordant harmonies : a new ecology for
the twenty-first century / Daniel B. Botkin.
p. cm.   Bibliography: p.   Includes index.
ISBN 0-19-505491-1
1. Nature conservation. 2. Environmental protection.
3. Environmental policy. I. Title.
QH75.B67   1990
333.7'2–dc20   89-32890

1 2 3 4 5 6 7 8 9

Printed in the United States of America
on acid-free, recycled paper

This book is dedicated to my father, Benjamin A. Botkin,
who in the language of the folk story and song
sought his own knowledge and understanding.

Preface

In the mid-1970s, I confronted several curious contradictions that I attempted to explain: decisions about managing nature were based on ideas that were clearly contradicted by facts, yet those who continued to advocate those outdated policies were acquainted with the facts; in my own field of ecology, those same ideas dominated, yet the facts that contradicted them were gathered by ecologists. We repeatedly failed to deal successfully with our environment, and we seemed to ignore the very facts that could most help us. In trying to discover how this could be, I began to work on this book. The pursuit of the answers led me to a kind of mystery story in which the mystery was not who committed a crime, but what caused the paradox. But as in a good mystery, the search for an explanation led down many paths and required peeling back layer after layer of impression and observation. At the surface were the activities of our society: scientists doing research; legislators signing bills; government officials dealing with policies. Underneath these was a layer of belief, myth, and assumption, of symbol and metaphor: the clock, the tree, and the stars. Here were exposed four ancient questions about the fundamental relationships between human beings and nature: What is the character of nature undisturbed? How does nature influence human beings? How do human beings influence nature? What is the proper role for human beings in nature? At this level, the solution to the paradox lies with a shift in perception, the change in metaphor, myth, and assumption.

Peeling back this layer revealed another, perhaps closer to the level at which our minds function, a level of two fundamental world views that some philosophers have characterized metaphorically as those of Apollo, god of light and knowledge, and of Dionysus, god of music and dance, the

classical opposition of the analytic and the rational, which have characterized modern science and tend to deal with nature by freezing it conceptu-
ally so that it can be analyzed, and the intuitive and emotive, which deal
with nature through motion, sound, and action. At this level, the solution
to the paradox of theory and observation lies in a new blending of these
apparently opposed modes of thought; the question exposed is primitive:
What is the harmony of nature, and in what ways do human themes blend
with and oppose those of nature? Putting these layers back together leads us
to a new construction of our perception of nature and our role in it.

The solution to the mystery, the threads of understanding I discovered, I
have tried to sew up in this book. Each chapter provides a part of the
pattern, not as a final answer in itself, but as a set of clues that build toward
an explanation. I invite the reader to join in the discovery of the answers in
the spirit of solving a mystery, in reading the messages in the cloth of
nature.

Santa Barbara   D. B. B.
April 1989

Acknowledgments

I wish to acknowledge the help and comments of many friends and colleagues during the past decade on the subject of this book. They include Matthew J. Sobel, applied mathematician, who engaged in many conversations in the early 1970s that sharpened the concepts of stability; Charles F. Beveridge, historian, who introduced me to the works of George Perkins Marsh, Clarence J. Glacken, and Marjorie H. Nicolson; Lawrence B. Slobodkin, ecologist, who understood the issues and gave me encouragement in the pursuit of the answers; Harold J. Morowitz and Lucile Morowitz, who read early drafts of the first chapters and encouraged me to continue; Eric Van Horne, who gave me invaluable advice about the tone, level, and style; Thomas E. Lovejoy, ecologist, who reviewed the Wilson Center work; Roderick F. Nash, historian, with whom I discussed this work and its themes during the past nine years, and who kindly reviewed a nearly completed draft; J. Baird Callicott, philosopher, who provided an extensive review of the nearly completed manuscript and whose knowledge of environmental ethics and Aldo Leopold's career was invaluable; and my wife, Erene, who provided helpful comments as we read the drafts of this book. I would especially like to thank William F. Curtis, my editor at Oxford University Press, who has encouraged and supported the preparation of the manuscript and given me an excellent perspective on what worked and what did not in the drafts. I am also grateful to Irene Pavitt for her expert assistance in editing the manuscript. I am also indebted to Paul B. Sears, conservationist, who got me started in ecology; Murray F. Buell, ecologist, who gave me inspiration as a scientist and teacher; and Heman L. Chase, New Hampshire surveyor, for many hours we spent surveying in the woods of New Hampshire and Vermont.

The work that laid the basis for Chapters 4, 5, and 6 and that provides a foundation for the entire book was begun under a fellowship from the Woodrow Wilson International Center for Scholars, Washington, D.C. Later work on the structure of the book was made possible by a fellowship from the Rockefeller Foundation Bellagio Study and Conference Center, Bellagio, Italy. Aspects of the material are a result of research supported by the World Wildlife Fund and by several federal agencies, including the National Science Foundation, the National Oceanographic and Atmospheric Administration, the Marine Mammal Commission, and the National Aeronautics and Space Administration's Office of Life Sciences.

Contents

THE CURRENT DILEMMA

The church, Santa Maria della Salute, Venice, Italy, said to be built on a foundation of more than one million tree trunks (photograph by the author).

−1

A View From A Marsh:
Myths and Facts about Nature

> In the universe the battle of conflicting elements springs from a single
> rational principle, so that it would be better for one to compare it to
> the melody which results from conflicting sounds.
>
> Plotinus, *The Enneads* (third century A.D.)

Our Current Dilemma

One of the famous and often photographed sights in Venice is the baroque
church of Santa Maria della Salute, known as La Salute, which decorates
the outer Grand Canal, its graceful dome presenting an image to the casual
visitor of great solidity, of heavy but graceful architecture, set against the
constant motion of the coastal waters. It is said that the building of that
single church began with the driving of 1,106,657 trunks of alder, oak, and
larch, trees once common in the region, into the muds of the lagoon.[1]
Once the trunks were completely submerged, so that they were no longer
exposed to the air, the wood was protected from decay and remains as the
foundation for the church. So it is with the rest of the city. That most
famous example of human artifact, the architecture of Venice, survives in a
changing lagoon because of a foundation built of wood, a biological supporting structure, surprising in our modern age of steel and concrete.
Venice was founded in the fifth and six centuries A.D. as a refuge for people
fleeing Germanic tribes, primarily the Lombards, who were destroying the
Roman Empire.[2] Inhabitants of towns around the northern Adriatic fled to
the marshes, from which they could more easily defend themselves. At
first, they returned to their home cities after a raid, but eventually they
began to settle in the lagoon. The mud in the marshes was unstable and
shifted continually; to create a city, it was necessary to stabilize the ground.
The first Venetians did this by driving millions of saplings into the mud.

Several years ago, I was in Venice to attend an international conference,
"Man's Role in Changing the Global Environment."[3] That city was an

3

intriguing place to discuss environment and people, because its history provides an image in miniature of our current situation. Standing across the Grand Canal from Santa Maria della Salute, I could not help but compare my view at the end of the twentieth century with the view that must have confronted the first settlers more than one thousand years ago, a view of flat marshland that stretched disheartenly as far as the eye could see. I imagined what it might be like to begin to build the foundation for a great city by driving saplings into the salt marsh to hold the mud in place. What ideas, what views of nature, the "environment," and the relationship between people and nature did that take? While impelled by necessity, the first Venetians did not go to those marshes so long ago empty-handed, without the benefit of some knowledge of technology or of natural history, without the benefit of civilization. They brought with them three things: ideas, techniques, and a perspective of the world—how nature works, how people might change nature, and how the world in the future might be different from the world they had known in the past. Today, we are in a position in relation to the environment of our entire planet similar to that of the ancient settlers of Venice in relation to the marshes of the Adriatic. We see problems shifting before us whose solutions are unclear.

In the past three decades, there has been growing concern over the adverse consequences of our technologies on local and regional environments, at the scale of a city like Venice and its environs, which includes the lagoon and the farmlands and industries nearby. Today we are witnessing technological effects that may radically change the relationship between people and nature on a global scale and with greater potential power than ever before. But more hopefully, we can envisage not only the destructive effects that have received so much widespread publicity, but also the possibility of constructive management that, if implemented, could achieve long-term uses of natural resources and enhance the environment in a way that could be both pleasing to us and necessary for the survival of life on the Earth. Environmental issues continue to be, for most of us, both frightening and frustrating. Some environmental problems seem to be discussed in the newspapers and on television again and again, with experts warning us about more and more impending problems that have few concrete solutions. Other issues, such as the possible decline of the ozone layer in the atmosphere, seem to recur every decade, at first with great calls of alarm and warnings of disaster from experts, only to seem on further scientific inquiry to be less dire than originally thought, then to temporarily fade away, only to come back again in a new form even more alarming than the last. As the scale of these issues continues to increase from the local *Silent Spring* of Rachel Carson more than 20 years ago to the global climatic warming of today, something is lacking in the way that we deal with these issues. Solving our environmental problems requires a new perspective that goes beyond science and has to do with the way that everyone perceives the world.

But we are not empty-handed; on the contrary, we are the beneficiaries of a rich history in our own century in the development of science and ideas about conservation. We walk in the footprints of pioneers in biology, geography, and conservation: Charles Darwin, Alexander von Humboldt, and George Perkins Marsh. Just as the first Venetians had a history of technology, knowledge of how to cut and use wood and stone, so we have a rich history in techniques, the great and powerful technologies of computers, of satellite remote sensing, and of modern chemical analysis. Just as the first Venetians were not the first to walk on the Adriatic shore, so we are not the first to understand that the environment is of importance. It is more than 20 years since the phrase "spaceship Earth" was coined and made popular[4] and 20 years since the Apollo astronauts took their famous photographs of the Earth from space—a blue globe, enveloped by swirling white clouds, against a black background—creating an image of a small island of life floating in an ocean of empty space. With this view of our planet, we are like the first settlers in Venice standing on the Adriatic coast and seeing outward a flat marshland, unsure perhaps whether that vista is friendly or hostile. They began to use their knowledge and their technology to build a great city. So can we begin to build a new approach to our environment, but we seem repeatedly thwarted in this attempt.

We tend to think that our actions are limited simply by tools and information. But it is not for the lack of a measuring tape or an account sheet of nature that we are unable to deal with the environment. The potential for us to make progress with environmental issues is limited by the basic assumptions that we make about nature, the unspoken, often unrecognized perspective from which we view our environment. This perspective, ironically in this scientific age, depends on myth and deeply buried beliefs. In order to gain a new view, one necessary to deal with global environmental problems, we must break free of old assumptions and old myths about nature and ourselves, while building on the scientific and technical advances of the past.

Our rich experience in conservation, science, and technology presents opportunities to take positive approaches to environmental issues. The environmental movement of the past three decades is only the most recent emergence of older concerns about the relationship between human beings and their surroundings. Environmentalism of the 1960s and 1970s was essentially a disapproving, and in this sense, negative movement, exposing the bad aspects of our civilization for our environment. It played an important role by awakening people's consciousness, but it did not provide many solutions or even viable approaches to solutions to our environmental problems. That environmentalism was based on ideas of the industrial age, ideas that developed in the eighteenth century and expanded in the nineteenth, ideas that I will argue in the rest of this book, are outmoded. That environmentalism has been perceived as opposing engineering and technological progress, but both those arguing for progress and those arguing for protection of the environment have shared a world view, hidden assumptions, and myths about human beings and nature that dominated the industrial era. Neither point of view has gotten to the roots of the issues, which lie deep in our ideas and assumptions about science and technology, and go even deeper in myths and ancient world views. Only by exposing the roots will we be able to achieve a constructive approach toward our environmental problems. By gaining a deeper understanding of the implications of twentieth-century science and technology for the environment, we can find a way to combine technology with our concerns about our environment in a constructive and positive manner.

How Our Perception Of Nature Must Change

The changes that must take place in our perspective are twofold: the recognition of the dynamic rather than the static properties of the Earth and its life-support system, and the acceptance of a global view of life on the Earth. We have tended to view nature as a Kodachrome still-life, much like a tourist-guide illustration of La Salute; but nature is a moving picture show, much like the continually changing and complex patterns of the waters in the Venetian lagoon. In the past, nature has meant what was in our background; today, the Earth is our village. And in the past 20 years, it has become obvious that it is a special place, a planet revealed by modern science as strangely suited to support life. The ability of the Earth's environment to support life was written about beautifully and precisely almost 80 years ago by Lawrence Henderson in his book *The Fitness of the Environment*.[5] Henderson was struck by the characteristics of the Earth as a planet that together make life possible, such as the size of the Earth (large enough to hold an atmosphere), its proximity to the sun (close enough to be warm enough for life, but not too close), and its rotation (one side is not continually heated and the other cooled). He was also struck by the chemical and physical characteristics of the simple compounds so important in living things and common on the Earth, especially water. The odd combination of qualities of water, each of which is unusual among similar small compounds and each of which makes water peculiarly suitable to support life, perplexed Henderson. He wrote at length about the importance of the high latent heat of water in modulating the temperature of the Earth and of individual organisms, and of the unique capability of water to act as a solvent for a great many chemicals that make life possible. Henderson's insight has since become common knowledge, and in the past decade, something new and important has been added to it: a growing understanding of the extent to which life has influenced the environment at the planetary scale over the Earth's history, and a growing recognition that our planetary life-support and life-containing system, now called the *biosphere*, is deeply complex. The biosphere is unlike the mechanical devices of our own construction, and its analysis requires the development of new scientific approaches.

We are accustomed to thinking of life as a characteristic of individual organisms. Individuals are alive, but an individual cannot sustain life. Life is sustained only by a group of organisms of many species—not simply a horde or mob, but a certain kind of system composed of many individuals of different species—and their environment, making together a network of living and nonliving parts that can maintain the flow of energy and the cycling of chemical elements that, in turn, support life.[6] A system that can do this not only is rare, but also is peculiar, peculiar from the perspective that we have become accustomed to in our methods of analyzing and constructing the physical trappings of our modern civilization— automobiles, motor boats, radios, the devices of the industrial age.

We can imagine very simple, closed systems that sustain life—algae in a small glass vial with water, air, a little soil harboring a few species of bacteria or fungi. Such simple systems have been made, and they have generally persisted for only a short time. Claire Folsome of the University of Hawaii has created the longest enduring of such systems from the muds and waters of Honolulu Bay; life in his sealed flasks has survived for more than 20 years, undergoing occasional green booms and busts while resting in the quiet of a shelf on the north-facing window of a Honolulu laboratory. In striking contrast, life and its planetary support system, the biosphere, have persisted for more than 3 billion years, in spite of—or perhaps because of—the biosphere's immensely greater complexity. In the biosphere, some 1.4 million species have been named, and my colleagues estimate that much greater numbers are as yet unnamed—somewhere between five and 30 million, depending on who makes the estimate—

dispersed in tens of thousands of local systems that we call *ecological communities* and *ecosystems.*[7]

These ecosystems are of perhaps thirty major kinds, which ecologists call *biomes*—such as the tropical rain forest, coral reef, grassland. We find that our planetary life-support system is complex at every scale and at every time. In the aggregate, the crowds of species make up a complex patchwork of subsystems at many different stages and states of development spread across the Earth's surface. It is an intriguing and unsolved question how this dense complexity persists and has persisted for so long. In the answer is a key to the survival of our own species. The answer to this question is also an answer to the ancient question about the very character of nature. Our planetary life-support and life-containing system, the biosphere, is, after all, "nature" taken in its largest sense.

Current knowledge about the biosphere is out of step with current beliefs about nature, which is one of the main impediments to progress on environmental issues. It tends to blind us to the possibilities for constructive action. Our technology places before us a new vista, but our beliefs are forcing us to look backward; the result is that we believe repeatedly that we are mired in a barren conceptual mud. This confusion tends to lead those concerned with conservation of the environment to emphasize the benefits of doing nothing and assuming that nature will know best.

Ancient Themes Of Nature

Until the industrial revolution, there were two major beliefs about the character of nature: nature as organic and nature as divinely created. Divinely created nature was perceived as perfectly ordered and perfectly stable; it achieved constancy, and, when disturbed, returned to that constant condition which was desirable and good.[8]

We find the idea of the perfect order of nature in the writings of the classical Greeks and Romans, and it was probably in the minds of people at the time of the founding of Venice. This apparent orderliness of nature was well expressed in the nineteenth century by George Perkins Marsh, the intellectual father of American conservation, in *Man and Nature*:

> In countries untrodden by man, the proportions and relative positions of land and water, the atmospheric precipitation and evaporation, the thermometric mean, and the distribution of vegetable and animal life, are subject to change only from geological influences so slow in their operation that the geographical conditions may be regarded as constant and immutable.[9]

In his own life, Marsh epitomizes much of the Western intellectual history of the ideas of nature. His was an amazing career.[10] Marsh, who was born in Vermont, became the American ambassador to Italy and to Egypt; during the time he spent in those countries, he was struck by the effects of thousands of years of human settlement on the landscape in comparison with the relatively untouched forests of his native Vermont. Later, as the fish commissioner in Vermont, he gave remarkably insightful explanations of the causes of the disappearance of fish from Vermont streams, perceiving far beyond his time the complex interactions among groups of living things. Marsh's assertion about the constancy and stability of nature is a theme that runs throughout Western history, and has been the predominant perspective of environmentalism during the past 20 years. This is an easy and comfortable viewpoint to take. Imagine the first Venetians looking out from the marshes to the Adriatic coast, which stretched as far as they could see. Although the muds shifted within the marshes, the marshes and the coast themselves must have seemed as permanent as any rock or mountain. We know now that this coastline has changed over time, that its present location is the product of the history of the great Pleistocene ice ages, and that the seas along the coast of Italy are the consequence of one of those slow but definite changes that are characteristic of nature.

While there have always been those who, like the classical philosopher Lucretius, have seen nature very differently, not as constant, but as organic, always changing, their views have been in the minority. George Perkins Marsh's idea of nature as undisturbed by human influence is the one generally advocated; this point of view is dominant in textbooks on ecology and in the popular environmental literature. Perhaps even more significant, this idea of nature forms the foundation of twentieth-century scientific theory about populations and ecosystems. It is the basis of most national laws and international agreements that control the use of wild lands and wild creatures just as it was an essential part of the 1960s and 1970s mythology about conservation, environment, and nature. Until the past few years, the predominant theories in ecology either presumed or had as a necessary consequence a very strict concept of a highly structured, ordered, and regulated, steady-state ecological system.[11] Scientists know now that this view is wrong at local and regional levels—whether for the condor and the whooping crane, or for the farm and the forest woodlot—that is, at the levels of populations and ecosystems. Change now appears to be intrinsic and natural at many scales of time and space in the biosphere. Nature changes over essentially all time scales, and in at least some cases these changes are necessary for the persistence of life, because life is adapted to them and depends on them.

The quality of change is illustrated by the history of climate, which can be reconstructed with much accuracy. The patterns of temperature change during the past million years—which encompass the time that our own species, *Homo sapiens*, has been on the Earth and therefore is the period that should concern us most in our attempts to interpret the character of nature—are illustrated in Figure 1, which shows changes in the average surface temperature of the Earth for four time scales. The patterns of temperature from about the time of the founding of Venice to the present are shown in Figure 1(d). Since the ninth century, when the Franks stormed inland Italian cities and forced their inhabitants to the lagoons of Venice, the temperature has varied without any obvious pattern, except that for most of the time average temperatures have been colder than those of the twentieth century. There are periods of small variation and periods of large variation, but there is no constancy or any simple pattern or regular cycle. Although we can calculate an average temperature during the past thousand years, as one can calculate an average for any set of numbers, there has not been an "average" temperature for the Earth during the past millennium in the sense of a fixed average about which the temperature varied in a regular way.

Moving back in time and taking a longer view, we see in Figure 1(c) the change in average temperature for the past 30,000 years, a period of time reaching back before the growth of civilizations, back to the time of the mammoth. Again we can discern a trend, a gradual warming, but not constancy and not even a regular cycle of temperatures.

Figure 1(b) shows the temperature patterns for the past 150,000 years. From this longer perspective, the warming trend of the past 30,000 years is merely one of many fluctuations. Finally, looking back almost 1 million years in Figure 1(a), we see for this largest scale of time a wandering of the Earth's surface temperature—up and down, mostly colder than the present climate, but with periods of little variation and periods of great variation, times with apparent cycles and times without cycles.

These graphs illustrate that change appears intrinsic and natural at many scales of time and space in the biosphere, and that nature changes during all time scales. The idea that change is natural has created problems in natural-resource management. How do you manage something that is always changing? And of even more concern is the possibility that by admitting to some kinds of change, we may have opened a Pandora's box of problems for environmentalists. The difficulty is simple: once we have acknowledged that some kinds of change are good, how can we argue against any alteration of the environment? There are several answers to this question. First, the failure to accept change leads to destructive, undesir-

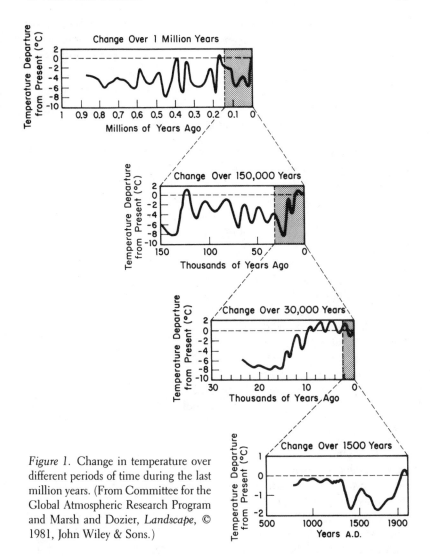

Figure 1. Change in temperature over different periods of time during the last million years. (From Committee for the Global Atmospheric Research Program and Marsh and Dozier, *Landscape,* © 1981, John Wiley & Sons.)

able results. It is only by understanding how nature works and applying this understanding in our management of nature (or to speak more generally, understanding our proper role in nature) that we can successfully achieve our goal: people living within nature, neither poisoning it nor destroying its reproductive capabilities.

The second answer is that to accept certain kinds of change is not to accept all kinds of change. Moreover, we must focus our attention on the rates at which changes occur, understanding that certain rates of change are natural, desirable, and acceptable, while others are not. As long as we refuse to admit that any change is natural, we cannot make this distinction and deal with its implications.

Ideas Of Nature In Transition

Before the seventeenth century, the image of nature as divinely ordered seems to have dominated explanations about how nature worked, but the only metaphors that people had to describe the Earth were organic; they were metaphors derived from animals and plants, from the phenomena of life with which they were familiar, including human life. The Earth was described as a kind of fellow creature, and these metaphors were apparently taken quite literally.

Beginning in the seventeenth century, with the rise of Newtonian mechanics and the work of Kepler and other scientists, powerful new ideas developed; along with the invention of machines such as the steam engine, they led to new metaphors, to the idea that the Earth and the solar system operate like clockwork, like a machine. Hence, from the human perspective, in the nineteenth century there was what Marjorie Nicolson, an expert on literature and nature, has called the "death of the Earth" —the death of the idea of an organic Earth.[12] Although little discussed today, this change had a profound impact at the time.

Today we analyze ecological systems looking backward, as though they were nineteenth-century machines, full of gears and wheels, for which our managerial goal, like that of any traditional engineer, is steady-state operation. To us, the mechanical view of the Earth, nature as a machine, seems an old and permanent one. But it is not. The mechanical Earth is a seventeenth-century idea that developed in the eighteenth, blossomed in the nineteenth, and carried into the twentieth century. This concept of nature and of the Earth would not have been familiar to the first Venetians. They would have known about and been comfortable with other, much more ancient ideas about nature—either the idea of an organic Earth or that of nature as divinely created order.

These three images of nature—the machine, the creature, and the divine—dominate our thoughts about the environment, although we are not usually aware of them. It is important for us to examine these three images both as explanations and as metaphor. As explanations of how nature works, the divinely ordered image and the mechanical image share much in common. Both lead to the idea of nature as constant unless unwisely disturbed, and as stable, capable of returning to its constant state if disturbed. Both lead to the conviction that undisturbed nature, or perhaps a nature with human beings playing their "natural" roles, is good, while a changing nature is bad. In contrast, the organic image as an explanation of how nature works focuses on change and processes, with change seen as inevitable, to which, like it or not, human beings must yield.

I believe that we are living through a time of change: a transition in our civilization from the mechanical age, that of gears and wheels, to a new era that appears to us as the space and computer age. As we engineer genetics and talk about the use of computers for "artificial intelligence," and as our children play games on a computer screen, we are moving away from the mechanical view to a different set of perceptions in which the distinction between organic and inorganic is no longer very clear. We have not settled on the right metaphors, images, and symbols. That is to say, we have not settled on a set of assumptions about "nature" that is so well accepted that it becomes an unspoken and unconscious complex of beliefs.

This, then, is the heart of the matter that confronts us. Like it or not, computers have changed our view of life and observations from space have changed our perceptions of our planet. We can no longer rely on nineteenth-century models of analysis for twenty-first-century problems. More than any other factor, confronting and recognizing these changes in our deep-seated assumptions is the major challenge that faces us in interpreting nature and in dealing with environmental issues.

When we do recognize, confront, and change these assumptions, we will be able to achieve a more comfortable relationship with nature. Only then can we proceed much more rapidly to develop a constructive approach to solving environmental problems. In this way, we can move on from the view of George Perkins Marsh, well aware of his warnings about the negative effects that our civilization can cause on our surroundings, but also ready to look ahead. Ahead of us lies the potential to build a great civilization in which our role in the environment is a positive one, managing sustainable natural resources and enhancing the quality of our environment. Only political will and our basic perspectives prevent us from moving constructively toward that new environment. The purpose of this book is to help begin the transition to a new perception of nature. The chapters that follow expand on the ideas I have introduced here. Let us hope that, although the future of our global environment may sometimes seem as gloomy as an unending sea marsh on a gray day, we are really viewing the foundation of a truly new development, a new advance in understanding our surroundings that leads to an advance in our civilization.

The border of Tsavo National Park (East), photographed in 1977, shows the effect of drought and elephant die-off of the late 1960s (photograph by the author).

–2

Why The Elephants Died: Breakdown in the Management of Living Resources

> Animal populations must exist in a state of balance for they are otherwise inexplicable.
>
> A. J. Nicolson (1933)[1]

> The balance of nature does not exist, and perhaps has never existed. The numbers of wild animals are constantly varying to a greater or lesser extent, and the variations are usually irregular in period and always irregular in amplitude. Each variation in the numbers of one species causes direct and indirect repercussions on the numbers of the others, and since many of the latter are themselves independently varying in numbers, the resultant confusion is remarkable.
>
> Charles Elton (1930)[2]

Views of Tsavo East

A Landsat satellite image taken in the late 1970s from 140 miles above the Earth over East Africa shows a curious geometric feature—two straight lines, each stretching 50 miles or more, one north and the other south-southeast, meeting at an obtuse angle, as though a planetary engineer had sketched the lines with a triangle and pencil at a drafting table. To the east of the lines, a dull brown indicates an area so thinly vegetated that an almost bare soil dominates the reflectance of light from the surface. To the west, a garish red indicates dense vegetation in infrared wavelengths, which are invisible to the naked human eye.

About the same time that the satellite orbited silently far overhead, I flew a few hundred feet above the ground in a single-engine aircraft, a Cessna-182, from whose noisy cockpit one of the boundaries was clearly visible. What appears as one line in the satellite view was revealed from this nearer vantage point as four: a railroad, a highway, and two fire breaks stretching into the blue haze of the horizon toward Nairobi. On the east of the line lay one of two parts of Tsavo, one of Kenya's largest national parks, covering approximately 5,000 square miles. It was the park land that appeared brown from the satellite and could be seen now as a desertlike dusty soil with a thin scattering of live and dead shrubs and trees, among which almost no game was visible. The land outside the park, to the west, which is red in the Landsat image, contained dense thickets of dark green trees and shrubs. The scene was strange from this elevation, just as it was from the satellite, appearing as a photographic negative of one's expectation of a park. Rather than an island of green in a wasted landscape, Tsavo appeared as a wasted island amid a green land.

The character of Tsavo was the result of 30 years of interplay between people and nature; of vagaries of climate, including a major drought that persisted through 1969 and 1970; and of a controversy over management that involved issues as old as Western civilization—the character of nature undisturbed by human influence and the proper role of human beings in nature.[3] Perhaps nowhere else was the impact of well-meaning management of wild nature so visible from a planetary perspective. Something had failed at Tsavo, in spite of the best intentions, and the failure of management of living resources was an example of a breakdown not merely in management, but also in myths, beliefs, and fundamental paradigms that modern technological civilization held about nature.

The Elephants and Lessons of Tsavo

Tsavo became a park in 1948. Its first warden, David Sheldrick, looked at its dry flat landscape, thickly vegetated by *Commiphora* trees and wild sisal, and knew that the park could attract tourists only to see wild game, not other scenic beauty. But much of the big game had been shot around the turn of the century by European settlers, and of the remaining wildlife, black rhinoceros and elephant were under intense pressure from poachers.

Sheldrick devoted years to building roads, providing year-round water for the wildlife, and eradicating poaching by catching and driving off poachers through a kind of antiguerrilla effort using Land Rovers, aircraft, and World War II repeating rifles. A thousand miles of roads were built to increase tourists' access. The Galena River was dammed, and artesian wells were dug. These measures resulted in a rapid buildup of elephants that took their toll on the vegetation, knocking down and killing trees and shrubs. The land seemed on its way to becoming desert. By 1959, areas where the vegetation had once been so thick that elephants were visible only if they actually crossed a road in front of tourists began to resemble a "lunar landscape," Sheldrick's wife, Daphne, wrote years later.[4] Sheldrick became concerned. He wrote in a report that

> during the past few years, the destruction of vegetation by elephant has reached serious proportions. If present trends continue, it is doubtful if the Park can continue to support the existing population much longer. What effect this will have on other species remains to be seen, but I think it is important that we should seek scientific advice regarding this problem as soon as possible.[5]

As with so many of these cases, the effects of human actions and the vagaries of the natural environment, including recurrent droughts, were confounded, and it was difficult to decide what to do. By 1966, most people believed that the park could be saved only by removing many elephants, and for a while Sheldrick agreed.[6]

But the rains came again, and the park seemed to recover; instead of the thicket of trees and shrubs, grasses sprouted and seemed to promise better food for the wildlife. The elephant population continued to grow, and the resource-management controversy worsened. The Ford Foundation agreed to sponsor a scientific study, and Richard Laws, one of the world's foremost experts on elephants and other large mammals, who had been studying elephants in Uganda, agreed to head the project. He and other scientists and some conservationists soon concluded that about 3,000 elephants should be shot to keep the population within its food supply and protect the game from the dangerous effects of its intrinsic capacities for growth. Sheldrick at first favored such action, but in the end reversed himself and returned to the very old idea that nature can take care of itself and that human interference is undesirable. He decided that "the conservation policy for Tsavo should be directed towards the attainment of a natural ecological climax, and that our participation towards this aim should be restricted to such measures as the control of fires, poaching, and other forms of human interference."[7] At that time, the phrase "natural ecological climax" was taken to mean nature in a mature condition, the result of a long series of stages that occurs after a catastrophic clearing of the landscape and, once attained, persists indefinitely without change. Many, like Sheldrick, accepted the "climax" condition as the truly natural and most desirable state of wilderness. When the trustees of the park sided with Sheldrick and concluded that more studies, especially of the vegetation, were needed, Laws resigned and returned to England.

Sheldrick had come to believe that the die-offs of elephants during the droughts could be regarded as a natural culling, bringing the number of elephants "in line with the carrying capacity of their particular dry weather feeding grounds," producing a selective death of the weaker, ensuring a healthier population, and allowing the regeneration of vegetation.[8] In short, he believed that nature used the droughts to maintain or restore its proper balance. But the drought of 1969 and 1970 was much worse than previous ones of the century, and as an estimated 6,000 elephants starved to death, they destroyed the vegetation, producing the scene still visible a decade later from the air and from space. Elephants and human beings together had drafted the lines on the Landsat image.

Here was a controversy very different from the better publicized environmental issues of the 1960s. Then, as environmentalism was achieving worldwide recognition, most environmental issues seemed to produce two extreme camps that disagreed on goals: the environmentalists seeming to argue that the salvation of civilization and the human spirit lay in the preservation of nature, and their opponents seeming to respond that environmentalism threatened industry, economics, progress, and perhaps civilization. In a quite different way, the disagreement at Tsavo was among conservationists who shared basic goals and a fundamental love of wild nature: they wished to conserve in perpetuity fine examples of wild nature for their own sake and for people to view. But they disagreed on methods.

Daphne Sheldrick defined her husband's position strongly in her book, *The Tsavo Story.* "Hasn't man always had a regrettable tendency to manipulate the natural order of things to suit himself," she wrote,

> With amazing arrogance we presume omniscience and an understanding of the complexities of Nature, and with amazing impertinence we firmly believe that we can better it. . . . We have forgotten that we, ourselves, are just a part of nature, an animal which seems to have taken the wrong turning, bent on total destruction.[9]

The story of Tsavo illustrates several important issues. The idea of the character of nature undisturbed by human influence is complex and open to numerous interpretations. There were two dominant opinions about what had happened at Tsavo. One was that undisturbed nature always achieves a balance, a constancy, a stability—the "natural ecological climax" that Daphne Sheldrick referred to in her book—and human beings only interfere with and destroy that balance. Therefore, the proper role for people is hands off. The other interpretation was that nature varies greatly, and human actions are required to create a balance. In regard to Tsavo, as with most other environmental issues of our century, the former belief won out, and the devastation of Tsavo was a product, at least in part, of this policy.

There is a third possibility: even Tsavo, large as it is, is too small to sustain an elephant population "naturally," and before the European colonization of Africa and the establishment of modern African nations, the elephants, when subjected to one of the recurrent droughts, would have migrated from Tsavo to another part of Africa. This possibility accepts change as intrinsic at a scale as large as Tsavo and is not consistent with the old idea of a balance of nature at that scale, but is consistent with the new perspective toward which we are moving. Even so, one who insisted that a balance of nature must exist could still argue that at the scale of the entire African continent, the elephant population must have achieved a constancy over time before the imposition of a political geography over an ecological geography.

Twenty years after the great Tsavo drought, elephants in Africa are in great danger from rampant illegal poaching that is reducing them to a threatened fraction of their former abundance. Clearly, the direct control of poaching, as Sheldrick did so well, is necessary if elephants are to survive. But the lesson of Tsavo is that wise management cannot stop simply with the eradication of poaching. Wise management in the future might require harvesting excess elephant populations when or if they occur again in parks and preserves, but would also control killings that impose a rate of decline that exceeds the reproductive capacities of elephant populations, a rate that is occurring because of the illegal poaching. The rate of change is the problem, not the harvesting per se. In the last analysis, the survival of elephants will depend on our perception of them within the context of their total, variable environment.

Failing Fisheries

Tsavo was just one of many examples in the twentieth century of attempts to manage the environment that somehow did not succeed. About the time of the great elephant die-off at Tsavo, it was becoming clear that the management of living resources was in trouble in many parts of the world. For example, far from Tsavo but linked by a common set of ideas about nature, the management of another kind of wildlife, the major commercial fisheries of the world, seemed to be foundering. The allowed catch of these fisheries was determined by international agreements, and various mechanisms were tried to institute the agreements. But in spite of them, major fisheries failed. A classic case was the Peruvian anchovy fishery, once the world's largest commercial fishery. In 1970, 8 million tons of anchovies were caught, but 2 years later the catch dropped by 75 percent, to 2 million tons. The fishery continued to decline and has not yet rebounded to its pre-1970 abundance, although some analysts say that a recovery is finally beginning. Yet this fishery was intentionally and actively managed with the goal of achieving a "maximum sustainable yield."

The story was repeated elsewhere. In the 1950s, Pacific sardines, once a major species off the California coast, suffered a catastrophic decline which continued through the 1970s. The Atlantic menhaden catch reached a peak of 785,000 tons in 1956, dropping to 178,000 tons in 1969. Atlantic herring and Norwegian cod showed the same kind of decline. The North Atlantic haddock catch, which had averaged 50,000 tons for many years, increased to 155,000 in 1965. The haddock population crashed, and the catch declined to a mere 12,000 tons, less than 10 percent of the peak, by the early 1970s. The International Commission for the Northwest Atlantic Fisheries established a quota of 6,000 tons. Apparently, haddock had been able to sustain a 50,000-ton catch; but when the catch was tripled, the population decreased so greatly that only a much smaller catch could be sustained.[10] The decline in elephants in Tsavo was curiously echoed by the decline in fish harvests and fish populations in faraway oceans.

Estimates of allowable catches—those that were believed sustainable—were made from a well-known equation developed in the study of populations, the S-shaped logistic growth curve. First proposed in 1849 by Pierre-François Verhulst,[11] a Belgian scientist, the curve is a description of how a population grows from a small number to its final limiting and sustaining abundance, which is known as the *carrying capacity*. In the twentieth century, several experiments demonstrated that populations of bacteria or certain insects grow according to Verhulst's equation if they are maintained in a laboratory vessel under constant environmental conditions and provided with a constant supply of food; the results of one such experiment are shown in Figure 2. The mathematics that generates this curve includes the idea that the population is stable in a classic sense: it will achieve an abundance that will remain constant forever unless disturbed, and once disturbed (increased above or decreased below its carrying capacity), the population will return to the same abundance. Scientists extrapolated from these experiments to the world outside the laboratory windows and assumed that the logistic could describe the growth of populations in the wilderness.

The logistic equation leads to a simple calculation of the population size that has the maximum growth, which turns out to be the population that is

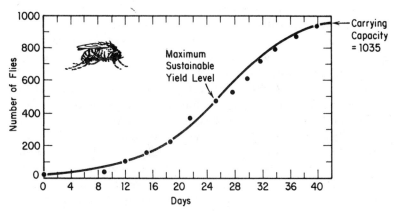

Figure 2. The growth of a population of fruit flies in a laboratory container. When kept in a constant environment and provided with a constant supply of food, a population of fruit flies increased following the classic S-shaped curve shown here, called the "logistic." (Revised from D. B. Botkin and E. A. Keller, *Environmental Studies: Earth As a Living Planet.* Originally revised and reprinted by permission of Yale University Press from *An Introduction of Population Ecology* by G. E. Hutchinson, 1978, Fig. 12, p. 25).

exactly one-half as large as the carrying capacity. This population size is known as the *maximum-sustainable-yield* population. If the mathematics were a true description of nature, the population could be allowed to grow each year above the maximum-sustainable-yield level and then be harvested down to it. Like clockwork, the population would grow back exactly the same amount each year, and a precisely sustainable harvest could be obtained year after year.

For the maximum-sustainable-yield concept to work, several things must be true. The population must have an exact and single carrying capacity, and its growth must follow exactly the logistic curve. It must be possible to know precisely both the carrying capacity and the present population size. It must be possible to obtain complete cooperation from all harvesters so that exactly the right number is harvested each year.

For the maximum-sustainable-yield concept to be employed successfully a measurement problem must be solved. But this is rarely solved in the management of wild populations to the level of precision required. In addition, economic issues must be addressed. These are issues that extend beyond science into the field that has become known as *environmental economics* and involve what are referred to as "policy instruments," meaning social, political, and economic mechanisms whose purpose is to create a situation in which, when a harvester acts in his own best interest he is also acting in a way that will lead to the desired total harvest.

The ideas underlying the maximum-sustainable-yield concept are the same as the ideas that were behind the management of Tsavo: the belief that nature undisturbed by human beings achieves a constancy that remains indefinitely, and that if disturbed, nature recovers its former status. The formal management of marine fisheries was based on the belief that nature undisturbed is constant and stable.

One might ask, of course, if the fisheries crashed not so much because of a theory but because real fishermen in a real world did not follow that theory. In the Philippines, for example, fishermen use dynamite and cyanide to catch fish; these practices kill huge numbers of fish in an area, and the dynamite also destroys their habitat. Such practices will destroy a fishery with or without a theory. International agreements could be compromised by fishermen circumventing them and harvesting amounts in excess of the allowed catch. Regulation has taken the form of inspectors on boats and inspection of boats on their return to harbor. To believe that major, managed world fisheries declined only because fishermen did not follow the maximum-sustainable-yield rule is to believe that the theory is correct that I am arguing fundamentally wrong. If the compliance of fishermen with established harvests were the only issue, management policies could have been set that take excess catches into account by estimating the amount by which fishermen would exceed the actual catch and then adjusting the official allowed catch downward so that the actual take would be at the maximum-sustainable-yield level.

There were attempts to get away from this tightly constraining point of view. For example, the Marine Mammal Protection Act passed by Congress in 1972, grew out of environmental concern with whaling and the declining numbers of most marine mammals to the point of their becoming endangered. The act states that the primary objective for management of marine mammals should be "to maintain the health and stability of the marine ecosystems" and that "whenever consistent with this primary objective, it should be the goal to obtain an optimum sustainable population keeping in mind the optimum carrying capacity of the habitat." What was this new idea, an *optimum sustainable population*? The act defines it as "the number of animals which will result in the maximum productivity of the population of the species, keeping in mind the optimum carrying capacity of the habitat and the health of the ecosystem of which they form a constituent element."[12] An advisory panel of scientists, headed by Douglas Chapman of the University of Washington, an expert on fisheries management, was formed to recommend a scientific basis for management of marine mammals under the new law. But in their recommendations, the scientists returned to the same logistic growth curve that they had used in fisheries management, defining an optimum sustainable population in terms of this curve. One interpretation the law allows is that the optimum population is close to, but somewhat larger than, the maximum-sustainable-yield population of the logistic. Another interpretation possible under that law is that an optimum sustainable population is at the carrying capacity, modified slightly to consider the idea of an optimum.[13] In practice, however, an operational definition of optimum sustainable yield was chosen that retreats from the attempt to move away from the concept of the logistic growth curve and that avoids the fundamental philosophical issues. This definition focuses instead on a single requirement of the maximum-sustainable-yield concept: that the carrying-capacity and the current size of the population must be known exactly. Recognizing that it is generally impossible to satisfy that requirement, the officials who determined harvest policies settled on the idea that the allowed harvest should not bring the population all the way down to the supposed one-half carrying-capacity level, but should instead maintain the population at 10 percent above that level. This choice of a meaning for an optimum sustainable population implicitly retained the assumption that the population follows the classic logistic growth curve and that it does in fact have a fixed carrying-capacity and absolute maximum-sustainable-yield level, but that they are difficult, if not impossible, to determine exactly.

This law illustrates that even as recently as the early 1970s, the scientific conservation of endangered marine species was based on the idea that nature undisturbed is constant and stable. The use of this concept for marine mammals seems especially peculiar because the Marine Mammal Protection Act was passed at a time when it was quite clear to fisheries experts that the logistic curve had not succeeded as the basis for the management of fisheries. Why, then, was it used when an opportunity to go beyond it had presented itself?

Myths of Nature and Management of Resources

The elephants of Tsavo, the management of fisheries, and the assumptions behind the Marine Mammal Protection Act raise a number of questions about the management of living resources during most of the twentieth century, including that as recently as the early 1970s. This management by and large failed to achieve its goals, even in those cases where good intentions prevailed and there was agreement among all parties about the goals.

What accounts for these failures? An important factor was that the management was based on beliefs that, although contradicted by facts, were so firmly rooted in our culture that they served as the basis for action and policy. These beliefs had two roots. One was in the science of ecology, which had begun in the late nineteenth century. The other lay with prescientific beliefs about nature. In his management of Tsavo, Sheldrick seemed motivated primarily by the latter, although he was influenced to some extent by the science of ecology. The management of fisheries and the Marine Mammal Protection Act were based on ecological theory first and on prescientific antecedents second.

It is worth repeating that the discussion of the roots of these beliefs has an importance that goes beyond the particular examples of Tsavo and marine fisheries. The failure of management of living resources was a symptom of the breakdown in myths, beliefs, and fundamental paradigms that modern technological civilization held about nature.

Some of these myths concerned the character of nature undisturbed by human influences—the character of wilderness. The qualities of a wilderness *without human beings* are crucial for us to understand so that we can know what is needed to preserve our surroundings, preserve ourselves, and understand the effects of our actions on nature. But at a more personal and deeper level, nature is our mirror. The way in which we view ourselves—as individuals and as members of societies—is in part a reflection of how we see ourselves in relation to nature. Later in this book, I will challenge the reality of the idea of wilderness as it has come to be interpreted in the twentieth century, the idea that between the time of the evolution of human beings and the beginning of written history most of the Earth was uninfluenced by human action.

Since the beginning of Western civilization, philosophers have held up the mirror of nature and found in it four questions about the biological realm of existence. What is the character of nature undisturbed by human influence? What are the effects of nature on human being—on individuals as well as civilization and culture? What is the role or purpose of people in nature? And what are the effects of human beings—as individuals and as societies—on the living nonhuman world?[14]

In prescientific Western culture, wilderness was perceived in several ways. At one extreme, wilderness was an idealization of divine order—a place of perfect order and harmony to be worshipped or to serve as a source of spiritual awakening. At the opposite extreme, wilderness was a place that was chaotic, dangerously powerful, and to be feared or challenged.[15]

In addition, since ancient times, discussions of the character of nature have focused on the amazing adaptations of organisms to their needs, on the diversity of species and their connections one with another, and on the appearance of a balance of nature. *Balance of nature* has meant not only the constancy and stability referred to earlier, but also the idea that every creature has its place in the harmonious workings of nature and is well adapted to its niche.

Flying just above the ground over Tsavo, my ears filled with the roar of the Cessna-182's engine, I focused on the desolate scene below, a scene that illustrated as clearly as I could imagine that our attempts to manage wildlife and other renewable natural resources had failed. But when that conclusion seemed so obvious in any snapshot of Tsavo, why, I wondered, were we still applying outmoded ideas to elephants and anchovies?

The conclusion that was apparent then and is worth repeating now is that the answer did not lie in facts alone—in the view of Tsavo alone—but in beliefs hidden from view. We had taken Pierre-François Verhulst's imaginative suggestion of a century before—an advance in scientific thinking at that time—and fixed it as though it were a permanent and final explanation. During its first hundred years, the science of ecology, along with its application in the management of living resources, viewed nature like a snapshot of Tsavo, as though it were fixed in time and space, as constant as the environment of a modern scientific laboratory. By the 1970s, when I was soaring and turning and circling over the dry bones of elephants on the barren plain at Tsavo, a curious situation had arisen, in which the accepted theories were failing to provide a successful basis for the management of living resources. It seemed to me that it is one thing to play games in a laboratory and pretend that nature is like an artificial container of fruit flies, but quite another to fool ourselves that such a game should be played out with the remaining treasures of wildlife and wild habitats in the realities of our complex and discordant world.

We must change what we have been doing, but we cannot do so if we stick to the surface level of things, merely observing the view through the plastic window of a single-engine airplane. To change the ways in which we manage these resources and the framework within which my colleagues and I, as scientists, make our measurements, we must revise our ideas at a deeper level. We must accept the contradiction between fact and theory, and understand that to resolve this contradiction we must move to a deeper level of thought and confront the very assumptions that have dominated perceptions of nature for a very long time. This will allow us to find the true idea of a harmony of nature, which as Plotinus wrote so long ago, is by its very essence discordant, created from the simultaneous movements of many tones, the combination of many processes flowing at the same time along various scales, leading not to a simple melody but to a symphony at some times harsh and at some times pleasing.[16]

A bull moose feeds on water plants in Washington Harbor, Isle Royale National Park, Michigan (photograph by the author).

–3

Moose in the Wilderness:
Stability and The Growth
of Populations

> The ecologist and the physical scientist tend to be machinery ori-
> ented . . . the machinery person tends to see *similarities* among phe-
> nomena as opposed to *differences*.
>
> Robert H. MacArthur (1972)[1]

Nature Undisturbed

One year around 1900, a small number of moose left the shore of Lake
Superior near the border of Minnesota and Ontario and crossed 15 miles
over the lake's frozen waters to a large forested island called, since the
arrival two centuries earlier of the first French explorers, Isle Royale. With
their poor eyesight, the moose may not have realized that they had reached
an island rather than just another promontory on the lake's wooded shore,
for Isle Royale is large, covering 210 square miles, an area 10 times that of
Bermuda and almost 9 times that of Manhattan. But the moose had migrated from a region heavily influenced by civilization to one that was then
and still is one of the best examples in the world of a wilderness undisturbed
by human influence, or what many would call the forest primeval.

People had visited Isle Royale during the past several thousand years, but
had never settled. The American Indians occasionally had crossed the icy
waters of the greatest of all lakes to collect "native" or pure copper, which
could be found at or near the surface in some rock outcrops. Europeans
also had tried copper mining, but found it uneconomical. The island had
seen a few small but short-lived farms, occasional resorts, and vacation
cabins. Moose had never been there before, but the commercial fishermen
who sought whitefish and trout in the deep lake waters and spent the
summers in shoreline cabins on the island knew that changes were taking
place as the twentieth century opened. For reasons the fishermen could not

explain, caribou, which had been common, were fast disappearing, apparently moving northward from the island into Canada. Now the moose had arrived, just as inexplicably.

From the air, Isle Royale appears as a series of parallel ridges and valleys lying southwest to northeast. They are made of sedimentary rocks laid down as early as 300 million years ago, interlaced with volcanic flows that covered sedimentary layers and then were themselves overlaid by sandstones and conglomerates. Today, the harder volcanic basalts form ridges that are forested with species of trees and shrubs that moose prefer. Along the cold shores are forests of white birch and fir—which provide spring, autumn, and winter food for the moose—and spruce—which the moose do not eat. In the interior, where the ridges are warmer because they are protected from the cold winds that blow off Lake Superior, grow yellow birch, maple, aspen, wild cherry, and other trees and shrubs that are summer forage of the moose.

In the island's valleys are forty-five large lakes, beautiful stretches of open, shallow water that on a clear day are deep blue against the dark green of the hills. Some of them grade into large marshes with patches of open water, floating mats of moss and sedge, and dense thickets of bog cranberry, Labrador tea, and graceful northern cedars. Many small streams are dammed by beaver ponds. Near the coast, the valleys end in long harbors whose shallow waters teem with water lilies, rushes, and many other aquatic plants that moose feed on in midsummer.

As the twentieth century opened, the moose had arrived at an ideal habitat for them, lacking at that time their principal predator, the North American timber wolf. They had arrived at what is for us a primeval wilderness, the reality of an ideal that has played a central and important role in the thoughts of human beings since the origin of Western civilization. Here was nature undisturbed—indeed less directly disturbed by human influence than the African plains and savannas, where *Homo sapiens* and their ancestors have been residents for several million years, and much of the North American arctic, which has experienced the impact of human hunters for thousands of years. Isle Royale was undisturbed, but it had been observed, the subject of a natural history survey in 1846, and it had been visited repeatedly by botanists who studied its forests and zoologists who studied its wildlife.

After the moose were first observed on the island in the early years of the twentieth century by fishermen and naturalists, their number increased rapidly. In less than a decade, the moose began to change the vegetation greatly, as reported in a series of scientific papers about the ecology of the island by William S. Cooper. Although there was not an accurate count of the animals, the increase in numbers was apparent from the effect of the moose on the vegetation. Two of their favorite foods—water lilies, which had almost completely covered some of the ponds, and yew, an evergreen shrub that had been the dominant ground cover in much of the island's forest—began to disappear. Both plant species were threatened with extinction on the island because of the moose.[2]

By the late 1920s and early 1930s, the impact of the moose on the vegetation was so great that Adolf Murie, a well-known naturalist, warned that they were about to run out of food, and a major die-off was imminent. This die-off did occur in the mid-1930s. Murie estimated that the number of moose dropped from more than 3,000 to fewer than 500.

Soon after the die-off, a fire burned more than one-third of the island. The forest that regenerated after the burn contained many low, young stems of species that moose favor, such as white birch. The moose population began a second increase, which continued until the mid-1940s, when the island became a national park. After the island was established as a national park, the moose again became numerous enough to have a great effect on the vegetation, and the park personnel became concerned that a second major die-off might occur. They wondered what should be done and therefore had to determine the character of a *natural* area. The national park was supposed to be natural. Was it natural to have the moose dying in large numbers? If so, should this really be allowed to happen when the moose were one of the park's main attractions? Indeed, one could ask whether the presence of the moose was natural at all, since they had not been on Isle Royale, as far as was known, prior to European settlement of North America.

It seemed clear to the park personnel that the population of moose was in an "unnatural" situation in one sense: its major predator, the timber wolf, was missing from the list of species on the island. It is an old belief that a predator is necessary to maintain the balance of the population of its prey. Following this belief, the National Park Service decided it would be beneficial to introduce wolves into Isle Royale.

Six wolves obtained from zoos were brought to the island in 1946. The zoo wolves were not accustomed to life in the wild, though, and instead of hunting moose, they were said to have hung around the Park Service headquarters looking for handouts. Although this intentional introduction failed, it was followed a few years later by a natural introduction—the arrival of a pack of wild wolves that probably crossed the lake during a particularly cold winter when the water froze across to the mainland. This pack, living mainly on the moose, increased from about a dozen in the 1940s to more than twenty in the early 1960s. Meanwhile, the moose population appeared to remain around 1,000 adults—a high but comparatively constant size—suggesting that indeed the wolves were holding the moose population in check and that Isle Royale, nature undisturbed, was indeed also an illustration of a constancy or balance of nature in the wilderness. But was the balance of nature really established there in a constant number of moose and wolves and in a constant abundance of the plants the moose ate?

It was in the late 1960s that I began a study of the moose and their wilderness ecosystem at Isle Royale, with the idea that here was a place where we could come to understand how a balance of nature might be achieved by the interaction of many species with one another and with their local, nonliving environment, the assumption being that the entire island was in such a balanced state. Our purpose was to determine the factors that controlled the population of the moose. We had an idea that some aspect of mineral nutrition would put an upper limit on the moose population, and we hoped to determine just which chemical element would be so limiting to the moose.

Others believed that the wolves provided the key to the apparent constancy of the moose population. The interaction between wolf and moose is complex. Packs of wolves have been observed to ambush moose. A wolf pack was once seen to divide into two groups, one of which hid along a heavily wooded and narrow pass in a moose trail, while the other drove a moose toward that point.[3]

After an initial scouting trip one spring, my colleagues (Peter Jordan, who had studied the moose on the island for years, and several students who made up a field crew) and I arrived at Washington Harbor, on the western end of the island, where we set up a research camp. We were accompanied by a large pile of equipment; in addition to the usual camping gear, we had carted to Isle Royale a large electromechanical Friden calculator, which must have weighed about 15 pounds and which we could plug into a single outlet that the Park Service provided to us at our camp site. We had brought the calculator along to help us make certain statistical computations. The calculator worked slowly, with a great deal of whirling and clicking. The Friden was especially slow at long division, and while it whirled and clicked over those calculations, I had time to pause and listen to the musical minor thirds being trilled by many white-throated sparrows or to the haunting call of the loons across the harbor. That calculator was unwieldy and seemed out of place in the wilderness, but the machinery within it was an apt metaphor for the concepts that dominated the science of ecology at that time. With that calculator; a pile of forestry field devices; some plastic laboratory chemical flasks, bottles, and graduated cylinders;

and a peculiar orange plastic, 18-foot, double-ended twentieth-century version of a whaling dory to haul our heavy gear around the island, we felt prepared for our scientific study.

In the second year of our study we upgraded our equipment and brought with us one of the very first pocket electronic calculators, one that could add, subtract, multiply, divide, and store one number, in absolute silence. This new calculator worked off a small battery, weighed only a few ounces, and had cost us only $450, a bargain at the time for a device that we could carry with us into the woods where we took measurements and samples. In one year our equipment had made the transition from a device based on gears and wheels to a device based on solid state computer logic. Our ideas evolved more slowly.

Not long after our study began, the moose and wolf populations began to change again. First the moose population began to increase; then the wolf population doubled to more than forty; later in the 1970s, the moose population began to decline. Variations in the two populations have continued ever since. These complex patterns, which show great variations over time and in which the individuality of the wolves and moose seemed to play an important role, did not conform to the theories that had predominated in the twentieth century about populations or the interactions between predator and prey, theories similar to the ideas that underlay David Sheldrick's management of the elephants at Tsavo.

We learned a lot about the moose, vegetation, and soil in the several years we worked on the island. By collecting samples of leaves and twigs of the plants that the moose ate and samples of mud, water, and moose tissue, we found that sodium was the most likely factor limiting the population of moose.[4] But this was a factor that could set an upper bound, not one that could neatly fix the moose abundance at a single level.

In the autumn, I began to set down some of what we had learned on the island in a computer program that I developed to provide a primitive model of the moose population. We needed a way to calculate what the total size and weight of the moose population would be for different birth and death rates. In the program, the moose were divided by age, and each age had a fixed rate of death and a fixed rate of reproduction. Since there were seventeen ages of moose, determining how the number of moose changed from year to year took many calculations, more than one would care to do by hand or even with the old-fashioned Friden mechanical calculator that we had carted out to the island.

The concepts that underlay that primitive computer program forced the computer-moose population to achieve, inevitably, a constant condition in which the number of moose and their total weight remained the same year after computer-generated year. A balance of nature was achieved within the computer, consistent with the ideas then prevalent about natural populations and with what we thought was correct for the moose on Isle Royale. It did not seem strange to us that the computer program, by design, forced this constancy on the population.

In spite of the laborious and troublesome character of computer programming at that time and the skepticism with which such an activity was viewed by most of my colleagues, I felt that there was a potential link between computer programs and field studies of wilderness, between the contemplation of the numbers and artificial "languages" of the computer and the contemplation of the character of nature as we observed it at Isle Royale. But the computer was yet a minor factor in our work, studying the character of the wilderness in 1970, dealing with ancient questions about the character of nature undisturbed by human influence, about the idea of a balance of nature.

Modern Ideas About The Balance Of Nature

The modern science that deals most directly with the ancient questions about human beings and nature is ecology, the study of the relationship between living things and their environment. That was the science I pursued in the work at Isle Royale, and in this book the term *ecology* is used to mean this science. The word has acquired other connotations connected to environmentalism, which is the social, political, and ethical movements that concern the use of the environment, and the original meaning of ecology is sometimes lost.

The word *ecology* was coined in 1866 by the German biologist Ernst Haeckel, less than ten years after the publication of Charles Darwin's *Origin of Species* which, Haeckel wrote, provided the basis for his new science, and only two years after the publication in 1864 by George Perkins Marsh of *Man and Nature*, which was the first major modern book suggesting that human activities were leading to negative effects on the environment.[5] From the mid-nineteenth century through the end of World War II, mechanical metaphors dominated people's ideas of beauty, progress, architecture, and home furnishings, even to the point of machines becoming the objects of art and the subjects of painting, as illustrated by the painting "Suspended Power," by Charles Sheeler, which appears as the introduction to Chapter 7. Ecology developed primarily in the twentieth century and, like the Friden calculator, was a child of the machine age, which began with the Industrial Revolution but flowered between the two world wars. Mechanical metaphors and machine models dominated the science of ecology until the early 1970s, when radical changes began to occur whose effects are only now beginning to be felt and understood.[6]

Ecology began in the latter part of the nineteenth century with three background elements: new observations of natural history, including the development and acceptance of the theory of biological evolution; pre-scientific beliefs about nature, including the age-old desire to find order and stability in nature; and a dependence on the physical sciences and engineering for theory, mathematical approaches, concepts, models, and metaphors. The last led to an increasingly sophisticated growth of mathematical theory (formal models) that required and led to exact equilibria, and to a world view of nature as the great machine. These foundations led to an untenable situation: the predominant, accepted ecological theories asserted that natural, undisturbed populations and ecological communities (sets of interacting populations) would achieve constancy in abundance, an assertion that became inconsistent with new observations. The mathematical theories developed in ecology about individual populations asserted the same ideas we have met before: that a natural population left undisturbed would achieve a constant number called the carrying capacity, that the population would remain at that abundance until disturbed, and that, once the disturbance was removed, the population would return to that same abundance. Theories for vegetation ecology maintained similar ideas: that a set of interacting species, such as trees and shrubs in a forest, would, if undisturbed, also achieve a constancy, not only in the numbers of each of the species, but also in the total number of species and in the total amount of organic matter stored in the forest.[7]

These assertions of the ecological theory of the period are reminiscent of the old idea of a balance of nature. Although the phrase "balance of nature" was not commonly used by ecologists, their desire to find constancy and stability in observations is apparent and revealing. This perception of order was stated by Stephen A. Forbes in "The Lake As A Microcosm," in which he wrote that "no phenomenon of life . . . is more remarkable than the steady balance of organic nature, which holds each species within the limits of a uniform average number, year after year, although each one is always doing its best to break across boundaries on every side." This balance is all the more remarkable because, on the one hand, "the reproductive rate is usually enormous," while, on the other, "the struggle for existence is correspondingly severe;" each individual has its enemies, and "nature seems to have taxed her skill and ingenuity to the utmost to furnish these enemies with contrivances for the destruction of their prey." In spite of these opposing forces, life continues and, Forbes believed, does not "even oscillate to any considerable degree, but on the contrary," a small lake is "as prosperous as if its state were one of profound and perpetual peace."[8]

In the simplest natural-history terms, there are two threats to such a balance of nature, one from within and one from without. The external threat is from the physical and chemical forces of the environment that erode and degrade: on the land, wind, storms, rain, fire, and slow chemical leaching of waters; in oceans, lakes, and ponds, the irrepressible force of gravity pulling nutrients down, away from life at the surface. All these forces exist at Isle Royale and were quite apparent when I was there doing field studies. There were days when the wind blew so strongly that the firs and cedars near the harbor shore bent low like old men away from the storm. Large areas of the island were difficult to cross; in some places much time was spent climbing and stepping up and down over logs, the remains of trees downed in storms. Fires occurred after summer thunderstorms and were watched for with great care and caution by the park personnel. How fragile nature's balance might be against these forces depends in part on the strength of biological forces of growth, and their ability to resist the forces of erosion—nature's finger in the dike—or to replace what has been pulled away. These are the power of the trees and shrubs to grow and fix roots in the soil.

The internal danger to a balance of nature is the same power of growth, the potential for exponential growth, with which the moose population at Isle Royale may have threatened the island at the beginning of the twentieth century. The capacity of a population for such rapid growth is probably best illustrated in our century by a population that is found on islands far from Isle Royale: the northern elephant seals that breed on the Channel Islands, just off the coast of southern California and Mexico. Hunted in the nineteenth century, the seals were reduced to about a dozen individuals around the turn of the century and were believed to be doomed to extinction. Instead, the population rebounded, and counts of the population show that elephant seals have increased in number quite steadily at about 9 percent per year (Figure 3). The population had consistently doubled approximately every 8 years and reached more than 60,000 in the mid-1970s.[9] If this rate were to continue, there would be 500,000 elephant seals around the turn of the next century, almost 500 million elephant seals in about 100 years, and in a little more than 400 years, the mass of elephant seals would equal the mass of the Earth. Making such calculations became quite fashionable in the 1960s, when environmentalism became popular and discussions about the limits to growth of the human population were common; obviously, such growth cannot continue for long. Even 500,000

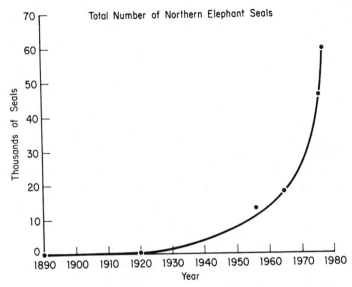

Figure 3. History of the elephant seal population, showing an exponential growth of 9 percent per year which has taken place since the population was reduced by hunting to about a dozen individuals around the turn of the twentieth century. (From D. B. Botkin and E. A. Keller, *Environmental Studies: Earth as a Living Planet.* [Columbus, Ohio: Charles Merrill Pub.])

elephant seals would have difficulty finding a place to sleep on the sand, and would likely destroy their breeding grounds.

Although many ancient philosophers and theologians believed in an absolute balance of nature, the incredible potential for the growth of biological populations has long been recognized; if it could occur, it could disrupt any balance or harmony. Aristotle, whose writings contain the oldest discussions of longevity and other fundamental population phenomena, recounts the story of a pregnant mouse that was shut up in a jar filled with millet seed, and "after a short while" when the jar was opened, "120 mice came to light."[10]

Of course, it has long been recognized that this potential—known as the potential for exponential, geometric, or Malthusian growth—could never be realized for a long time by any natural population, for it would soon be limited by some necessary life requirement. An exponential growth assumes that the population increases by a constant percentage in each time period, just as does money in a fixed-interest savings account. (It is interesting that the human population has grown faster than an exponential in recent times because since the beginning of modern medicine the rate of increase itself has increased.) Thus we arrive at the famous Malthusian statement that organisms have the potential for geometric increase, while their resources can increase only arithmetically.

Machine-Age Moose and Wolves

Much of the theory in ecology, from the origin of this science until the 1970s, relied on two formal models of population growth: the logistic for the growth of a single population, and the Lotka-Volterra equations for predator-prey interactions. Although a population has the capacity for exponential growth, it was believed in reality to grow smoothly and continuously along an S-shaped curve called the *logistic*, eventually reaching a fixed, maximum size called the carrying capacity. Two populations, a predator and a prey, were supposed to oscillate regularly, either continuing forever, or dampening to a constant abundance, like two swinging pendulums. The two populations swing out of phase—the prey at a peak when its predator is at a minimum; the predator at a peak when its prey drops to a minimum—following equations known as the Lotka–Volterra, after two of the first scientists to apply them to explain population growth.

Implicit in the logistic equation are several assumptions about the characterization of a population. The logistic equation expresses in the simplest form our intuitive notions about the limitation of the growth of a population with finite resources, and this simplicity has an appeal to scientists. The equation views all individuals as equal: the population is described by only its total number, and an individual has no other attribute than its presence or absence. Every individual is thus assumed to contribute equally to reproduction, mortality, and growth, and to reduce the available resources by exactly the same amount. Moreover, a "logistic" individual decreases the availability of resources for its fellows regardless of how many others there are. In logistic terms, the elephant population at Tsavo should have grown smoothly to an equilibrium.

Thus a logistic population appears metaphorically like a collection of identical colliding balls, the collisions resulting in a certain rate of destruction and the balls capable of identical rates of division. A logistic moose is never a calf or senile; the equation cannot distinguish between a population composed primarily of young, nonreproducing individuals and a population composed primarily of reproductively active adults.

Although the logistic equation is supposed to be an ecological formula, the environment of a population does not appear in it in an explicit way. Strictly speaking, the logistic can accurately describe only a population to which all required resources are available at a constant rate, and whose members are exposed to all toxins (except those generated by themselves) at a constant rate. A logistic moose responds instantaneously to changes in the size of the population; there is no history, no time lags, no seasons; a logistic moose has no fat.

Pencil and Paper Predator and Prey

The major original contributions to the application of these mathematical models to populations occurred in the first decades of the twentieth-century and were carried out by Alfred Lotka in the United States, Vladimir Vernadsky in Russia, and Vito Volterra in Italy, with some elegant experimentation conducted in the same period by the Russian Georgii Frantsevich Gause.

The equations were based on physics and chemistry, and the derivation of their ideas from physics and chemistry was made quite explicit by these scientists. "If we cause to hesitate in defining life," wrote Lotka in his classic work, *The Elements of Physical Biology*, let us "pass from legend to the world of scientific fact" and "borrow the method of the physicist."[11] His fifth chapter was entitled "The Program of Physical Biology," and he divided it into sections on statics and kinetics, as would a textbook in mechanics. His discussion of kinetics investigated the solutions of simultaneous differential equations, which he applied to population growth.

Lotka gave a nonmathematical explanation of the idea of the stability of populations. He considered as an example a "perfectly screened dwelling" that could be kept indefinitely free from flies and, as such, has an equilibrium of zero flies. This is an unstable equilibrium, for if only a few flies break through the screens, they will breed, and the room will become filled with flies. The number of flies will be determined by the amount of food, by "measures taken to combat the pest," and so forth. The population will "attain some approximately steady number (for a given season)."

Vito Volterra, an Italian, became interested in the reports of his son-in-law about Mediterranean fisheries. A decline in the catch of fish during World War I led to an increase in the abundance of predatory fish. This suggested the idea that predator and prey fish would undergo opposing changes in abundance, with the prey decreasing as the predators increased, and vice versa.[12] Volterra recognized that a representation of such an interaction could be described by two simple mathematical equations, which also describe the interactions between two chemicals in a liquid medium. These two equations (one for the predator and one for the prey) have become famous as the Lotka–Volterra equations for predator–prey

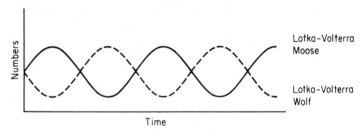

Figure 4. The Lotka–Volterra equations result in symmetric, out-of-phase oscillations between predator and prey.

interactions. It is impossible to overestimate the influence of these equations in twentieth-century population-biology. They, like the logistic, occur in every ecology and population biology text, underlie hundreds of papers, and have been the subject of repeated, extensive mathematical analyses in long monographs and treatises.

A set of Lotka–Volterra populations is much like a logistic population, except there are two colors of colliding balls. A collision between balls of different colors results in the disappearance of one (the prey) and an increase in the number of the other (the predator). In the absence of "predator" balls, the "prey" balls increase either exponentially or, in later formulations, following the logistic. The predator balls simply die away at an exponential rate in the absence of the prey.

It is worth repeating that with the Lotka–Volterra equations, two kinds of stability are possible: unending constant oscillations or dampened oscillations that lead to a fixed single equilibrium. The swings of predator and prey are out of phase, with one reaching a peak when the other reaches a minimum, as illustrated in Figure 4. A Lotka–Volterra Isle Royale wolf population would increase and decrease, chasing over time the similarly oscillating moose population, each population reaching its peak while the other descended to its trough. Interestingly, in the Lotka–Volterra formulation, predator and prey population oscillate *because* of their interactions.

As with the logistic, the Lotka–Volterra equations do not distinguish individuals within either population. All Lotka–Volterra prey would be like a logistic moose; similarly, a Lotka–Volterra predator would be equally identical to its fellows. A wolf pack would not be divided into lead male and female; there would be no wolf pups playing at the adults' heels. The populations are viewed as though from afar, as though through the wrong end of a telescope, reduced to their simplest single character, each animal indistinguishable from others of the same species. These equations reduce the biological world to a mechanistic system.

Nature In A Test Tube

The growth of a single population and the effect of predators on prey were studied in the laboratory by Gause, who used two species of single-celled microbes of the biological Protista: *Paramecium caudatum* as the prey, and *Didinium nasutum* as the predator. Gause conducted scientific research at its best, combining formal theory with laboratory experiments, which he described in his famous book, *The Struggle for Existence*. The theory he chose for population growth was the logistic equation and the Lotka–Volterra equations.

In Gause's experiments, the microbes were grown in laboratory flasks under constant conditions, with a uniform environment, and a steady supply of food. In one experiment, he grew paramecia alone and found that as long as the food supply was constant and the environment constant in every other way as well, the growth did follow a logistic (Figure 5). The artificial conditions of his laboratory experiments and the unicellular paramecia match the assumptions of the logistic about as closely as is possible. Gause's successful single-species experiments were influential, and the terms "Gausian curves" and "Gausian experiments" became common. Although other laboratory experiments with insects such as fruit flies

Figure 5. The growth of a population of *Paramecium caudatum* as studied by Gause in his famous experiments (from G. F. Gause, 1934, *The Struggle For Existence*, [Baltimore: Williams and Wilkins Co., 1934]).

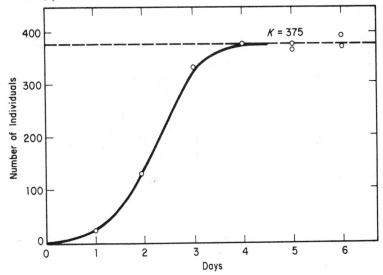

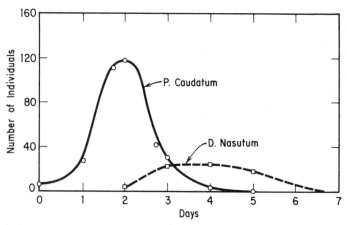

Figure 6. The interaction between a microbial predator and prey in a famous laboratory experiment by Gause (from G. F. Gause, *The Struggle For Existence*, Baltimore: Williams and Wilkins Co., 1934).

kept in closed containers in a constant environment with a sustained food supply also yielded logistic growth curves, logistic growth has never been so observed in nature.

In another set of experiments, five *Paramecium* prey were introduced into each of several tubes; two days later, three *Didinium* predators were added. The *Paramecium* increased in abundance, reaching 120 individuals by the second day, and then declined rapidly after the predators were introduced. The predators increased to about 20 individuals. By the fifth day, the *Paramecium* were completely eliminated by the *Didinium*, which eventually died of starvation (Figure 6).

In other experiments, Gause repeatedly tried to obtain the Lotka–Volterra oscillations, but could not. At best, he was able to sustain several cycles before one or the other species went extinct. Furthermore, the swings were not properly out of phase, as predicted by the Lotka–Volterra equations (Figure 4). Gause concluded that the periodic oscillations were not a property of the interaction itself, as predicted by the equations, but seemed to result from "interferences." Gause's analyses are among the most scientifically complete in the history of ecology in that he considered concepts, formal theory, and experimental tests. In spite of the fact that his tests falsified the theory, the Lotka–Volterra equations continued to be used widely throughout the decades that followed.[13] In a concluding statement in his book, Gause wrote,

We expected at the beginning . . . to find "classical" oscillations in numbers arising in consequence of the continuous interaction between predator and prey as was assumed by Lotka and by Volterra. But it immediately became apparent that such fluctuations are impossible in the population studied, and that this holds true for more than our special case. . . . It is to be hoped that further experimental researches will enable us to penetrate deeper into the nature of the processes of the struggle for existence. But in this direction many and varied difficulties will undoubtedly be encountered.[14]

Mechanical Stability Applied to Nature

Gause's predator–prey experiments, the elephants of Tsavo, the crashes of marine fisheries, and the conservation of marine mammals are a few illustrations among many of the deficiencies of the earlier theories in ecology that asserted a constancy of nature. At the heart of the issues are ideas of stability, constancy, and balance, ideas intimately entwined in theories about nature. Perhaps one reason that the deficiencies of the theories were not examined or tested adequately by observations in the field—out in nature—was that ecologists were typically uncomfortable with theory and theoreticians. Doing science and creating theory were commonly distinguished as separate activities. Although theory was typically considered not to be necessary or important to the practicing ecologist—formal models were considered unnecessary, and conceptual models were typically not discussed explicitly—theory played a dominant role in shaping the very character of inquiry and conclusions about populations and ecosystems (i.e., about nature). As Kenneth Watt wrote in 1962, ecologists had tended to believe that their science had lacked theory, while in fact it had "too much" theory—in the sense that the theory had been utilized and was influential even though it was not carefully connected to observations.[15] "Field ecologists," those making measurements and observations in the forest and field, generally did not understand the mathematics of the logistic and of the Lotka–Volterra equations. But since physicists and mathematicians had the highest status among scientists, and since what physicists and mathematicians generally said was generally right, field ecologists tended to regard the logistic and the Lotka-Volterra equations as true. Lacking the understanding to analyze and thereby criticize these equations, they accepted them on the basis of authority.

In the scientific literature of ecology, the idea of ecological stability is often vague and implicit, but where it is stated explicitly, it is almost invariably equivalent to, and usually consciously borrowed from, the physical concept of the stability of a mechanical system, phrased in terms used in engineering, physics, and chemistry. Three concepts of stability were important to ecology and its applications in the first half of the twentieth century (actually extending into the 1970s): static equilibrium, quasi-steady-state, and classical static stability. Static equilibrium means absolute constancy of abundance of all species over time (like a clock pendulum at rest); quasi-steady-state refers to variations that are persistent but small enough to be ignored (like a shaking clock pendulum); classical static stability has two attributes: constancy unless disturbed, and the ability and tendency to return to the state of constancy following a disturbance (like a pendulum in motion).[16]

An equilibrium is a fixed rest point—a condition of constancy. The idea of stability is often confused with the equilibrium or constancy itself, but an equilibrium can be stable or unstable. A metal rod balanced on end is in an unstable equilibrium. As long as it is not pushed, it remains in a constant vertical state. A pendulum, in contrast, has a stable equilibrium in its vertical position.

These ideas suggest, at least metaphorically, the possibility of fragile and resilient balances in nature. It is possible that there can be balance without stability. Conversely, the ability to return to an original condition might be quite strong, whether or not the original condition had the appearance of perfect order or relative chaos. There are many physical or mechanical examples of fragile and resilient stability. Imagine a traveler on a train who is sitting in a club car with a drink and building a house of cards. The house of cards has considerable order, but it will collapse at the slightest vibration; one could not expect the house of cards to last very long on the journey. The liquid in the glass may jostle about considerably, but not spill unless the train hits a particularly violent bump. Is Isle Royale like the house of cards or the liquid in a glass?

It is comparatively easy to consider the characteristics of constancy and stability of physical entities: a ball, a pendulum, a tower, or an airplane. It is much harder to attach clear meanings to the ideas of constancy and stability for populations, communities, and ecosystems, and the difficulty increases in that order. But with the machine metaphor for the balance of nature expressed in formal mathematical models, these became the basis for the management of fisheries, wildlife, and endangered species. In the social and political movement known as environmentalism, ideas of stability may have been less formal, but the same underlying beliefs of a balance of nature dominated. Although environmentalism seemed to be a radical movement, the ideas on which it was based represented a resurgence of prescientific myths about nature blended with early-twentieth-century studies that provided short-term and static images of nature undisturbed.

Rabbits, Cats, and Trappers

I realy [sic] do not know what we should have done for Victuals, as not one partridge has been served out this winter nor Rabbits, nor Fish to be got.
> George Atkinson, January 9, 1785.

There are in some seasons plenty of rabbits, this year in particular, some years very few, and what is rather remarkable, the rabbits are the most numerous when the cats appear . . . the cats are only plentiful at certain periods of about every 8 to 10 years.
> Peter Fidler, report to the
> Hudson's Bay Company, 1820.

Might I turn your attention to the remarkable circle of increase and decrease that each decades [sic] exhibits. In nearly all the Furbearing animals this is observable, but particularly so in the Martens. The highest years in the decade 1845–55 being the extremes and the lowest 1849.
> Bernard Ross, letter to Spencer Baird of the
> Smithsonian Institution, November 26, 1859.
> (All above quoted in L. B. Keith, *Wildlife's Ten-year Cycle*,
> [Madison: University of Wisconsin press, 1963], p. 6.).

Analysis of fur returns and pelt collections using autocorrelations and spectral techniques demonstrates that some populations exhibit unequivocally regular oscillations while others exhibit fluctuations which are either non-cyclic or questionably cyclic. In Canada, lynx in the Mackenzie River district and snowshoe hare oscillate with a period in the neighborhood of ten years.
> James P. Finerty, Ph.D. thesis,
> Yale University, 1971.

Another approach to determining whether nature really is constant over time is to examine long-term histories of populations, ecological communities, and ecosystems. However, ecology is barely 100 years old, and a century is too short to resolve by direct observation whether populations are constant or stable. And among the small number of scientific observations, there are few in which the methods of observation have been consistent for more than a decade. Few scientists have maintained an interest in one population for more than a decade. And in the cases where they might have, it has been rare that any government or private organization has been willing to fund such long projects.

Counting the number of animals of one species for a long time is a rather idiosyncratic activity, best illustrated by a study of thrips in Australia. The thrip is an insect about 1 millimeter long that lives in the petals of flowers, where it feeds on pollen. Two Australian biologists, James Davidson and Herbert Andrewartha, went for a walk every morning between 1932 and 1946, except on Sundays and "certain holidays." They collected roses at precisely 9:00 A.M. and counted the number of thrips per rose, making this one of the longest direct scientific counts of a single population of insects. Over the 14-year period, there was great variation in the population size, with the peak number of thrips per rose varying

Figure 7. The number of the thrips per rose, as measured over a 14-year period (from H. G. Andrewartha and L. C. Birch, *The Distribution and Abundance of Animals* 1954 [Chicago: Univ. of Chicago Press]).

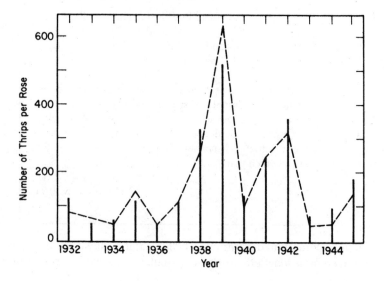

from as few as 100 in 1934 to as many as 500 in 1939. Variation, not
constancy, was the rule (Figure 7), with the number of thrips changing
both annually and seasonally, in which case the largest number was found
in midsummer.[17]

Insect populations are in general highly variable, as suggested by outbreaks of locusts and short-term observations of other insects that attack
crops and trees. However, the dearth of long-term scientific studies prevented any definitive conclusions about the constancy and stability of
insect populations. For many years, censuses were made of insect pests in
German coniferous forests. According to one record, the lasiocampid moth
maintained a comparatively low and constant population in all but 2 years
during an 80-year period, but in those 2 years the population increased to
epidemic numbers. At the peak, the insect was 10,000 times as numerous
as it had been at the minimum. There are a few other studies, including
150 counts of the moth *Lymantria monacha*, of which there were six
outbreaks in Germany. Highly erratic fluctuations in the chinch bug population were observed in the Mississippi valley between 1823 and 1940, and
similarly erratic variations have been observed in wheat-blossom midges in
England and tsetse flies in Africa.[18]

Amateur bird watchers and the participants in annual American Audubon Society Christmas counts have made shorter-term direct observations
of some species of birds. The longer records of breeding bird populations
are from Europe and are on the order of decades; they also show great
fluctuation rather than constancy.

Perhaps surprising to our scientifically sophisticated views, trappers in
northern Canada provide us with the longest continual records of animal
populations. Moravian missionaries began trading for furs with the Indians
around Hudson Bay in 1770. The trade grew. The Hudson's Bay Company
entered the fur trade around 1830, and records have been kept since.
Charles Elton realized the importance of these records and examined them
in the 1940s. His analysis made them among the best known and most
studied population histories, mentioned in every ecology textbook. In the
1970s data accumulated since Elton did his study were obtained from the
Hudson's Bay Company. We can examine these records to see whether the
animal abundances were constant over time. We can also, as some scientists have tried to do, analyze these historical records to find out if predator
and prey oscillated as would a Lotka–Volterra pair of populations.[19]

A 220-year history of one of the animals, the Canadian lynx, is shown in
Figure 8. The number of lynx pelts obtained varied tremendously, from
fewer than 1,000 in the 1790s to more than 80,000 in 1885, but oscillated

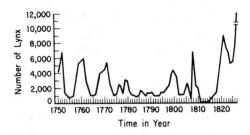

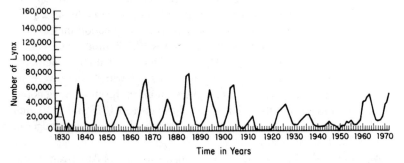

Figure 8. The 220-year history of the Canadian lynx based on fur trading records from the Hudson Bay Company (data until 1940 from W. S. Allee, A. E. Emerson, O. Park, T. Park and K. P. Schmidt, *Principles of Animal Ecology*, [Philadelphia: W. B. Saunders Co. 1949] data since 1940 kindly made available to the author by the Hudson Bay Company).

fairly regularly, with peaks about every decade. Other fur-bearing animals showed the same kind of variation, and fell into two groups: herbivores (such as the arctic hare, that is a prey of the lynx), whose abundance cycled approximately every 4 years; and carnivores (such as the lynx), whose abundance cycled about every 10 years. The obvious conclusions to draw from this history are: that animal populations are not constant and that predator and prey do not oscillate as would a Lotka–Volterra set.

But the data might be faulty. The number of animals trapped might have varied even though the abundance of the animals was constant. For example, the number of trappers and traps and the interest in catching animals might have changed, perhaps with some kind of 10-year economic cycle. Elton considered this, but concluded from the records that there were always more trappers and more traps than animals to be caught, and on this basis the trapping would be an accurate reflection of the animal populations. The observations of the trappers and other residents over the years support Elton's conclusion. But it is not certain that this was the case, and it would be much better to have records that were independent of trapping intensity. Recently, it has come to light that the data are faulty in another way: the major trapping of arctic lynx took place in a different area of Canada from that of hare, and so the Hudson's Bay Company's records are not in fact a record of the populations of a predator and its actual prey, but only of a predator and an animal that it could have preyed on if the two were in the same habitat.[20]

In the cases I have discussed, predators do not seem to control the abundance of their prey in an exact sense. However, predators and parasites do have large effects on prey and host populations; the evidence is especially strong for parasites, which are used routinely today in the biological control of pests. A plant spray containing *Bacillus thuringiensis*, a bacterium that causes disease in garden insect pests, is widely available. Parasitic wasps are used to control caterpillars. As for predators, mosquito fish are placed in rice paddies to control the growth of mosquitoes. Herbivores can devastate the vegetation that is their prey, as is clear for the moose at Isle Royale. Thus predators and parasites can greatly reduce the abundance of their prey and hosts, but there is little evidence that the result is a constancy of nature, a perfect balance in the classical sense.

Fitting Facts to Theory

By the 1950s and 1960s, evidence indicated that variation in population size is the rule, that animal populations are not in a static equilibrium. Some argued that the data show merely minor variations and are therefore proof of a quasi-steady-state. This was the view stated in the 1950s, by David Lack, a British ecologist, in an influential book, *The Natural Regulation of Animal Numbers*. Lack reviewed the evidence available then, just as we are doing now, and concluded that "most wild animals fluctuate irregularly in numbers between limits that are extremely restricted compared with what their rates of increase would allow."[21] This means that each population is capable of exponential growth, and the fact that exponential growth did not occur over the entire period of observation was taken to be sufficient evidence that the variations are not different from constancy: the pendulum may be shaking, but it is fundamentally stable.

But this is an unfair argument, made on shifting grounds. There are two meanings of the word *regulate*: to maintain an exact constancy, and to remain within some general range. One starts the argument with the first meaning, by stating that nature undisturbed is constant and therefore is regulated. Turning to the evidence of lynx pelts, for instance, one finds variations in number from 800 to 80,000. But, Lack would say, in a 220-year period, an exponentially growing lynx population would have used up all the available resources on a huge portion of the Earth. In comparison, the variations in the lynx population are small, and therefore there must be some mechanism at work to keep the population in check. The second meaning of *regulate* is invoked. The discussion ends with the conclusion that the population is regulated, suggesting that the first meaning of the term is meant.

The fallacy can be illustrated by analogy. This argument would not be acceptable for a stability analysis of an airplane in flight as viewed by a passenger. Suppose a pilot guaranteed that an airplane was stable and very constant in flight, but its path through the air traced out the curve of the lynx's population history, varying from 800 to 80,000 feet in altitude. Who would want to call that airplane stable? Lack's interpretation violates the assumptions of the logistic and the more qualitative assumptions about animal populations generally held by ecologists at the time he wrote his book. In addition, his interpretation violates ancient and modern ideas of a balance of nature that assume and require strict constancy and tight regulation. The facts were made to fit the theory, not vice versa.

When I first went to Isle Royale, it was generally accepted that animal populations in undisturbed wilderness are unchanging over time. But the evidence that was available, the evidence discussed in this chapter, leads to a different conclusion. The dominant ecological theory of the machine age implies and predicts that populations achieve a constant abundance or undergo exacting periodic oscillations and that the growth of populations is stable; that is, populations return to their original constant abundances or exact predator–prey cycles if disturbed. But, variation, rather than constancy, in the abundance of animal populations was evident in observations and experiments. In only the simplest possible case—the growth of a single population of Paramecia under constant laboratory conditions—is the theory supported by experiment. Even two-species laboratory populations fail to support the theory, and long-term records of predator and prey populations in the wild show cycles that are not similar to those predicted by theory, with huge variations in amplitude and periodicities of different lengths. In spite of the absence of agreement between theory and fact, the theory was used in science and as a basis for resource management.

So far, however, I have considered rather short-term histories of populations. Perhaps a longer history of nature involving larger groups of species than predator and prey will provide additional insight about the character of undisturbed nature and its stability or lack of stability.

"The Forest Dwellers," of Hutcheson Memorial Forest, New Jersey (*Life* November 8, 1954, copyright W. L. Maier).

4

Oaks in New Jersey:
Machine-Age Forests

The individual trees of those woods grow up, have their youth, their
old age, and a period to their life, and die as we men do. You will see
many a Sapling growing up, many an old Tree tottering to its Fall, and
many fallen and rotting away, while they are succeeded by others of
their kind, just as the Race of Man is. By this Succession of Vegetation
the Wilderness is kept cloathed with Woods just as the human Species
keeps the Earth peopled by its continuing Succession of Generations.

Thomas Pownall (1784)[1]

[The new settlers of Pennsylvania take] little account of Natural History, that science being here (as in other parts of the world) looked
upon as a mere trifle, and the pastime of fools.

Peter Kalm (1750)[2]

A Virgin Forest Begins to Change

In 1701, Cornelius van Liew, a Dutch settler, purchased land near what
became New Brunswick, New Jersey, clearing all of it but one small area of
magnificent old trees, which he kept as a woodlot. Half a century later, the
forests of this locale were viewed by Peter Kalm, a Swedish botanist sent to
the New World by Carolus Linnaeus to collect plants. Traveling from
Philadelphia north to New England in 1749, Kalm described the forests as
composed of large oaks, hickories, and chestnuts, so free of underbrush
that one could drive a horse and carriage through the woods.[3]

By the mid-1950s, the chestnut blight had eliminated the chestnut as a
major tree of the eastern United States, and all the original oak-hickory
forests of New Jersey had been cut except for van Liew's small woodlot,
barely 65 acres. Recognized for its uniqueness as the sole remaining virgin
forest of the region, it was purchased in the 1950s by Rutgers University
and became known as the Hutcheson Memorial Forest. The establishment

of this unique preserve became a minor media event. An article in *Audubon* in 1954 described this wood as

> a climax forest . . . a cross-section of nature in equilibrium in which the forest trees have developed over a long period of time. The present oaks and other hardwood trees have succeeded other types of trees that went before them. Now these trees, after reaching old age, die and return their substance to the soil and help their replacements to sturdy growth and ripe old age in turn.

The replacements for the current mature trees were thought to be "largely white, red and black oaks," with some hickories—that is, the same species that dominated the current forests.[4]

A major national magazine advertisement by Sinclair Oil, which had helped in the purchase of the forest, referred to the woods as a place where "nature has been working for thousands of years to perfect this 'climax' community in which trees, plants, animals, and all the creatures of the forest have reached a state of harmonious balance with their environment. Left undisturbed, this stabilized society will continue to perpetuate itself century after century." In the advertisement appeared a picture of Rutgers University's leading ecologist, Murray Buell, examining the cross section of one of the huge logs that were the remains of an old tree.

A major article in the November 8, 1954, issue of *Life* repeated the theme. This woodland "stands as a 'climax' forest community, which means that it has approached a state of equilibrium with its environment, perpetuating itself year after year essentially without change, secure against the invasions of all other forest types that might seek to displace it."[5]

The article went on to describe what the scientists believed about "how long nature might take to recreate the woods were they now despoiled and converted to cropland." Buell and his contemporaries regarded populations of trees as complex assemblages made up of individuals of different sizes and different rates of growth, reproduction, and mortality. Beginning with bare ground, a forest was believed to develop through a series of stages, each following the preceding one in clockwork fashion, until a final permanent form—the "climax stage"—was achieved. This process was called *succession*, a term perhaps first used by Thomas Pownall in 1784 (which I quoted at the beginning of this chapter) and reintroduced in 1860 by Thoreau to describe the development of pine woodlands following the logging of hardwood stands in New England and used again in 1864 by George Perkins Marsh. This succession, which led inevitably to the same climax forest, was described in *Life*. It was assumed to be so exact that even the duration of each stage was regular and predictable, with the entire process taking "no less than four full centuries."[6]

Such a climax forest would make a pleasant still-life painting, composed of trees of many sizes. Dominating the landscape would be the old, 100-foot trees, beneath which would grow younger trees, then saplings, and, close to the forest floor, seedlings. As the old trees died, they would be replaced by vigorously growing younger trees, and so on, so that the view of the forest at any one time would be identical to the view at any future time.

But Hutcheson Forest did not stay constant. By the late 1960s it was clear that something unexpected was happening: the forest, contrary to expectations, was changing. There were few young oaks beneath the dying giants. Instead, saplings of sugar maple were everywhere. The future forest would be maple, not oak and hickory. What had happened to the forest of permanent form and structure? The answer lay within the trees themselves. Trees that had fallen during a hurricane in 1950 were cut, and their growth rings were counted and studied.

These studies showed that fire had once been common in Hutcheson Forest. When a fire burns through a forest, trees not killed may be wounded, with patches of bark burned away, leaving scars, over which new wood grows. Annual growth rings allowed Rutgers scientists to date each fire and determine the average time between fires. Buell found that before European settlement in 1701, fires had occurred about every decade, but none had burned after European settlement, when they had been intentionally suppressed.[7]

Oaks and hickories, it turned out, dominated the forest because they are more resistant to fire than sugar maple. Other evidence suggests that the American Indians occasionally may have set fires. The effects of fire were visible in another way: instead of the open woods that Peter Kalm had seen, the forest was a dense thicket of shrubs and saplings crowded against the tall trees. The forest had taken more than 200 years to respond to the suppression of fire in a way that people could recognize. The forest primeval was revealed as, in part, a human product.[8]

Exotic species from other continents—including Japanese honeysuckle, Norway maple, and the Chinese tree of heaven—were abundant as young plants. These exotics have been brought to North America for various purposes, usually decorative. Norway maple had become a fashionable urban tree; Japanese honeysuckle was planted in many urban gardens. Once they were established in the New World, their seeds were transported by natural means—wind, birds, or mammals—and spread into Hutcheson Forest. The future forest would be one that no one had ever seen, dominated by native and introduced maples and dense with exotic species.

The perception of forests was the same as the perception of animal populations. Among scientists as well as in the public one finds a belief in the constancy of nature and the ability of nature to recover exactly its former structure following a disturbance. In the 1950s these ideas were presented as the result of modern science; they were in fact an exact repetition of nineteenth-century ideas.[9]

Static Theories

The classic statement of the belief in the constancy and stability of nature had been made in 1864 by George Perkins Marsh in *Man and Nature*:

> Nature, left undisturbed, so fashions her territory as to give it almost unchanging permanence of form, outline, and proportion, except when shattered by geologic convulsions; and in these comparatively rare cases of derangement, she sets herself at once to repair the superficial damage, and to restore, as nearly as practicable, the former aspect of her dominion.

He went on to write that "in countries untrodden by man," all factors balance one another, so that "the geographical conditions may be regarded as constant and immutable."[10]

A century later, formal scientific statements about succession had changed little. For example, Robert Whittaker, one of the major plant ecologists of the twentieth century, wrote in 1970 that where a climax community has been destroyed the vegetation "communities go through progressive development of parallel and interacting changes in environments and communities, a succession" and that "the end point of succession is a climax community of relatively stable species composition and steady-state function, adapted to its habitat and essentially permanent in its habitat if undisturbed."[11] In a paper that summarized the current major beliefs—the mechanistic beliefs—about ecology even as the machine age waned, Eugene Odum, who many consider to be the father of modern ecosystem ecology, wrote in 1969 that succession is "an orderly process of community development that is reasonably directional and, therefore, predictable" and that succession "culminates in a stabilized ecosystem."[12]

Hutcheson Forest did not conform to these ideas. The character of nature, or the interactions of human beings and nature, or both, led to different dynamics. Was this merely a peculiar exception or the general case? Trees would seem more likely than animals to remain in constant abundance over long periods, not only because individuals cannot migrate, but also because the characteristic lifetimes of many major tree species greatly exceed those of animals.

Botanists divide the landscape into vegetation associations, or groups of species that occur together over wide geographical areas. They are defined in terms of those species that are believed to be the dominant ones in undisturbed conditions. Until recently, scientists believed that these groups had persisted for a long time before the European colonization of America, with little change; that is, the vegetation was in static equilibrium. Once again, we can turn to Isle Royale, our American wilderness, for an example. In 1909, William S. Cooper, a biologist from the University of Chicago, went to Isle Royale to study its forests and their development following natural disturbances from windstorms and fires. The result was one of the classic studies of forest ecology of the early twentieth century. [13]

Cooper studied primarily the northeastern part of the island, which he found was largely a forest of balsam fir, white spruce, and white birch, with some bogs and areas of maple. The forest, he wrote, "is the final and permanent vegetational stage, toward the establishment of which all the other plant societies are successive steps," and "both observational and experimental studies have shown that the balsam-birch-white spruce forest, *in spite of appearances to the contrary* [my italics], is, taken as a whole, in equilibrium; that no changes of a successional nature are taking place within it," even though "superficial observation would be likely to lead to exactly the opposite conclusion." The statements are reminiscent of Nicolson's comments about animal populations, quoted in Chapter 3. [14]

Cooper saw this forest as stable in three ways. First, it had classic stability: when disturbed, any patch recovered to its original condition, which persisted until disturbed again. Second, any bare surface—be it a barren, dry, rocky ridge top; an open-water bog; or a fertile, well-drained soil— would, if given long enough time without disturbance, develop into the same final balsam-spruce-birch forest: "In other words, those phases of the vegetation that are not uniform in character with the main forest mass are plainly tending toward uniformity." Third, although there were natural disturbances, such as fire and windstorms, they were local and balanced out in the larger picture: "The climax forest is a complex of windfall areas of differing ages, the youngest made up of dense clumps of small trees, and the oldest containing a few mature trees with little or no young growth beneath" but "the changes in various parts" balance each other so that "the forest as a whole" remains the same. Every disturbed area returned to the same final condition, which remained constant until disturbed again. Moreover, the forest was believed subject to a uniform rate of small disturbances so that its average composition was always the same. Any small area was thus characterized by a stability like that of a pendulum; if upset or pushed, it returned to its former condition. The forest as a whole, on a large scale, was composed of a constant number of patches of any one stage at any time, and was, therefore, uniform. Nature without human influence was constant in both the small and the large. Cooper's study and conclusions were being repeated in other areas and this concept of succession was expounded by major botanists in the first decades of the twentieth century.

A Dynamic Past

The view of nature that we have been talking about is rather local, about what you can see in a casual day's walk around Hutcheson Forest or in a hike of several days at Isle Royale. When we fail to find constancy at that scale, the natural thing to do is to take a broader perspective, hoping that conditions will average out or that there are features of a larger area that are constant even if the local scene is not. And so we need to take a longer look back in time and a broader scan beyond the horizon.

Trees and higher plants provide much better evidence about long-term patterns than do animal populations. With vegetation three kinds of data are available. First are written historical accounts. In North America, for example, there are the accounts written by early explorers, notes of land surveyors, and studies by natural historians. Because forests are important as economic resources and forest lands were often cleared for farming, ranching, and human settlement, there is a considerable written history of the conditions of forests.

Second, many species of trees produce annual growth rings, from which their age and how well they grew during each year of their lifetimes can be determined. By extension, the age and history of the development of an entire forest can be determined by direct measurement of the growth rings of sample trees, as was done in Hutcheson Forest, making possible a reconstruction of the history of a forest for hundreds and sometimes thousands of years.

Third, tiny grains of pollen provide the longest record of the history of forests. Pollen is widely dispersed, and the outer casings of pollen persist for very long periods. When pollen grains are deposited in lakes, they drift to the bottom and become part of the lake sediments. As a lake gradually fills in, the sediments form a history of the local and regional vegetation, with the oldest sediments at the bottom and the most recent at the top. Scientists study these records by driving long corers into the lake sediments, and preserving the cores by freezing and using radioactive isotopes to date the samples. The patterns on pollen grains are distinct, and the grains are inert; thus grains millions of years old can be used to identify the species that were present and to estimate their relative abundance at each time.

It is well known that the Earth has gone through major periods of glaciation during the past two million years, and they have caused great disruption in the distribution of life on the land, but continental glaciation is a comparatively recent discovery, not known to modern science until the nineteenth century and not influential in the study of natural history until the twentieth century.[15]

The farthest extent of the continental ice is demarcated by terminal moraines, hills of mixed deposits of soil and rocks that extend for hundreds and thousands of miles. There are a number of distinct terminal moraines in Europe and North America. Four predominant moraines suggested to nineteenth and early twentieth century scientists that there had been four major eras of glaciation. (More recent evidence suggests that there were perhaps as many as sixteen major periods of glaciation.)

The last great Pleistocene continental glaciers, which formed and expanded between 70,000 and 5,000 years ago, had an impact on the Earth that is difficult for us to imagine. As it is now reconstructed and generally accepted among scientists, the continental ice sheet covered 6 million square miles in North America, 2.3 million in Europe and 6 million in Asia at the time of its greatest extension.[16] The North American ice sheet exceeded in size that of modern Antarctica, and the ice was as much as 4,000 feet thick. Its southernmost extension, along latitude 37°30'N, ran from Cape Cod through Long Island, Lake Erie, central Ohio, Indiana, Illinois, approximately along the Missouri River valley to the Rockies.

The effects extended beyond these limits. Decreases in temperature and increases in rainfall created large lakes to the south of the glaciers. One was Lake Bonneville, which 12,000 years ago covered 20,000 square miles, an area ten times its current remnant, Utah's Great Salt Lake. Large parts of the midwest of central North America were covered with loess, wind-blown sands and silts, as much as twenty feet thick, forming the very fertile soils of the Great Plains, from Louisiana to eastern Colorado, including 20,000 square miles of sandhills in Nebraska and South Dakota, and other sandhills in Texas and New Mexico.

The evidence of continental glaciation raised several major questions. How can a balance of nature incorporate the history of the periods of glaciation? What can be said about the constancy and stability of nature since the last glaciation or during interglacials, the warmer periods between times of glacial expansion? Is there any time period for which one could talk about a constancy of nature if the climate of the Earth has gone through these major disturbances? These questions are of particular interest to us for the Pleistocene epoch, usually estimated to have begun approximately 2 million years ago, because it corresponds closely with contemporary scientific estimates of the origin of human beings.[17] Thus our species appears to have emerged during the Pleistocene, and man the toolmaker appears to have arisen near the beginning of the modern glacial ages.

In this context, our original question can be rephrased: what is the evidence that there has been any kind of constancy or stability of nature since the origin of *Homo sapiens* or since the appearance of hominid species who were toolmakers? Until very recently, it was generally accepted that periods of glaciation represented atypical climatic conditions, while the interglacials represented the typical or average climate of the Pleistocene. The normal climate of the past 2 million years was thought to be much like the present. The duration of the interglacial periods was believed to be much longer than that of the glacial periods, so that the glaciations were viewed as comparatively short anomalies or disturbances of a climate that was otherwise comparatively uniform. Furthermore, the impact of glaciation was thought to have been limited to the higher latitudes, leaving the subtropics and tropics untouched. Now we know that climate changed at all latitudes, and that throughout the tenure of our species on this planet climate has varied. With this in mind, we can ask what was the natural state of the vegetation in temperate and higher latitudes since the end of the last glaciation.

Wilderness History

A little more than 100 miles west of Isle Royale lies a million acres of lakes, streams, marshes, and forests, set aside as a legally designated wilderness known as the Boundary Waters Canoe Area, extending from Minnesota to an adjacent area in Ontario. Moose meander here as they do on Isle Royale, and people come every summer to canoe and hike and to discover wilderness. But what is the true character of this wilderness that they seek? The history of the vegetation holds some clues for us. That history has been reconstructed using all three kinds of evidence: written history; existing forests; and lake sediments. Pollen deposits from the Lake of the Clouds within the Boundary Waters Canoe Area indicate that the last glaciation was followed by a tundra period in which the ground was covered by low shrubs now characteristic of the far North, as well as reindeer moss and other lichens and lower plants.[18]

The tundra was replaced by a forest of spruce, species that are now found in the boreal forest of the North, where they dominate many areas of Alaska and Ontario. About 9,200 years ago the spruce forest was replaced by a forest of jack pine and red pine, trees characteristic of warmer and drier areas. Paper birch and alder immigrated into this forest about 8,300 years ago; white pine arrived about 7,000 years ago, and then there was a return to spruce, jack pine, and white pine, suggesting a cooling of the climate. Thus every thousand years a substantial change occurred in the vegetation of the forest, reflecting in part changes in the climate and in part the arrival of species that had been driven south during the ice age and were slowly returning.

Which of these forests represented *the* natural state? If one's goal were to return the Boundary Waters Canoe Area to its natural condition, which of these forests would one choose? Each appears equally natural in the sense that each dominated the landscape for approximately 1,000 years, and each occupied the area at a time when the influence of human beings was non-existent or slight. The range of choice is great, representing kinds of vegetation communities now distributed thousands of miles apart and some that no longer exist. Thus the idea of keeping the Boundary Waters Canoe Area in a constant state leads us to a blind alley. We know that allowing this area to become tundra is not what we had in mind. Nor do we want it to become an open prairie. It is my impression that what most people really want from a visit to the Boundary Waters Canoe Area is the sense of wilderness as it was experienced by the voyageurs 200 to 300 years ago, not only the feeling of wilderness as a place that has been untouched by human beings, as it has been expressed in recent decades, but also the feeling of the north woods. That goal is a much less stringent one than a constant nature. It requires that we manage the forest to allow for a natural range of variations in space and time. It would not allow us to strip mine the area or suppress fires to the point that the forest changes its character.

Let us consider in some detail the goal of managing a particular spot in the Boundary Waters Canoe Area to retain its constant, single "natural" state. This creates a quandary not only in the short term, but also in the longer term because as the glaciers receded and the climate changed the vegetation communities also changed. Thus the abundances of forest-tree species over time at a particular location were not constant. In light of this history, what meaning can we now attach to a stability of nature? Or, as a manager of a wilderness, what would we recommend as the *natural forest* for Minnesota or Isle Royale?

One answer that ecologists proposed during the first half of the twentieth century was the idea of the "climatic climax" forest. This idea is that, even if the forests moved around during the ice ages, they did so as units that remained intact, just as when one moves snapshots around in the family album: the location of a picture changes, but the people in each picture remain the same. Granting that the glaciers caused a great displacement in the location of vegetation communities, these communities were assumed to have migrated intact southward in front of the advancing ice, and then migrated northward again as the ice retreated. For example, for many years a standard text about ice age geology pictured vegetation communities during the height of the glaciation as having been pushed south, un-changed.[19] It showed a tundra border just below the edge of the ice, spruce forests to the south of the tundra, and temperate mixed-species forests to the south of the spruce.

If the "climatic climax" idea was true, then the communities had a continuous existence throughout the Pleistocene, and the *natural* condi-tion of a particular spot would be the biological community that was characteristic of the present climate. But unfortunately, this idea has also been shown to be false. Margaret B. Davis studied pollen deposits from twenty-six sites scattered across the eastern and central United States and reconstructed the paths of migration of the major tree species as they returned north during the last 13,000 years as the North American conti-nental ice sheet melted.[20] The trees migrated at different rates, depending on the size and mobility of their seeds. Light seeds, like those of poplar, are readily blown over long distances by the wind, and they moved northward most rapidly. Heavy seeds, like those of beech, are moved by squirrels and other small animals, and thus they migrated much more slowly.

The different species not only moved northward at different rates, but also moved northward from different directions. The hickories returned to Hutcheson Forest by moving northeastward from a refuge in the southern Midwest or West, while chestnut moved westward from a refuge east of the Carolinas, in what is now the Atlantic Ocean, but was dry land during the glaciation. (The glaciers contained so much of the Earth's waters that the ocean level was several hundred feet below its present average.) Thus the forest composition itself changed markedly over the millennia, and the species that seem most important in the modern forest had been scattered in different directions, forming forest communities that no longer exist.

In our search for constancy in nature, we have had to abandon the ideas of local constancy and of a climatic climax, but we still have a few more possibilities. Perhaps the vegetation recovered very quickly to its present condition after an ice-age. If this were the case, then one could talk about an interglacial forest that would be constant throughout its entire range for most of the interglacial period. But the evidence is against this possibility also. A map of tree-migration routes indicates markedly different rates of return for different species. Hemlock reached Massachusetts 9,000 years ago, approximately 2,000 years before beech, although now beech and hemlock grow in the same region.[21]

The migration process seems not to have reached its limit. Hemlock reached the Upper Peninsula of Michigan 5,000 years ago, and moved westward slowly, reaching the western shore of Lake Superior 1,000 years ago near where the moose of Isle Royale must have entered the waters of that great lake at the turn of the century. Beech, however, seems to be still migrating westward, with the present western boundary of its range in the middle of the Upper Peninsula. Given that information, one could make a last-ditch attempt to hold on to a belief in constancy of nature, arguing that recovery is still taking place and a true equilibrium in the distribution of the forest trees has yet to be reached. But this interpretation forces us to conclude that the true and constant state of nature will be achieved in the future and has never been seen by human beings. This is a peculiar and undesirable idea of a natural condition. The point is academic anyway, because the migration rates of trees during the previous interglacials show that such an equilibrium never was reached at the middle and high latitudes even by the end of an interglacial.

As I mentioned earlier, the interglacial periods themselves are now interpreted as interruptions of a more normal climate. One might therefore conclude that the conditions that exist during interglacials, i.e. the conditions familiar to human beings since the beginnings of civilization, are unnatural, but this would be a peculiar and undesirable interpretation.

The pollen evidence contradicts the beliefs that prevailed among ecologists through the mid-twentieth century. A cynic could argue that the ice, being the most common feature during the past 2 million years, is the natural condition and the true description of nature undisturbed north of the moraines. Obviously, the line of reasoning we have attempted to follow, searching for a constancy of structure, is in error.

There is still one last possibility: if the vegetation is not constant, perhaps the pattern of change repeats itself so that vegetation still responds like a clock pendulum to climatic change. If this were true, then the pattern of re-establishment would have been repeated in every interglacial. For example, beech would always retreat to the same refuge during an ice age and return from it following the same routes at the same times. If so, then one could claim that the natural state of the forest would be the appropriate stage in the sequence that occurred following the end of each glaciation.

But this idea does not seem to work either. Pollen records from England, where the history of the trees has been studied for six interglacial periods, show that the pattern of migration of species does not repeat itself from one ice age to another. For example, as the glaciers melted at the end of the most recent period, hazel became very abundant very rapidly in East Anglia, Great Britain and then essentially disappeared. But in the previous interglacial hazel in Great Britain became abundant slightly later, and slowly decreased in abundance throughout the period. In the oldest interglacial, hazel in Great Britain was never very abundant, but did persist throughout the period. The apparent disappearance of hazel in Great Britain during our own time could be attributed to human activities. But the great differences in patterns of re-establishment of hazel in the earlier interglacials argues against regularity in the pattern of recovery during interglacials. The evidence, as far as the picture is complete, is consistent for the forested regions of North America and Europe.

To further complicate the picture, forests also change slowly in response to changes in soils, which develop continually throughout interglacial periods, suggesting perhaps that interglacials are too short to produce soil in a steady-state, and providing another reason that vegetation might fail to achieve a constant condition even over a long period of time between glaciers.

Wherever we seek to find constancy we discover change. Having looked at the old woodlands in Hutcheson Forest, at Isle Royale, and in the wilderness of the boundary waters, in the land of the moose and the wolf, and having uncovered the histories hidden within the trees and within the muds, we find that nature undisturbed is not constant in form, structure, or proportion, but changes at every scale of time and space. The old idea of a static landscape, like a single musical chord sounded forever, must be abandoned, for such a landscape never existed except in our imagination. Nature undisturbed by human influence seems more like a symphony whose harmonies arise from variation and change over every interval of time. We see a landscape that is always in flux, changing over many scales of time and space, changing with individual births and deaths, local disruptions and recoveries, larger scale responses to climate from one glacial age to another, and to the slower alterations of soils, and yet larger variations between glacial ages.

Tropical Wilderness

There is so much concern today about the fate of natural areas in the tropics, especially the rain forests and the great plains and savannas of eastern and southern Africa, that it is important to turn our attention to the character of nature in these latitudes.

It was commonly believed among ecologists before the 1960s that, even more so than in the middle and high latitudes, the tropics had been characterized by climatic constancy and that the patterns of vegetation in the tropics had varied little in the past millennia. This concept of the tropics changed in the 1970s when sufficient evidence from pollen studies became available.

What, for example, has been the history of the great dry savannas at Tsavo, in the Serengeti, and down to the Cape of Good Hope, land that has felt the elephants' massive but gentle stride for centuries and has been considered by some the last place on Earth for wild nature? Although the great plains and savannas of Africa are often portrayed as the last natural wilderness, they have been influenced by human beings for millions of years through hunting and through fire. Contrary to popular myth, the populations of wildebeest and other large herbivores have varied greatly in the twentieth century, first decimated by rinderpest, a viral disease usually fatal to cattle, introduced from Europe at the turn of the century, recovering only in recent decades, and undergoing rapid population increases ever since.[22]

While much less is known about the history of Africa than that of regions in the northern latitudes during the Pleistocene, the picture that is emerging is similar to the one for the north. Some of the evidence comes from the study of mountain glaciers in East Africa. In the land of the elephant, as in the land of the moose, the climate has changed greatly. Daniel Livingstone, an expert on African lakes and their history, studied pollen cores from Lake Victoria and wrote that "The African environment is capricious, not stable, and apparently has been so for at least several million years."[23] At times in the past, glaciers existed in the equatorial mountains and the climate was much wetter and cooler than it is today, with rain forests growing where there are now dry grasslands. At other times, the rainfall decreased and lakes dried up.[24]

If the vegetation changed, so must have the soils, the soil organisms, the large mammals, the insects, and the birds. Rain forests lack the great number of large mammals found in the tropical savannas and grasslands of Africa. Thus the changes in the sediments of Lake Victoria and the other African lakes, the variations in the extent and distribution of the African mountain glaciers, suggest that Africa too has been subject to biological change rather than constancy. Over the past thousands of years, the deserts, grasslands, savannas, and woodlands have marched slowly across the landscape to the beat of the changing climate.

As in Africa, the ice-age history of the vegetation in other tropical areas is confounded by the effects of human civilization, so that only the earlier periods are useful in seeking to uncover the pattern of nature without human beings. In the tropics, as in the north, it is not easy to find wilderness undisturbed. One likely area that has been subject to some study is the Western Highland District of New Guinea, where mountains reach an elevation of 14,000 feet. Here cores of sediments from swamps and ponds have been collected along a 60-mile distance, from elevations of 5,200 to 8,300 feet, providing information about conditions back as far as 30,000 years ago.[25]

Hiking down from these summits today, a traveler passes through alpine grasslands at the highest elevations, a subalpine forest between 13,000 and 11,000 feet, and a transitional forest called mixed montane, which changes at 9,000 feet to a southern hemisphere beech forest and to a southern hemisphere oak forest below 8,000 feet. The five ponds and swamps studied, which lie below 9,000 feet, fall within either southern hemisphere oak or beech forests that are affected by the distribution of pigs and fire, the effects of human agriculture. The pollen in the sediments show that it was much colder on the mountains more than 22,000 years ago than it is today; alpine and subalpine plants, which occur now above 11,000 feet, grew between 6,000 and 7,000 feet, where today there are oak forests. Between 22,000 and 18,000 years ago, the climate warmed and the tundra was replaced by beech forests. At 8,000 feet, where now grow beech forests, alpine grasses grew 16,000 to 12,000 years ago; subsequently, beech and mixed montane forests, typical of the colder climates, alternated over thousands of years.

There is also evidence of an opening up of the forests at the lower elevations during the past 5,000 years, suggesting human influence, and human artifacts have been found at two sites dated at 2,300 years old. D. Walker of the Australian National University concludes from these studies that change not only is likely, but is a demonstrable fact even in vegetation formerly thought to be more stable than most, and change has been continuous.[26]

Almost 1,200 miles directly to the south of Mount Hagen lies Lynch's Crater at an elevation of almost 2,000 feet above sea level in Australia. Lynch's Crater is one of Australia's few natural lakes. Now filled with a swamp, this natural basin was formed by an ancient volcanic explosion. The crater lies in the Atherton Tableland of northern Queensland, which today is in the subtropics, wetter than much of Australia, with an average rainfall of approximately 100 inches per year.

In the swamp, little of the pre-British settlement vegetation remains, most of the region having been cleared for cattle grazing. However, a tropical rain forest exists several miles to the east of the crater, suggesting the character of the presettlement landscape. A sediment core taken from the swamp tells a story of change similar to those for New Guinea and Lake Victoria. [27] The oldest sediments from Lynch's Crater, 60 feet below the present surface, indicate that forests occupied the surrounding areas between 60,000 and 38,000 years ago, but the species included some that no longer occur in northeastern Queensland and the relative abundances of others are not like those found today. Similar forests grow today in areas that receive less than half the rain that falls in the region of Lynch's Crater. Between 38,000 and 27,000 years ago, the rain-forest species gradually diminished and were replaced by plants of dry woodlands. Thus the area near Lynch's Crater appears to have undergone a slow, long warming and drying.

From 27,000 to 12,000 years ago, the plants of dry woodlands were dominant. Then rain-forest species returned, but the collection of species has no known modern equivalent in northern Queensland. For example, small plants typical of the understory of modern rain forests were much more abundant than they are in modern rain forests.

Other studies in Australia and New Guinea suggest a similar vegetation history. [28] Some allow an even longer history to be reconstructed. Taken together, the various studies conducted in the past several decades suggest that the climate in the tropics between 60,000 and 40,000 years ago was drier than it is now, became colder during the next 10,000 years, and even colder in the subsequent 10,000, with the greatest extent of mountain glaciers in New Guinea occurring about 17,000 years ago. Like the glaciers in East Africa, these glaciers, it has been estimated, would have formed as a result of a 6 to 10°F lowering of the average annual temperature. The temperatures rose rapidly beginning around 15,000 years ago; by 10,000 years ago, lakes filled in southern Australia and most of the ice was gone from the New Guinea mountains. Between 8,000 and 5,000 years ago, the climate was somewhat warmer than the modern one.

The evidence from Australia and New Guinea is consistent with that from East Africa. Thus the tropics, which had been believed to be constant throughout the past 2 million years, are known to have varied greatly. This seemed obvious to Walker who concluded that if the naturalness of change is not taken into account in planning the future, those plans are doomed to failure in one way or another: "Planning which is ecologically rational needs a measure of flexibility simply because ecosystems are dynamic, evolving all the time and at varying rates. . . . Once we have determined our aims," he continued, "we must look forward to the need for continuous management to achieve and maintain them. And a knowledge of the processes of vegetation change, on all time scales up to tens of thousands of years at best, is likely to prove important in that management." [29]

Thus near the end of the machine age, the available evidence over-whelmingly opposed the idea that populations or communities have been constant in abundances or in the relative importance of species. Until 10 or 20 years ago, scientists believed that the low latitudes had escaped the catastrophic changes brought about by the Pleistocene glaciations and therefore offered the best hope of finding a constancy in nature. During the past 20 years, a radical change has taken place in the interpretation of the Pleistocene history of the tropics. Everywhere that careful studies have been made, from Africa to New Guinea and Australia, a similar picture emerges: alternations of times of cool and wet climate with times of warm and dry; changes in the distribution of communities of plants and in the kinds of plants that made up these biological communities. The picture, although cruder, is like the one we found for the higher latitudes in the Northern Hemisphere. And thus those land areas that would seem most likely to be the home of nature's biological constancy appear not to be so.

The classical areas of wilderness, those last outposts of nature undisturbed—the forest of Isle Royale, the grasslands and savannas of East Africa, the mountains of New Guinea, the marshes of Australia—show a temporal mutability that we cannot ignore. The sediments in lakes are evidence of the great mutability of biological communities: changes in the combination of species; differences in the migration rates of species; trans-formations in biological communities with changes in climate; differences among the interglacial periods in the species that composed the forests and grasslands, and in the relative importance of the species that have existed throughout the Pleistocene. Thus in both temperate forests and tropical regions, nature is not constant, it is not like a single tone held indefinitely, but is composed of patterns that themselves change, like a melody played against random background noises.

Sometimes Change Is Necessary

Local changes sometimes are necessary for life for two reasons: the chemi-cal clock sometimes runs down and chemicals become unavailable; and species evolve with change, and many are specifically adapted to it.

In Australia, there are sand dunes that have existed for 100,000 years; this is highly unusual because dunes are typically subjected to intense storms and are eventually blown open by the wind. The Australian dunes form a sequence with the youngest, nearest the shore, and the oldest, the farthest inland. One can trace the history of a typical area by walking inland from the coast, from one dune to another. Because the dunes are older the farther they are from the ocean, this walk is a journey back through time and should therefore take one to older and older stages in ecological succession. At first, the vegetation seems to follow the classical model of succession: from dune to dune, the plants become larger and more dense. Near the shore are few scattered hardy plants, small and with shallow roots, that hold the sand in place, which allow seeds of other plants to sprout. Farther inland grow larger woodland plants of greater diversity. But at the oldest dunes, the pattern deviates from the classical one: the vegetation becomes smaller and less diverse as woodlands give way to a shrubland.[30]

Studies of this sequence of dunes have shown that chemical elements needed for life can build up in the sandy soil from salt spray from the ocean and from organic matter added by the plants as they die. As the dunes age, however, the chemical elements are leached downward by rain, and plants need deeper and deeper roots to survive. Eventually, most of the chemicals settle in a layer below the reach of most kinds of plants; a scrubland of relatively few species survives. Only an intense disturbance will turn the sand over and bring the chemical elements necessary for life back to the surface.

A similar story can be told for rain forests along the west coast of New Zealand's South Island, where one can follow ecological succession by walking from the edge of a glacier toward the shore, a brief walk. Near the glaciers, where plants are just beginning to become established, the normal pattern of ecological succession occurs: first lichens and mosses, then low flowering plants, then trees, then temperate rain forest with a dense growth of many species. But this is not the last stage; farther toward the shore, the rain forest disappears and is replaced by scrubby grass and shrubs. Here, as on the Australian dunes, chemical elements necessary for the plants have been leached downward into the soil, below the reach of the trees; only a few plants adapted to very low nutrient soils can grow. Another glaciation that would turn over the soil could bring these elements to the surface.

A third example is the natural regrowth of forests along the Alaskan coast as the glaciers have melted back in the twentieth century. Again, the succession of plants at first seems to fit the classical pattern. Alders are among the first trees to become established; they have nitrogen-fixing symbiotic bacteria in their roots, and together the alders and their bacteria enrich the soil. In the enriched soil grow other trees, including spruce, which eventually grows taller than the alder, shading that species and preventing its reproduction. Slowly, lacking the alder and its bacteria, which adds nitrogen to the soil, the soil becomes less fertile. When spruce trees die, beds of sphagnum moss develop. They make the soil acid and soak up water, making the area uninhabitable for trees, and what was forest becomes bog, not at all like the "climax" forest of spruce that was supposed to be the final stage.[31]

Another ice age would start the Alaskan forests again. Even a slight cooling period, perhaps no more than existed during the little ice age, from the mid-sixteenth to the mid-nineteenth century, could rebuild the glaciers enough to cover Glacier Bay and locally renew forest progression. Similarly, the New Zealand rain forests will not occur again without another ice age. A smaller, shorter change in the environment might be enough to restart the progression of dunes along the Australian coast, perhaps an episode of severe storms. But in all three cases, an environmental change is necessary for the recurrence of what used to be thought of as the climax stage, which would remain indefinitely under undisturbed conditions.

If we want to keep some of these stages frozen in their current conditions, we can change the soils by turning them over or adding fertilizers. That is, we can substitute our own energy, time, and resources to replace nature's natural processes. We can do this in some cases for a long time and in all cases for a short time, but we cannot freeze all of nature indefinitely in a single state.

Conserving a Small Warbler: A New Direction in the Management of Living Resources

In the 1960s, the facts about the naturalness of change and the adaptations of living things to change finally began to force their way through the myths of constancy to affect the management of living resources. One of the first and classic examples of the beginnings of this new direction was the attempt, still ongoing, to save a small friendly bird, the Kirtland's warbler.

In 1951, a survey was made of the Kirtland's warbler, making it the first songbird in the United States to be subject to a complete census. About 400 nesting males were found. Concern about the species grew in the 1960s and increased when only 201 nesting males were found in the third census, in 1971.[32] Conservationists and scientists began to try to understand what was causing the decline, which threatened the species with extinction.

The Kirtland's warbler winters in the Bahamas and then flies north to Michigan, where it breeds in an exacting set of conditions in jack pine woodlands. Although jack pine grows widely throughout the boreal forests, especially in Canada, Kirtland's warbler nests only in jack-pine woods on one soil type, called Grayling sands, which occurs in central Michigan at the very southern end of the range of jack pine. These warblers build their nests on the ground and, apparently because the nests must remain dry, prefer to build them on dead tree branches still attached to a tree at ground level, and only on coarse sandy soil that drains away rain water rapidly. Young jack pines provide the dead branches at the ground surface, and Kirtland's warblers are known to nest only in jack-pine woodlands that are between 6 and 21 years old, ages when the trees, 5 to 20 feet tall, retain dead branches at ground level. Males are territorial, and each defends an area as large as 80 acres in a uniform jack-pine stand.

These requirements leave the warbler with few nesting areas, all the fewer because jack pine is a "fire species," which persists only where there are periodic forest fires. Jack-pine cones open only after they are heated by fire, and the trees are intolerant of shade, able to grow only when their leaves can reach into full sunlight. Even if seeds were to germinate under mature trees, the seedlings could not grow in the shade and would die. Jack pine produces an abundance of dead branches that promote fires, which is interpreted by some as an evolutionary adaptation to promote those conditions most conducive to the survival of the species.

The Kirtland's warbler thus requires change at a rather short interval— forest fires approximately every 20 to 30 years, which was about the frequency of fires in jack-pine woods in presettlement times.[33] But then where was the warbler in ancient times, when the continental ice sheets were retreating during the past 10,000 years? With such specific nesting habits, the warbler must have followed the jack pine as it migrated northward and nested in the trees on outwash plains, where the roaring rivers created by melting ice deposited coarse sands. At best, the warbler could have reached Michigan no sooner than 6,000 to 8,000 years ago, when the jack pine returned to this area. But the males seem unwilling to set up new territories away from old ones. They nest only a short distance from where they were born. Thus the species might have migrated northward even more slowly than the forests.

At the time of the first European settlement of North America, jack pine may have covered a large area in what is now Michigan. Even as recently as the 1950s, the pine was estimated to cover nearly 500,000 acres in the state. European settlers first reached the warbler's habitat in 1854 when Tawas City was founded on Lake Huron, after which lumbering of red and white pine in the area began in earnest. Jack pine, a small poorly formed tree, was then considered a trash species to the commercial loggers and was left alone, but many large fires followed the logging operations when large amounts of slash—branches and twigs and other economically undesirable parts of the trees—were left in the woods. Elsewhere, fires were set in jack-pine areas to clear them and promote the growth of blueberries. Some experts think that the population of Kirtland's warblers peaked in the late nineteenth century as a result of these fires. After 1927, fire suppression became the practice, and control of forest fires reduced the area burned and the size of individual fires. Where possible, it was the practice to encourage the replacement of jack pine with economically more useful species. These actions reduced the areas conducive to the nesting behavior of the warbler.[34]

Although it may seem obvious today that the warbler requires forest fire, this was not always understood. In 1926, one expert wrote that "fire might be the worst enemy of the bird."[35] Only with the introduction of controlled burning after vigorous advocacy by conservationists and ornithologists was habitat for the warbler maintained. The Kirtland's Warbler Recovery Plan, published by the Department of the Interior and the Fish and Wildlife Service in 1976 and updated in 1985, calls for the creation of 38,000 acres of new habitat for the warbler for which "prescribed fire will be the primary tool used to regenerate non-merchantable jack-pine stands on poor sites."[36] In this case, the facts had become unavoidable and could not be hidden in myth: unlike trees that may seem to extend indefinitely to the horizon or fish in the oceans whose numbers are difficult to count, the Kirtland's warbler population consisted of a small number of individuals, including males that were subject to a complete census and whose habitat requirements were absolutely clear. Those who wanted to save this species acted from observation. This episode, perhaps small in the grander scale of the Earth's millions of species, marked a turning point in the modern perception of the character of nature and the requirements to manage and maintain nature. Within a decade after an article in *Audubon* described Hutcheson Forest in New Jersey as "a cross-section of nature in equilibrium," the same magazine contained an article, "A Bird Worth A Forest Fire," which explained the necessity of fire for the persistence of a bird, marking as well as any two statements the beginning of the transition in ideas about nature within which we now find ourselves.[37]

A breakdown was occurring in the old ideas, which were no longer tenable. Even today, the lesson of the Kirtland's warbler is not widely heard or widely accepted for other forests and their animals. It is worth repeating that the breakdown in ideas and myths is discomforting, even frightening. And in this case, the conclusion that one must manage at least one species by promoting change may seem to some who want to make wise use of our natural resources to open up a Pandora's box of terrible consequences. With the warbler, we must now confront the question I raised before: If one admits that some changes are acceptable, how can one reject any changes? It is also worth repeating that there are clear answers to this question, for the fact that some changes are natural and necessary does not imply that all changes, regardless of time, intensity, and rate, are desirable. There are both natural and unnatural changes, and there are natural and unnatural rates of change. To recognize that melodies and themes are made up of changing tones does not imply that any noise is music. The key to a new but wise management of nature is to accept changes that are natural in kind and in frequency, to pick out the melodies from the noise. To understand these distinctions requires that we explore the origin and history of those beliefs that have so dominated our treatment of nature; only by doing so can we free ourselves from these myths and create a new mythology consistent with facts and science and appropriate for our time.

BACKGROUND TO CRISIS

The Creation of the Animals. Engraving by Charles Heath in *The Holy Bible* (London: White, Cochrane, and Co., 1815 [Courtesy of Library Special Collections, University of California, Santa Barbara]).

–5

Mountain Lions and Mule Deer: Nature as Divine Order

> Everything in the world is marvellously ordered by divine providence
> and wisdom for the safety and protection of us all. . . . Who cannot
> wonder at this harmony of things, at this symphony of nature which
> seems to will the well-being of the world?
>
> Cicero, *The Nature of the Gods* (44 B.C.)

An Orderly Universe

One of the themes that runs through twentieth-century ecology is the idea
of a highly ordered universe with several characteristics important to life:
the orderliness is itself extremely well suited to support life, and life forms
part of the ordered structure, with every species having its role in nature, a
necessary function as a part of the entity. The perception that the universe
is remarkably structured and ordered to support life was expressed in the
early part of the century in the book *The Fitness of the Environment* by
Lawrence Henderson.[1] As I mentioned briefly in Chapter 1, Henderson
reflected on the many ways the Earth has just the right characteristics to
support life. For example, he discussed the unusual qualities of water that
make life possible, including its excellent heat-storage capacity and the
high temperatures required to melt ice and boil water, both of which allow
water to act as a temperature stabilizer both in the environment and within
organisms. Water melts at a very high temperature in comparison with
other small compounds. Since the rate of chemical reactions increases
with rise in temperature, reactions can take place in water at rates sufficient
to support life as we know it. In contrast, other small compounds, such as
ammonia, melt at much lower temperatures ($-103°F$ for ammonia), and
chemical reactions would therefore take place extremely slowly in liquid
ammonia. Unlike most materials, water expands (i.e., is less dense) when it
freezes, so that solid water floats on liquid water, which has important
implications for life. Henderson recounted an old experiment that had

shown that if a vessel with ice at the bottom was filled with water, the water above the ice could be heated and boiled without melting the ice. If this were the case in nature, ice would gradually build up on the bottom of lakes and oceans until "eventually all or much of the body of water . . . would be turned to ice." Since liquid water is necessary to sustain living cells, to support the "meteorological" cycle, and to stabilize the temperature of the Earth, which, in turn, is important to life, then "no other known substance could be substituted for water as the material out of which oceans, lakes, and rivers are formed" or "as the substance which passes through the meteorological cycle, without radical sacrifice of some of the most vital features of existing conditions."[2] Water is the "universal solvent," able to maintain many chemicals in solution so that the complex chemical processes of life can take place. Simply analyze human urine, Henderson suggested, within which there may be eighty dissolved compounds, to see that water is a wonderfully perfect liquid to support life. Among the other remarkable life-support properties emphasized by Henderson are those of our planet, which is large enough to hold an atmosphere within which life can evolve and persist, is near enough to the sun to be warm but not too close to be too hot, and rotates on its axis so that one side does not become very hot while the other remains very cold. Henderson's book evokes an image of a universe of extraordinary order at every level, from the biochemical to the astronomical, beyond the likelihood of mere chance, and it leaves the reader with a puzzling contradiction: science was supposed to explain the world around us without recourse to purposefulness and religion, and yet an analysis of nineteenth- and early twentieth-century scientific discoveries, those available to Henderson at the time he wrote his book, implies that the character of our planet and of our universe seems too perfectly designed for life to have happened by chance. The universe appears to be an elegantly complex machine suited to life's needs.[3]

Order and Disorder on the Kaibab Plateau

The perception of nature as highly ordered has been common among scientists, naturalists, and conservationists in the twentieth century. Not only was the environment thought to be highly ordered, but species were perceived to interact in a highly ordered way. This orderliness was exemplified by the role of predators in nature, as revealed by a famous case in predator control. A rapid decline in mule deer on the Kaibab Plateau, whose edge forms part of the North Rim of the Grand Canyon, was the focus of a widely known controversy in American conservation during the first decades of the twentieth century. According to an account made famous by the great American conservationist Aldo Leopold, the decline was the result of an earlier irruption of the deer, during which these browsing animals had destroyed the trees and shrubs on which they fed and depended. Having destroyed much of their food, the deer starved and the population crashed. Leopold blamed the problem on "overcontrol" of the major predator of the deer, the North American mountain lion which had, he believed, kept the population of the deer in check, so that the two species had existed in a natural balance. This account of the Kaibab mule deer, first made famous by Leopold, was repeated in many standard ecology and wildlife-management textbooks and scientific papers, in which Leopold's account was accepted as true.[4]

The trouble began, Leopold wrote, around the turn of the century, which was a time of "predator control;" large predators were considered to pose a danger to domestic stock, and there was considerable hunting of mountain lions. From 1906 to 1931, hunters hired by the government killed an estimated 781 mountain lions, 30 wolves, 4,889 coyotes, and 554 bobcats on the Kaibab. One hunter, "Uncle Jim" Owens, claimed to have taken 600 lions himself between 1906 and 1918.[5] The small population of mule deer, estimated to have numbered 4,000 in 1904, was said to have increased rapidly after the removal of the lion.[6] By 1930, a population peak was reported, with estimates as high as 100,000. Then 50 percent of the herd was said to have starved to death during the two following winters, and the population suffered a decline to only 10,000 animals, according to some reports.

From Leopold's perspective, the lion, along with the wolf and other major predators, played an important and necessary role in the workings of nature. "The cow man who cleans his range of wolves does not realize that he is taking over the wolf's job of trimming the herd to fit the range," wrote Leopold in his famous and influential book A Sand County Almanac. "When wolves are removed from mountains the deer multiply," he continued, and "I have seen every edible bush and seedling browsed, first to anaemic desuetude, and then to death. . . . In the end, the bones of the hoped-for deer herd, dead of its own too-much, bleach with the bones of dead sage, or molder under the high-lined junipers."[7] In saying that predators are required in nature to regulate the abundance of their prey, Leopold was stating a belief common throughout the century in wildlife management and among conservationists and ecologists. These experts in general agreed with Leopold that in their undisturbed condition, the mountain lions and the deer lived in a natural balance, with the lions killing just enough deer to keep the population constant. Considerable policy had followed from this belief, including the National Park Service's attempt in the 1940s to introduce wolves onto Isle Royale in order to regulate the moose on that island, which were undergoing an irruption.

The facts of the Kaibab Plateau story were pieced together by Graeme Caughley (Figure 9), an Australian biologist who had studied patterns in populations of wild ungulates (the herbivorous, cud-chewing mammals, which include deer and cattle).[8] Leopold had based his analysis on a paper written by D. I. Rasmussen, another wildlife naturalist, who had given not one, but three sets of estimates of the size of the mule deer population: a forest supervisor's estimates that were made each year, but not by a quantitative method; observations of others who visited the Kaibab Plateau; and Rasmussen's own estimates.[9] These three sets of figures differed markedly from one another. Whereas one source estimated the peak abundance in the 1920s to be 100,000, others estimated the peak abundance to be 70,000, 60,000, 50,000 and 30,000. The last number was, in fact, simply that believed to be "sustainable" by most naturalists, meaning that the annual vegetation growth available on the plateau each year would be sufficient to sustain a population of 30,000 deer indefinitely. If the population had actually been 30,000, there would have been no irruption and no crash; the population would have been essentially constant.

And even if there had been an irruption, the role of predators was not clear. If it occurred, the growth of the population of Kaibab mule deer coincided with the reduction of the number of sheep and cattle on the plateau. As recently as 1889, there had been 200,000 sheep and 20,000 cattle grazing on the plateau, but there were only 5,000 sheep and few cattle by 1908. Thus the increase in the deer population might have been the result of a reduction in competition rather than a decrease in predation. Other experts suggested that the increase in the mule deer population may have resulted from changes in the frequency of fire and other disturbances or in the weather patterns, which increased the supply of edible vegetation.

Caughley analyzed all known cases of the introduction of large ungulates into new habitats, and found that a population irruption and crash had occurred every time, regardless of the presence or absence of predators. Following a severe disruption of a habitat, such as could have occurred under the grazing pressure of the cattle in the nineteenth century, the response of the deer could have been very similar to that experienced by ungulates following their introduction into a new habitat.

Thus an examination of the facts about counts of the number of animals leaves us up in the air. The famous "irruption" of mule deer on the Kaibab Plateau may or may not have occurred, and if it did occur the causes may

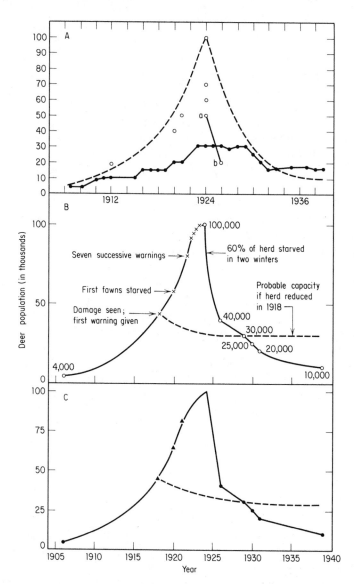

Figure 9. Evolution of the Kaibab deer herd eruption. A. Population estimate of the Kaibab deer herd, from Rasmussen[5]. Linked solid circles are the forest supervisor's estimates; circles give estimates of other persons, those labeled a and b being those of Mr. B. Swapp; and the dashed line is Rasmussen's own estimate of trend. B. A copy of Leopold's[4] interpretation of trend. C. A copy of trend given by Davis and Golley[8], after Allee et al.[4], after Leopold[4] from Rasmussen[5] (source: G. Caughley, "Eruption of ungulate populations, with emphasis on Himalayan Thar in New Zealand," *Ecology* 51[1970]: 54–55).

have been completely unrelated to the presence of predators. It is surprising that such careful and observant naturalists as Leopold, Rasmussen, and the others who examined the Kaibab history and to whom the study of nature was important would have accepted one explanation among many when the facts were so ambiguous. Many interpretations are possible, yet for many years, until the publication of Caughley's article in 1970, only one of the possible stories was accepted, a story that painted a clear picture of highly ordered nature within which even predators had an essential role.

The story of the mule deer on the Kaibab Plateau is only one of many from the first half of the twentieth century regarding the removal of predators, irruptions of prey, and the role of people in these processes. To proclaim that we do not have enough information to know if an irruption of mule deer was caused by the removal of the mountain lion, or even if the irruption occurred at all, is to speak against deep-seated beliefs about the necessity for the existence of predators as well as all other creatures on the Earth. For the role of predators in the balance of nature was regarded as only one, albeit outstanding, example of the incredible and wonderful order of nature, with each species having its place in the great working of the whole system.

In the context of this book, the justification for protection of predators is revealing because these animals are otherwise among those most disliked by people and most often considered as pests whose existence on the Earth has been viewed as undesirable. To argue that even they have a necessary role in nature, worthy of their conservation, is to argue from an extreme case, but the general context is the one that was seen at its most universal by Henderson.

Echoes of the Idea of Order

The explanation for the existence of predators, if unsupported by twentieth-century facts, had curious echoes in the past. Two centuries before Leopold, for example, Thomas Jefferson, who, among his many other interests, was intrigued by fossils and by natural history, gave the same justification for the necessity of predators as did Leopold. Jefferson wrote of a "benevolent persuasion that no link in the chain of creation will ever be suffered to perish." There is a reason for the comparative rarity of predators which Jefferson called the "ordinary economy of nature. . . . If lions and tygers multiplied as rabbits do, or eagles as pigeons, all other animal nature would have been long ago destroyed, and themselves would have been ultimately extinguished after eating out their pasture."[10]

Jefferson's statements, in turn, echoed ideas common in the eighteenth century. There are many writers one can quote. Among the most important was Thomas Derham, who wrote *Physico-Theology: or, a Demonstration of the Being and Attributes of GOD, from His Works of Creation.*[11] Derham's book discussed the discoveries by European explorers and naturalists of new species of animals and plants that had begun during the age of exploration and was continuing in his own time. First was the "discovery" of new lands—the Americas, Australia, the Pacific islands—followed by the increasing exploration of the wildlife of Africa and Asia. Derham's purpose was to explain the discoveries of natural history within a Christian context. He struggled with several issues, including the question: If there are so many kinds of creatures on the Earth and each kind has a great capacity for reproduction, what prevents the world from being overpopulated and falling into disorder?[12] "The whole surface of our globe can afford room and support only to such a number of all sorts of creatures," he wrote. These creatures could, by their "doubling, trebling, or any other multiplication of their kind," increase to the point that "they must starve, or devour another." That this did not occur, Derham took as evidence of divine order and purpose. The keeping of the balance of nature, he wrote, "is manifestly a work of the divine wisdom and providence." Order in nature is maintained because God gave creatures the longevity and reproductive capacity that are "proportional to their use in the world." Long-lived animals have a small rate of increase, and "by that means they do not over-stock the world," while those creatures that reproduce rapidly have "great use," as they are "food to man, or other animals."[13]

Derham tried to deal with the more difficult problem of why there should be, on an Earth made by a perfect God, vicious predators, such as the newly discovered Peruvian condor, which he called that "most pernicious of birds" and described as "a fowl of that magnitude, strength and appetite, as to seize not only on the sheep and the lesser cattle, but even the larger beasts, yea the very children, too." They were observed to be the rarest of animals, "being seldom seen, or only one, or a few in large countries; enough to keep up the species; but not to overcharge the world." He gave many other examples of predators, which in all cases were rare in comparison with their prey. Derham wrote that this was a "very remarkable act of the Divine providence, that useful creatures are produced in great plenty," while "creatures less useful, or by their voracity pernicious, have commonly fewer young, or do seldomer bring forth."

This, then, was the mechanism that maintained the "balance of the animal world," which is "throughout all ages, kept even." It is "by a curious harmony and a just proportion between the increase of all animals and the length of their lives, the world is through all ages well, but not over-stored."[14] This indeed was a divine order.

Although one of the more influential authorities of the time, Derham was not alone in his explanations, which were extended to many kinds of animals. Jacques-Henri Bernardin de Saint-Pierre wrote in the same century about the "noxious insects which prey upon our fruits, our corn, nay our persons." He regarded these unpleasant and undesirable events as the result of human activities, for "if snails, maybugs, caterpillars, and locusts, ravage our plains, it is because we destroy the birds of our grove which live upon them;" or, by introducing the trees of foreign countries into another "we have transported with them the eggs of those insects which they nourish, without importing, likewise, the birds of the same climate which destroy them." He believed that there is a natural balance within each country, which is upset by human actions; every country has birds "peculiar to itself, for the preservation of its plants."[15] Birds that feed on insects have their role in the divine order, just as do condors or lions, which feed on large mammals.

Derham's explanations, although presented in terms of the discoveries of his age, which forced a reconsideration of ancient issues, were merely a repetition of the argument given by earlier Christian writers, which, in turn, was the echo of the explanation by the philosophers of classical Greece and Rome. Derham restated what has become known as the "design argument." As C. J. Glacken described it,

> Living nature has been one of the important proofs used to demonstrate the existence of a creator and of a purposeful creation; in the pursuit of this proof there has been an intensification, a quickening, and a concentration of interest in the processes of nature itself. Proof of the existence of divine purpose involved consideration of the assumed orderliness of nature, and if this orderliness were granted, the way was open for a conception of nature as a balance and harmony to which all life was adapted.[16]

For the basis of this argument, Derham and other Christian writers relied most heavily on the ideas of four classical philosophers: Cicero, Seneca, Plato, and Xenophon.[17]

To the ancient question of the character of nature undisturbed, these theologians and philosophers had answered: a world of divine order, with its great chain of being. Again, there are many writers one can quote. Herodotus, for example, wrote in the first century B.C. that "timid animals which are a prey to others are all made to produce young abundantly, so that the species may not be entirely eaten up and lost," whereas the "savage and noxious" animals are "made very unfruitful."[18] While Derham and his contemporaries sought an explanation of nature in the universal purposes of the Christian God, Herodotus and the philosophers of his era had sought the same explanation in the universal purposes of their many gods. In the first half of the twentieth century, scientists, conservationists, and wildlife managers sought an answer to the same observations in universal laws of science; however, they arrived at a parallel explanation: nature is highly ordered, as illustrated by the existence of predators, which are necessary to regulate their prey.

Facts of nature other than the presence of predators are similarly explained from the assumption of a divine order. The writings of Cicero, who among the classical writers perhaps best summarizes many of these explanations, include the more general context. In *The Nature of the Gods*, Cicero wrote that there are "signs of purposive intelligence" in the anatomy and morphology of organisms.[19] The shape and form of animals and plants are miraculously well suited to their needs. Trees have bark to shield them from heat and cold. Animals have hides, fur, feathers, scales, and spines to protect and insulate them.

Similarly, the food habits of living creatures seemed to suggest a purpose behind the order in nature. Nature gave animals not only an appetite to seek the food that they need, but also senses to distinguish the right food and special structures to obtain it: "Some animals catch their food by running, some by crawling, others by flying or swimming. Some seize it with teeth and jaws, some snatch and hold it in their claws." Each has adaptations suited to its size: "Some are so small that they can easily pick it [their food] from the earth with their beaks," while the elephant "even has a trunk, as otherwise the size of his body would make it difficult for him to reach his food."

Evidence to support the ideas of order and purpose could be taken from the interactions among species, as in the way that one kind of organism captures another, or that two species cooperate. Cicero describes a shellfish that "by entering into an alliance with a small squill" obtains its food: "When a small fish swims inside the gaping shell, the squill with a bite signals it to close it. So two very different creatures combine to seek their food together." Sea frogs were said to cover themselves with sand and creep along the water's edge as bait for their prey. These adaptations were considered to be "marvelous," and many examples were repeated by the classical philosophers.

These observations of natural history—some more, some less accurate—suggest that the biological world is one of a marvelous order. "What power is it which preserves them all according to their kind?" Cicero asked. These ideas, so well summarized in the first century B.C., have been stated, restated, and argued about from the time of the early Greeks to the present day. In his dialogue *Timaeus*, which is often cited as a source of the design argument, Plato wrote that "nothing incomplete is beautiful" and that nature must be "the perfect image of the whole of which all animals—both individuals and species—are parts."[20] The arguments are sometimes justified on the basis of observations and sometimes on the basis of belief. Thus an argument can begin with a few observations that suggest balance, order, and perfection in the world, or from a belief that there *must* be such order, and if we can only study nature correctly we will discover it. Glacken has pointed out that there were three kinds of proof for the existence of a divine providence: (1) physiology and anatomy; for example, the eye is an amazing device to give human beings a way to view the world and thus to appreciate divine creation; (2) the cosmic order; and (3) the Earth as a fit environment for life, and the way that the Earth's creatures appear to have been given exactly those characteristics that they need to survive. Thus life and nature provided the basis for two of the three proofs. Aristotle, for example, argued that nature does nothing in vain. He made the comparison between a machine, which requires a person to make it, and the Earth, which is a divinely ordered entity that requires a divine creator. While Plato believed that nature is ordered and beautiful, Aristotle added the idea that nature was designed to meet humanity's needs. Similar ideas can be found in the Bible; for example, Psalm 104 suggests that God gave every creature its place in nature and order to the world.

Failure of the Divine Order

The assumption and the conclusion that there is and must be a divine order in nature leave a major question unanswered: If there must be such an order, how do we explain its absence? Two answers have been given to this question, both of which point the finger at ourselves. One answer claims that an imbalanced nature is the result of what we have done; the other claims that it is the result of what we have not done.

The first answer is that the absence of a balance of nature is not natural or God's will, but must be the result of human interference with this natural state of affairs. Although to environmentalists of the 1960s and 1970s this idea may have seemed new, it is quite ancient. Among the classical philosophers, for example, Pliny contrasted the beauty and bountifulness of the Earth without human interference with the imperfections of people who abused the Earth. He speculated that there was a purpose for wild animals that are hostile to humans. They were intended to be guardians of the Earth, protecting it from human actions.

Nature as the *"External Throne of the Divine Magnificence"*

The other major explanation of the failure of the divine order lay in a belief that human beings are the final cog in the machine to create the divine order. This is then interpreted as the purpose of people on the Earth, a purpose from which we have strayed when we either fail to do our job at all or incorrectly alter and thus destroy the divine order. As Alexander Pope put it in his "Essay on Man," the great chain of being extends from God to human beings to "Beast, bird, fish, insect, what no eye can see" and "From Nature's chain whatever link you strike, Tenth, or ten thousandth, breaks the chain alike."[21]

In the history of Western thought, nature has repeatedly been viewed as a wilderness in the worst sense, full of dangers and evils as well as lacking the symmetry, order, and therefore beauty of the domesticated landscape created by civilization. These ideas were given voice in the eighteenth century by Georges Leclerc, Comte de Buffon, in his *Natural History*, in which he wrote that although nature is the "external throne of the divine magnificence," people "among living beings" establish "order, subordination and harmony." Human beings are granted by God "dominion over every creature," and it is our role to add "embellishment, cultivation, extension and polish." It is man who "cuts down the thistle and the bramble, and he multiplies the vine and the rose."[22]

Nature without the proper action of human beings is not divinely ordered. Buffon describes the unpleasantness and the horror of nature undisturbed—that is, unhusbanded by human beings. "View those melancholy deserts where man has never resided," he admonishes. They are "overrun with briars, thorns, and trees which are deformed, broken and corrupted." Seeds are "choked and buried in the midst of rubbish and sterility." In wildness, nature has the appearance of "old age and decrepitude." Instead of the "beautiful verdure" of managed landscape, there is "nothing but a disordered mass of gross herbage, and of trees loaded with parasitical plants." The wetlands are a particularly awful example of nature undisturbed; they are "occupied with putrid and stagnating waters" and are impassable, useless, and "covered with stinking aquatic plants, serve only to nourish venomous insects, and to harbour impure animals." The unmanaged forests are equally unpleasant; they are "decayed," and in them "noxious herbs rise and choke the useful kinds." In savannas, there are "nothing but rude vegetables, hard prickly plants, so interlaced together, that they seem to have less hold of the earth than of each other, and which, by successively drying and shooting, form a coarse mat of several feet in thickness."

Human beings, forced to enter or live in such inhumane landscapes, experience horror and fear. Pursuing wild animals, a hunter is "obliged to watch perpetually lest he should fall victim to their rage, terrified by their occasional roarings, and even struck with the awful silence of those profound solitudes." Nature uncultivated is "hideous and languishing," and human beings alone can make it "agreeable and vivacious." Thus we must drain the marshes and transform the stagnant waters into canals and brooks. We should set fire to "those superannuated forests, which are already half consumed" and finish the clearing "by destroying with iron what could not be dissipated by fire." We are admonished to carry out our role in nature, just as every creature is meant to carry out its role.

Buffon's detailed description about a disagreeable wilderness is of interest to a twentieth-century naturalist, for it seems to contain merely the plants that grow in wetlands or in abandoned fields recently under cultivation or in pasture, rather than in the true forest wilderness that existed in Europe before any influence of civilization. For example, Buffon describes wild nature as having the thistle and bramble, "overrun with briars, thorns" which are generally characteristic of new woodlands that grow on comparatively open but abandoned fields, rather than of the dense shaded understory of old and undisturbed forests. Similarly, his description of "nothing but rude vegetables, hard prickly plants, so interlaced together . . . by successively drying and shooting, form a coarse mat of several feet in thickness," is reminiscent of abandoned agricultural fields or pastures within 10 or 20 years after their last use or of marshes, which are usually the last areas to be cleared for human occupation. Thus the "wilderness" of Buffon appears to have been simply the abandoned and poorest lands in an otherwise heavily domesticated landscape, not nature untrammeled by human beings, which is the meaning of wilderness in the twentieth century.

Whatever the reality of Buffon's surroundings, we find in his writings a repetition of a view of nature that predominated from the time of the classical Greeks through the Romans and to the nineteenth century— although there may be elements for order and balance in the biological world, the attainment of the order and its beauty requires the action of human beings to create symmetry and harmony. Cicero, for example, summarized this classical view of the human role in nature as "the protection of some animals and plants and indeed there are many which could not survive without human care."[23] Buffon's ideas can be also traced to the

Bible; Psalm 8, for example, says that God gave man "to have dominion over the works of thy hands."

Nature as Designed for People

From Plato, Aristotle, and others, the view developed that there is an order in nature and that there is a purpose behind the order. "Someone may ask 'But for whose sake has this mighty work of creation been undertaken?' " wrote Cicero. To assume it was for the trees and other plants would be "absurd, for though they are sustained by nature they are devoid of sense or feeling." Equally absurd would be to assume it was for nonhuman animals, for "it seems no more likely that the gods would have undertaken so great a labour for dumb creatures who have no understanding." And who then is left? "For whom then shall we say the world was made? Surely for those living creatures who are endowed with reason. . . . For reason is the highest attribute of all. We may therefore well believe that the world and everything in it has been created for the gods and for mankind."[24]

Not all the writers on nature believed this, of course. Perhaps the most famous, if not the first, of the classical philosophers to oppose the predominant view that the world was created for human beings (the design argument, as discussed by Glacken) was Lucretius, who wrote in *De Rerum Natura* that "this world of ours was not prepared for us by a god. Too much is wrong with it." Two-thirds of the world "that pair of thieves, fierce heat, insistent cold, have robbed men of," and of the rest, where human beings might live, "nature, as violent as either one, would occupy and homestead with fence of briar and bramble." Rather than life's necessities being given too easily to people, they must "groan as they heave the mattock" and "break the soil shoving the plow along," for without the plow "nothing at all could, of its own initiative, leap forth." Moreover, the vagaries of weather make it clear that the world was not made for people: "How many a time the produce of great agonies of toil burgeons and flourishes, and then the sun is much too hot and burns it to a crisp; or sudden cloudbursts, zero frosts, or winds of hurricane force are, all of them, destroyers." Also, if the world were made for people, why are there "the dreadful race of predatory beasts, man's enemies on sea and land?"

Indeed, the animals are better off than people; they grow without such care as we require, "they don't need rattles, they don't need the babbling baby-talk of doting nurses," nor do animals need clothes suited to each season or the protection of "weapons and walls" because for them "earth and nature, generous artificer, supply their every lack."[25]

From these ideas, Lucretius argued that if there is a purpose behind the order, and if there is an order, the goal of this purpose cannot be the well-being of human beings. In every century, there have been those who shared with Lucretius a skepticism about the perfection of nature, the design of nature, and the purpose for that design. But throughout the history of the West, one of the dominant themes about nature has been the belief that the universe, the solar system, and the Earth are incredibly well suited to the requirements of life, so well suited as to exceed the likelihood of mere chance. Throughout most of Western history, this belief led to another: that the design of the universe must be the result of some purpose and purposeful creation and is necessarily a realization of a divine order. In the twentieth century, these ideas became more complex, and the simple central belief in a divine order became obscured. Scientific observation was understood to deal only with what is, with the what and how of the universe, not with the why of metaphysics and religion. Scientists sought an understanding of the way in which the universe functions, an understanding of the rules that govern the phenomena that we observe. But ironically, the pursuit of these explanations brought Henderson, in *The Fitness of the Environment*, back to an ancient sense of wonder at the remarkable features of the Earth that are so peculiarly suited to the emergence, evolution, and continuation of life. Unable as a scientist—acting in his role as a scientist—to make the next step in the argument, Henderson merely wondered while Cicero had asserted that such an orderliness could not be the result of chance. But the sense of wonder at the orderliness of the universe has never disappeared from the ideas of Western civilization.

Although in the modern era and especially in the twentieth century, the role of science has been clearly differentiated from the roles of religion and metaphysics, the observations of modern science have reinforced the ancient idea of a wonderfully ordered universe and therefore the theme of nature as divine order. The belief in divine order carried with it a long history and therefore a kind of mental—intellectual and emotional—momentum. The powerful observations and theories of nineteenth-century science, which revealed amazing order in nature and suitability of the environment for life in realms never before known—the universal chemistry and physics of water, the size of and distance of our planet from the sun—were impelled by and, in turn, reinforced this momentum.

Reinforcing these powerful beliefs were the historical interpretations of biological nature—for example, the ancient explanation for the existence of predators in an otherwise perfect universe. These ancient ideas were repeated as though newly discovered in century after century, revived in the age of exploration and 200 years later in Derham's discussion of why a perfect God would have made that "most pernicious of birds," the Peruvian condor. Such explanations became codified in the twentieth century through eighteenth- and nineteenth-century mathematics, which seemed to explain and justify the beliefs. But, in fact, the equations had developed from the belief in a specific kind of order. It is perhaps ironic that the strong intentional separation of science from religion tended to obscure the underlying connections between them in the explanations about the character of biological nature. The idea of a divinely ordered universe that is perfectly structured for life has persisted, if often beneath the surface, influencing the development in an obscured way of the interpretations of environment, nature, and the role of human beings in nature in our own time.

In reviewing briefly the history of the idea of a divinely ordered universe and the scientific observations of order, it has not been my purpose to argue either for or against a religious interpretation of the character of nature, but merely to show the parallel and the historical connection between the ancient, religious, and metaphysical perspectives on nature and modern beliefs that have been accepted as scientific. This is a humanistic goal, necessary for us if we are to make wise use of nature and if we are to seek some kind of harmony with our surroundings in the future. What we learn from the mountain lion and the mule deer is about what we believed, not about what we know.

The interior of a volcano as drawn by Athanasius Kircher in his book, *Mundus Subterraneus*, published in 1665 (courtesy of the William Andrews Clark Memorial Library, University of California, Los Angeles).

—6

Earth a Fellow Creature: Organic Views of Nature

> Time does change the nature of the whole wide world; one state develops from another; not one thing is like itself forever, all things move, all things are nature's wanderers . . .
>
> Lucretius, *De Rerum Natura* (first century B.C.)[1]

> From Thales to Galileo, the world had been *animate*. It was permeated by mind, intelligent, alive. . . . The world and the universe lived as man lived; the world and even the universe, like man, was subject to decay and death. . . . With the death of an animate world and the breaking of the circles of the universe, old truths began to lose their force, gradually becoming the language of poets rather than of scientists.
>
> Marjorie H. Nicolson,
> *Mountain Gloom and Mountain Glory* (1959)[2]

Nature Within The Volcano

One of the first people to descend into the crater of an active volcano and return to write about it was Athanasius Kircher, a seventeenth-century Jesuit priest who later wrote a book, *Mundus Subterraneus*, that described what he had seen. Father Kircher descended into Mount Vesuvius in 1638 and then into Mount Aetna. Climbing to the summit of Vesuvius the night before he descended into it, he saw "a horrible combustion" and heard "horrible bellowings and roarings of the Mountain." There was "a stench of Sulphur and burning Bitumen," with "smoaks mixt with darkish globes of Fires." Descending into the volcano, he found underground passages with bodies of water and areas of fire, which together suggested to him a kind of order. "The underground world is a well fram'd House, with distinct Rooms, Cellars, and Store-houses, by great Art and Wisdom fitted together," he wrote, "not, as many think, a confused and jumbled heap or Chaos of things."[3]

Rather than explain the caverns and their fires and waters in terms of force, energy, and pressures that might have lifted water and rock, perhaps by an analogy with the internal belts and pulleys of a windmill or another machine—that is, in terms of principles of physics, as a modern geologist would do—Kircher began his explanation of what he had seen with a quote from Virgil, who had written that the "belching rocks" of volcanoes were the torn entrails of the mountains. Kircher believed that water and ashes were the food of the fires. Along with rain, hail, and snow, the fires were fed by "veins of the Sea." Fire and water thus "sweetly conspire in mutual service, and with an inviolable friendship and wedlock" mix together their "several and distinct private lodgings" for the "good of the whole."[4] "Out of ashes mixt with water, a new food and nourishment of everlasting fire is generated," he wrote. The water mixed with dust and ashes produced a continual "conception and birth" of fires. The fires then grew and matured and, becoming ripe, erupted. To Kircher the volcanoes were like a rose, nurtured of water and minerals, so that a seed could sprout, grow, mature, and burst into fiery bloom.[5]

In short, Father Kircher described the action of the volcanoes and the inner workings of the Earth in terms of organic, or biological, metaphors. In his drawing of the Earth, (reproduced at the beginning of this chapter) he pictured the planet as having a structure like that of a living creature or of a cell within such a creature. In his analysis of these subterranean phenomena, Kircher was a spokesman for the second major idea about nature that runs through the history of Western civilization: the organic view, that the Earth either is *like* a living creature or *is* a living creature.

What is the essence of the organic view? An idealized (that is, perfect) organism has certain attributes. It passes through the major life stages: birth, youth, maturation, maturity, reproduction, old age, senility, and death. An organism thus has a history; what it will be tomorrow depends on not only what it is today, but also what it was yesterday. An organism proceeds through its existence in a one-way direction, passing from stage to stage, each of which cannot be relived by the individual. The idealized organism in this sense is like a rose, which is first a bud, then a flower that is opening, a flower in full bloom, a fading flower, a fruit, and finally a new rose plant. A rose that lived forever would no longer be organic and would no longer have the same charm and beauty.

Such an idealized organism also has individuality—a personality, and thus idiosyncrasies, which are at the same time charming and trouble-some. An organism is subject to chance and has whimsical qualities; it is in some ways unpredictable, a creator of chance. Will this rose be beautiful? Will it live, or will it die prematurely? The uncertainty is an essential organic quality, adding to the rarity of other special individual qualities and thus to their value. Even an idealized organism lacks continuing perfection, since it eventually ages, dies, and decays. This process is natural, and gives organic entities individuality, charm, and attractiveness, enhanced perhaps by a touch of sadness at the fleeting nature of organic beauty.[6]

The Idea of a Living Earth

The idea that the Earth might be viewed as organic in this sense may seem quaint and strange to us in the twentieth century, but it has been one of the predominant views throughout human history—perhaps more common than the idea of divine order—and has a much longer history than our own scientific explanation of nature. The organic view has been traced back by archaeologists and anthropologists to early cultures, prescientific and non-Judeo-Christian. It can be found in many contemporary non-Western "primitive" societies. In the history of the West, the organic view was important in ancient Greek and Roman thought and in Judeo-Christian thought.[7] The organic view fit in with and helped justify the biblical stories of the change of the Earth, including the loss of the Garden of Eden and the Flood. Disorder and other aspects of the world, both physical and biological, that were hostile to people were the result of man's fall from grace. The physical chaos represented by mountains, oceans, and marshes, as well as the existence of fossils, were taken to be the direct result of the Flood and a consequence of the expulsion from the Garden of Eden. As late as the seventeenth century, Thomas Burnet, a contemporary of Kircher, wrote in his influential book on theology, *Telluria Theoria Sacra*, that the Earth before the Flood had been "smooth, regular and uniform; without Mountains, and without a Sea." Divine order, harmony, and balance were evident everywhere, so that

> the smoothness of the Earth made the Face of the Heavens so too; the Air was calm and serene; none of those tumultuary Motions and Conflicts of Vapours, which the Mountains and the Winds cause in ours; 'Twas suited to a golden Age, and to the first innocency of Nature.

The Flood created the "ruins of a broken world." Where there had been a "wide and endless plain, smooth as a calm sea" there was after the Flood "wild, vast, and undigested heaps of stone and earth," from which developed geographical variations, oceans, mountains, and even "stagnant fens and bogs."[8]

Burnet believed in a golden age like that described by the Greek and

Roman writers, and in an aging, thus organic, Earth. But Burnet also
argued that the discoveries of science concerning the history of the Earth
could be fitted into the older views and provided further revelations of
God's works. Thus from Burnet's seventeenth-century perspective, a belief
in the organic Earth was consistent both with explanations offered by the
new sciences and with the idea of a divine order. The wounded Earth had
slowly recovered to a certain extent by Burnet's time, in part, he argued,
because people had undertaken the husbandry of nature.[9]

The European Renaissance forced a reexamination of ideas about nature
and a renewal of the ancient controversy about the balance of nature.
Many developments forced this reexamination, including: discoveries of
new worlds—with their wildernesses, exotic and curious creatures, and
peoples living a stone age life; discoveries about the physical universe,
making clear that humanity is not at the center of the universe and that the
planets do not revolve around the sun in perfectly circular orbits; and
discoveries of geology, including fossils and the composition of the surface
of the Earth. A controversy arose: much of the new knowledge about
nature seemed to contradict the belief in a divinely ordered universe and a
balance of nature. How could these new observations be reconciled with
old beliefs? One solution was to return to the organic idea of nature, which
included a belief that the Earth had aged and, although perhaps perfect at
one time, was no longer so. Some scientific findings in the seventeenth
century seemed to reinforce the organic view. For example, Nicolaus
Steno, who was the first to recognize that the Earth's surface is made in
part of water-deposited sediments, which were laid down horizontally and
later made irregular by subterranean forces, wrote in 1671 that "all present
mountains did not exist from the beginning."[10] The metaphor of the Earth
like a living creature was sometimes taken quite literally, as in a poem of
the sixteenth century, *The Purple Island*, by Phineas Fletcher in which he
described the Earth's analogues of bones, heart, stomach, and all of its
bodily organs.

Such views can be traced back to the Greeks and Romans. Empedocles
thought that the sea was the sweat of the Earth. Lucretius, as mentioned in
Chapter 5, was the most famous opponent of the idea of divine order and
the most important proponent among the classical philosophers for the
organic idea. "In the beginning," Lucretius wrote, the "earth covered the
hills and all the plains with green, and flowering meadows shone in the
rich color." The Earth—that is, nature—had gone through stages in its
life, just as a person does. "When the earth and air were younger, more and
larger things came into being," and then the "earth was indeed prolific,
with fields profuse in teeming warmth and wet." The Earth "deserves her

name of Mother," because the rich fields were like wombs, the creatures were like embryos. There were "pores or ducts of Earth, channels from which a kind of milklike juice would issue, as a woman's breasts are filled with the sweet milk after her child is born." But the Earth had aged; "of parturition, Earth has given up like a worn-out old woman."[11] Change is recognized as inevitable, but as leading unavoidably only to decay and death.

The mortality of the Earth was evident in its erosion, with the soil washed away by heavy rains, and the riverbanks "shorn, gnawed by the currents." Erosion was regarded as part of a process of losses and gains: "For every benefit, requital must be given. Earth's our mother, also our common grave. And so you see Earth is receiving loss and gain forever."[12] Thus the mutability and decay of the Earth was recognized by the ancient philosophers. Furthermore, if the Earth was like man and man like the Earth, then one "had every reason to expect to find in the globe and in the cosmos exact analogies for the structure, functions, and processes of the human body."[13]

Analogies were made between the life history of human beings and other kinds of living things. For example, in *A Topographical Description of the Dominion of the United States*, Thomas Pownall wrote that trees in a forest "grow up, have their youth, their old age, and a period to their life, and die as we men do." A visit to a forest shows "many a sapling growing up, many an old tree tottering to its fall, and many fallen and rotting away, while they are succeeded by others of their kind, just as the race of man is."[14] In this way the Earth is kept vegetated just as people continue on the Earth.

New Technologies and An Aging Earth

The discovery of strange animals and plants and vast oceans and mountains in newly found areas of the Earth, as well as discoveries about life made possible by two new machines, the telescope and the microscope, forced a reconsideration of the theological arguments about the existence of God. Whereas in previous philosophical writings, the perfection of the Earth and the universe was taken as evidence that they were created by God—a perfect and infinite God could make only a perfect world—the mountains and oceans, with their fearsome irregularities became signs of the power of God. In the eighteenth century, Joseph Addison wrote in *Pleasures of the Imagination* that he saw in ocean storms an "agreeable horror" and that the power of the oceans "raises in my thoughts the idea of an Almighty Being and convinces me of his existence as much as a metaphysical demonstration."[15] With this, the proof for the existence of God had completely shifted from the demonstration of structural symmetry in nature to the demonstration of power in the (apparently) disorderly ocean storms.

In the seventeenth century, an organic idea of beauty also underwent a resurgence. In classical Greece and Rome, order, permanence, and regularity were beautiful; this view had predominated throughout the Christian era into the Renaissance. But at the end of the seventeenth century, ideas began to change. In 1690, Erasmus Warren wrote in *Geologia* that the present world, with its irregularities, was beautiful. Nature has asymmetries and "a wild variety," he wrote. "Without its irregularities, ruggedness and inequalities, the Earth would be not only less useful and less diverse but less comely." In a book first published in 1693, *The Folly and Unreasonableness of Atheism Demonstrated from the Origin and Frame of the World*, Richard Bentley wrote that "there is no universal reason that a figure by us called regular, which had equal sides and angles, is absolutely more beautiful than any irregular one." Sir Thomas Brown justified the ugliness of the toad, bear, and elephant on the grounds of their adaptation to their needs. Irregularity along with variation in time became beautiful.[16]

In the sixteenth-century poetry of Andrew Marvell, mountains are unjust, deformed, and ill-designed excrescences. By the late seventeenth century, mountains were perceived quite differently. For example, John Dennis, who traveled through the Alps in 1688, wrote that the mountains were a place where one experienced a "delightful horror" and "terrible joy." By the mid-eighteenth century a descriptive poetry had emerged that glorified the wildness of nature. James Thomson, for example, wrote in his poem, "The Seasons" of "Earth's universal face as one wild dazzling waste," which he viewed with "pleasing dread." Thus the irregular structure of the observable, biological world became beautiful.[17] The transition was not restricted to literary formalisms but included the actual appreciation of nature. In the eighteenth century, Addison, for example, admired Chinese gardens more than his own English gardens because the Chinese gardens were less artificially regular and appeared closer to nature.

In the nineteenth century, the organic perspective was celebrated in romantic poetry. The romantic perception was a shift from classical aesthetics—derived from the Greek and Romans and based on symmetry, balance, harmony, and structural order—to the aesthetics found most familiarly in the Romantic poets of the nineteenth century, but which was widespread. In part, the aesthetics of the nineteenth century can be seen as a reaction to the scientific age, a rejection of the machine-dominated world and to the mechanistic perceptions that accompanied the scientific advances of the eighteenth century, and in part as a result of the increased accessibility of remote regions, including rugged mountains, to more and more people, among whom were the poets themselves. Mountains became places where power dwelt in tranquillity, "remote, serene, and inaccessible," and a "secret strength of things Which governs thought," impressing the viewer of the scene with the power and infinity of God, in Wordsworth's poem "Mont Blanc." To Wordsworth, change and decay, lamented by earlier poets, are an inevitable part of the "enormous performances of Nature."[18]

But the nineteenth-century idea of beauty can also be regarded as an attempt to grapple with the deeper implications of the new sciences, primarily the idea that the world was held together not by structural symmetries, but by universal rules that from a religious point of view could be interpreted as evidence of the wisdom and power of God. In terms of an understanding of nature, the organic view was dismissed in the machine age. However, there is a strong theme of an organic aesthetic apparent in the Romantic poets, an aesthetic in some ways dependent on science, and in other ways dependent on the rejection of the sciences.

Underlying the shift from an argument that God must exist because his world looked perfectly ordered to the argument that God is evident in the power of natural forces is a shift from an explanation based simply on structural characteristics to an explanation based on processes and dynamic qualities. This is a key transition, which will come up again in later chapters.

Nature As Superorganisms

The organic viewpoint has not been important in the explanation of nature in the twentieth century, in contrast to the idea of a divine order. The closest one can find to this perception is in the ideas of F. E. Clements, a plant ecologist who was famous among his colleagues for his explanation of what he referred to as "plant associations." Clements worked in the first decades of the twentieth century, when plant ecologists were beginning to study major patterns in time and space of the major types of vegetation, such as: the oak–hickory–chestnut forests, which extended from Connecticut into the Appalachians; the maple–beech–northern hardwood forests, which were found in New England; and the boreal forests, the spruce–fir–birch–aspen forests of the north. Clements and his colleagues believed that each of these groups occurs under a certain range of climatic conditions; given the right climate, a particular kind of vegetation would be found. Analogous kinds of vegetation could be found worldwide: in North Amer-

ica, for example, desert plants were mainly of the cactus and yucca families; in Africa, plants that looked like cactus were members of the
Euphorbia family. In a specific kind of environment, plants evolve that are
similar in form—but to Clements not just single species. Whole "communities" of plants seemed to him to have evolved and adapted to the needs of
the climate.

From this perspective, Clements developed the idea of the plant
formation—a collection of species occurring together—as a "superorganism," arising, growing, maturing, reproducing, and dying. Its mature phase became known as the "climax" stage, and it had parents in prior
climax stages. Like other organisms, this "superorganism" could be an
object of scientific study. Clements thought that plant formations had an
evolutionary history, descending from a common ancestor. He imagined a
"panclimax," a "grouping of formations on different continents whose de-
scent from a common ancestor is indicated by possession of similar dominant growth forms."[19]

Clements's organic view of vegetation was rapidly challenged and by the
1940s had been completely dismissed in the United States, where it has
remained a historical curiosity, useful in explaining to students of ecology
why it is an inappropriate perception. The first challenges to Clements's
ideas occurred in the 1920s by botanists led by Leontii Ramensky of Russia
and Henry Gleason of the United States, who made two arguments against
Clements's idea of the superorganism:

1. Each species responds uniquely to environmental factors, and its
   distribution is determined solely by its relationship with the environment, not by its interaction with or dependence on other plant species; thus the co-occurrence of two species is simply an accident of
   similar adaptations, not a mutual dependency.
2. The type of species that dominates a landscape changes continuously
   in space; there are no sharp boundaries between communities. There
   is no inside and outside of a superorganism. If there are not sharp
   boundaries, then the superorganism cannot really exist.

Many studies done in the first half of the twentieth century concerned
the distribution of plants. They sought to determine if species are distributed in groups, as Clements's idea seemed to require, or if each species has
its own individual geographical pattern. Some of this research was carried
out as late as the 1950s by Robert H. Whittaker, John T. Curtis, and Robert
P. McIntosh, who showed that no two species that they studied had exactly
the same distribution. Whittaker put the superorganism idea to rest with
the statement that

species distributions cannot be "independent" in the sense that they are unaffected by competition and other interrelations. These interrelations, however, do not result in the organization of species into definite groups of associates. . . . species distributions are "individualistic" in the sense that each species is distributed according to its own way of relating to the range of total environmental circumstances, including effects of and interrelations with other species.

Thus "natural communities are not organisms."[20]

The key point here is the dismissal of Clements's ideas in the twentieth century; the organic view of nature, although one of the dominant perceptions throughout the history of Western ideas, was of minor importance and was vigorously dismissed when proposed in the scientific age. The organic view is incompatible with the perspective of the machine age. It seems clearly wrong and inadequate to us, which it is. However, the mechanistic view, which underlay the descriptions of animal populations and forest history discussed in earlier chapters, is also erroneous. It is my sense that 50 or 100 years from now, the simple mechanistic and simple organic perspectives will seem equally silly as explanations of nature. It is only our heritage of the machine age, the dominance of its metaphors, and the correspondence between the machine metaphor and the divine order that have made the mechanistic description seem so much more plausible to us than Kircher's idea of the marriage of fire and water or Clements's concept of a forest as a superorganism.

Suspended Power, painting by Charles Sheeler, 1939, oil on canvas, (courtesy of the Dallas Museum of Art).

_7

In Mill Hollow:
Nature as the Great Machine

Machines . . . machines . . . machines! This is the cry that, running
like a leitmotif through the modern world, echoes off along the highway of the future toward a goal that cannot be other than imagina-
tively foreseen.

Edward Alden Jewell (1927)[1]

Fixing Chase's Mill

Chase's Mill, on the outflow of Warren's Pond in East Alstead, New
Hampshire, is one of the few remaining working water-powered mills in
New England. An old-looking building with unpainted, weathered vertical
pine boards for siding, the mill stands on a site used for water power for
about two centuries. Rebuilt in 1917, the mill houses a turbine wheel, a
marvel of nineteenth-century engineering. Unlike the large picturesque
overshot or undershot wheels of romantic paintings, the turbine wheel is
quite small, occupying a space less than 3 feet in diameter. It is mounted
inside the mill rather than outside, in line with the flow of the water, just as
a jet-engine turbine is mounted in the flow of air passing the airplane.
Such turbine wheels are much more efficient than the older kinds, and had
a brief popularity. They were soon replaced by similar turbines connected
to electric generators.

The wheel is powered by water fed to it by a long flume about 18 inches
in diameter that starts at a small dam beside the mill. The flume goes
through the mill's basement and then drops vertically into a subbasement,
where the water enters the wheel. When the flume gate is opened, a rush
of water starts the turbine spinning, generating about 18 horsepower,
which is transferred by a spinning vertical shaft to the basement. In the
basement are a number of huge pulleys about 3 feet in diameter, mounted
on long horizontal metal shafts and connected to one another by leather
belts which transfer the power back and forth across the room—to the slap

slap slap of the leather belts, the whir of the pulleys, the rush of the water, and the rumble of the turbine, which vibrates the floor. Some belts transfer power upward once again to the main floor to run woodworking tools: a planer, a power saw, a joiner.

Heman Chase, whose family has owned the mill for 70 years, used to say that the mill basement—full of belts and pulleys—was the best place a young person could learn about machinery and the principles of physics and mechanics. That mill and its machinery were part of Chase's ideal of life, the nineteenth-century American village, almost completely self-sufficient, producing its own goods, generating its own power, growing its own food, and boasting a pond for recreation and water power. The village ideal is a self-sustaining and repairable, regenerating system, the whole community operating as smoothly as the mill.

One cold winter day, Heman and I worked to replace the flume, which, after 30 years of use, had rusted too badly to contain the water. Like other parts of the mill, the flume had been replaced before. On that morning, we moved in the last new galvanized pipe, and sealed and taped the sections together. The mill was as good as new, the machinery back together. The mill is a realization of the nineteenth-century mechanical ideal: parts that fit together and that are replaceable and readily comprehensible in their transfer of energy from flowing water to cutting tools. These are the qualities of the idealized machine, which never wears out; parts may age, but they can be replaced. On the day that I write this, I notice an article in which George M. Nelson, president of the Alyeska Pipeline Service Company, is quoted as saying that in some respects, the pipeline is "like an airplane, you keep rebuilding and replacing parts that need it, and the thing will go on forever."[2]

In addition, an idealized machine operates according to readily understood rules and laws of nature, in a way that is readily predictable. The machine exists in an idealized universe without chance. Thus it has no history: how it will be tomorrow can be predicted from how it is today; there is no need to know how it was yesterday, since that information is observable in its condition today.

The comforting aspects of a machine like Chase's Mill lie in its predictability, the capacity for repair, potential for indefinite continuation (as long as it is properly maintained) and timelessness. For these qualities, we give up individuality and the unpredictable charm of personality; in a sense, we also give up the notion of precious moments that characterize a living thing, moments that will never come again.

While machines cannot change themselves—they are not creative, they do not evolve—people can change them, improve them, re-engineer them. This too is comforting in one way; we are in control of the machine and can make it do what we want. So it was with Chase's Mill. The turbine mill had replaced a less efficient, although more picturesque, overshot wheel; it, in turn, became obsolete with the development of hydroelectric turbines. If a machine is not good enough or if a better one is invented, the old gives way to the new. At best, the old machine becomes a picturesque object and a hobby, an artifact to be displayed in a museum.

Chase's Mill may seem a bit of quaint history, but in the nineteenth century it was one of the modern advances of the age that had begun two centuries earlier with Kepler and Newton, with the rise of the new physics and the beginning of modern mechanical engineering. To us in the twentieth century, the mechanical view of the Earth seems an old and permanent one, but it is not. The mechanical Earth is an idea a few centuries old that has persisted far into the twentieth century. The mechanical view is consistent with the idea of a divine order in most of its particulars and consequences, and thus the mechanical perspective simultaneously reinforced the ideal of divine order and was reinforced by that theological perception. But the mechanical view of nature as it has been perceived in the past, and is still perceived by many, is antithetical to the organic view of nature.[3]

The Death of the Earth

A crucial philosophical change occurred in the seventeenth and eighteenth centuries when the perspectives of the new mechanical age replaced the organic view of nature. Marjorie Nicolson has called this transition the "death of the Earth,"[4] meaning that the Earth was no longer regarded as an animate creature, but as a vast machine. This change in perception was primarily a result of the new physics of Galileo, Kepler, and Newton, and new highly successful machines. Stars and planets moved like clockwork according to universal rules. The Earth itself obeyed these rules. To project its position and trajectory through space only its current state need be known. New machines made such discoveries possible: telescopes, improved clocks, machines with the same inherent qualities as the turbine wheel in Chase's Mill. The development of modern sciences, beginning with physics, led to a change in metaphors, but more profoundly to a change in explanation; from a belief in the Earth as an organism created by the Great Artist to a belief in the Earth as a magnificent machine invented by the Great Engineer.

With the new physics, beginning with Kepler's discovery that the orbits of the planets are not perfect circles and thus not ideal in a certain classical interpretation, but are explainable in terms of the beautiful symmetry of the laws of Newton, the "old truths began to lose their force, gradually becoming the language of poets rather than of scientists."[5] Descartes, in the *Principles of Philosophy*, provided a major turning point, departing completely from theories of divine creation and thus a divine origin of order to develop a theory from a basis in a *mechanistic* universe. Descartes and Newton built the foundation from which the organic idea was supplanted by the machine-age idea.

The wealth of new discoveries in physics and geology eventually overwhelmed the arguments that there was a perfect order in the observable architecture of the *physical* universe and the *physical* Earth. The awakening of interest in the natural surroundings made clear to some, particularly those students of the details of the landscape, that a varied, asymmetrical landscape was pleasing and that the new, strange creatures were fascinating to see. A new justification arose: instead of the existence of God being proved by the perfect balance in the world, the power of ocean storms and the awful perspective of the mountains were demonstrations of God's power and their purpose was to set people's thoughts onto this power of God.

The rise of the mechanical world view had several important consequences. First was the recognition of the power of the new laws of physics. Second was the rise of machines: the steam engine, the steam train, the paddlewheel boat, the sewing machine, the entire Industrial Revolution. The success of the machines and their ability to transform society and improve the standard of living reinforced the growing faith in the new sciences and the machine ideal.

Third, the mechanistic view offered a new kind of theological perspective. A perfectly working, idealized machine could be seen as the product of a perfect God. Thus we find the rise of the argument only too familiar to beginning students in philosophy, that the world is "like a watch" and not only is a perfect machine, but also must have a maker.

Fourth, a mechanistic explanation of nature on the Earth developed, including the Earth's geologic and biological processes. For example, George Wetherill and Charles Drake described "The Earth as a Machine" in a 1980 article in *Science*. "Looked at from the purely physical point of view, the earth has often been loosely described as a 'heat engine.' It is now clear that this is not simply a metaphor but that it is literally true."[6] This change in the perception of nature was accompanied and followed by greater and more precise observations of the Earth's geological and biological qualities.

A mechanistic "nature"—except in our own age, an oxymoron—would have the attributes of a well-oiled machine, including the capacity to keep operating, replaceable parts, and the ability to maintain a steady-state and thus to be in a balance, so that births and deaths, immigration and emigration, the input of sunlight and the loss of energy as heat, the uptake of nutrients and the loss of nutrients always happened in a way that maintained life in a constant state of abundance and activity.

A mechanistic "nature" can also be re-engineered by us; from this point of view, we can believe that we can tinker with nature and improve it, replace nature's equivalent of an overshot wheel with a turbine wheel. This is the other side of the coin of the mechanistic view, the side that has dominated much of our management of natural resources and the environment in the twentieth century. Not only has it been customary to use civil-engineering approaches to environmental issues, but it is consistent with the mechanistic perception of nature that, as a machine, nature is better improved by using novel engineering devices than by employing organic approaches. This point of view is consistent with much of our attitude toward the development of land and resources. As an example, a predominant approach to erosion control has been to use civil-engineering techniques, such as building concrete walls along steep slopes.

Ironically, those holding the most extreme positions in conservation and in economic development share a world view. The extremists among conservationists are known as preservationists. They believe that nature should be left completely alone, that the machinery of nature functions perfectly without human intervention. Some among them argue that even the scientific study of nature is an undesirable activity that is bound to affect and change nature. (Most conservationists believe in what is usually referred to as "wise use" of nature and natural resources, and among them there has been a wide range of opinions about how much people should interfere with natural mechanisms.) To both preservationists and engineers, nature is as malleable as heated iron. From the engineering perspective, this tractability is good and should be exploited; from the preservationist's perspective, it has allowed the abuse of nature. Operating from the same perspective, these two viewpoints gave rise to apparent conflict. But looking at it from outside the mechanistic paradigm, the contradiction appears more like a subtle difference in the assessment of our ability to successfully engineer that malleable and engineerable nature.

Finally, the idea of divine order declined from a "truth" to a metaphor, while the organic view, also reduced to a metaphor, was dismissed, no longer thought of as a serious notion.

A Mechanical View of Life

Seventeenth-Century Beginnings

The beginnings of the machine-age perspective on nature can be seen as early as the seventeenth century in *The Primitive Origination of Mankind*, in which Sir Matthew Hale wrote that the "Qualities of Natural things are so ordered, to keep always the great Wheel in circulation." That is, there is a reason to believe that, like clockwork gears, nature can be kept running and that the faith in this operation of nature lies in universal laws of science. In addition, the "vicissitudes of Generation and Corruption"— that is, the processes of birth and death—are "a standing Law in Nature fixed in things." Hale recognized the prime mover of nature and life as energy, the "influxes of the Heat" from the sun as well as "the mutual and restless Agitation of those two great Engins [sic] of Nature, Heat and Cold," which are the "great Instruments" maintaining the "Rotation and Circle of Generations and Corruptions, especially of Animals and Vegetables of all sorts."[7] Nature was beginning to appear as a machine driven by an engine of heat and sunlight.

The Growth of Science: Eighteenth-Century Advances

The discoveries and observations about the Earth's surface and the life on that surface reinforced the mechanical interpretation. In the geologic sciences, discoveries made it clear that the factors that had shaped the Earth's surface could be explained from an understanding of force, energy, power, and the laws of mechanics. The intellectual powerfulness of eighteenth-century physics could be, apparently, extended to explain how the mountains and valleys were formed, as with the explanation of how glaciers had altered the surface of the Earth in many places.

The climate during the past several centuries has fluctuated sufficiently to cause the mountain glaciers in the Alps to expand and contract repeatedly to a degree large enough to be apparent to long-term residents of the region.[8] No doubt, the Swiss inhabitants of the high Alpine valleys recognized long ago that the glaciers changed their shape and extension and that rocks not connected at one time to a glacier could have been deposited during a past extension of the ice. Large boulders composed of one kind of mineral are found on top of bedrock of a very different kind. Granite boulders, for example, rest on limestone bedrock in the Alps, and it would be apparent to a careful observer that these boulders must have been moved there by some large, external force. Some may have believed that they were placed there by pagan gods or were carried there by the waters of the biblical Flood, but others recognized a connection with the glaciers.

Nineteenth-Century

These observations, however ancient or recent they might have been, did not enter the intellectual thought of the West until the nineteenth century. For example, it was in that century that the idea of large-scale glaciation entered scientific discussions. The idea began in 1815 when a Swiss peasant, J. P. Peeraudin, suggested to a Swiss civil engineer, Ignaz Venetz-Sitten, that some of the features of the mountain valleys, including the boulders and soil debris, were due to glaciers that in a previous time had extended down the slopes beyond their present limits. Impressed with these observations, Venetz-Sitten spoke before a natural history society at Lucerne in 1821, and suggested that the glaciers had at some previous time extended considerably beyond their present range.

The famous geologist Louis Agassiz, who had traveled to the Alps to refute these ideas, had become so impressed with the correspondence between the glacial debris in the mountains and the topography he had seen at lower elevations that he formulated a theory of continental glaciation. It was soon recognized that glaciers had covered vast areas in Great Britain and North America. The theory of continental glaciation became generally accepted, although opposition to it appeared in the scientific literature until the very end of the nineteenth century. Thus in less than 3 decades, a mechanism had been suggested to explain local topographic features in the Alps and then extended as a widespread process that had occurred over large areas of the Earth. The presence of rocky fields was no longer viewed as the aging of Mother Earth, but as the result of mechanical processes with a universal character. Nature could be explained as a machine.

The mechanization of life was much more difficult to imagine than that of rocks and mountains, partially because of the great diversity of life forms. Alexander von Humboldt represents one of the major thinkers who, in the nineteenth century, attempted to confront the wealth of observations of life forms that had become available and to seek a general understanding of the order of nature. As he wrote in *The Cosmos*, his goal was "to combine all cosmical phenomena in one sole picture of nature," to find "great laws, by which individual phenomena are governed" so that he could "comprehend the plan of the universe—the order of nature," which must begin with "a generalization of particular facts, and a knowledge of the conditions under which physical changes regularly and periodically manifest themselves."[9] Humboldt was seeking to apply the scientific method to explain the diversity of biological nature.

Humboldt wrote about nature's capacity to achieve a steady-state more than a decade before George Perkins Marsh did. "We may easily comprehend how, on a given area, the individuals of one class of plants or animals may limit each other's numbers, and how, after the long continued contests and fluctuations engendered by the requirements of nourishments . . . a condition of equilibrium may have been at length established."[10]

Thus we arrive at the time of George Perkins Marsh, who, as I have mentioned, believed that nature has the ability to recover from any disturbance. As he wrote, nature has two key attributes. First, when "left undisturbed," nature "so fashions her territory as to give it almost unchanging permanence of form, outline, and proportion." Second, when disturbed, nature "sets herself at once to repair the superficial damage, and to restore, as nearly as practicable, the former aspect of her dominion." The net result is nature in a steady-state, at least in "countries untrodden by man," where all qualities, from "the proportions and relative positions of land and water, the atmospheric precipitation and evaporation, the thermometric mean, and the distribution of vegetable and animal life," are maintained in an almost perfect constancy, "subject to change only from geological influences so slow in their operation that the geographical conditions may be regarded as constant and immutable."[11]

This mechanization of the Earth and its life forms signaled a profound change in the perception of nature. The Earth must have seemed a friendlier place to those who viewed it as a fellow creature. No wonder we value whales all out of proportion to our contact with them or their importance to our own survival, for they represent, in the now-inanimate vastness of the oceans, a huge and benign entity, an almost humanlike presence, the gentle giant animating the immense and lonely oceans. If the rocks under our feet were yet alive and the ocean were Earth's blood, we might have less need to know the presence, beyond our horizon, of the leviathan.

Perfection Revised

The rise of the nineteenth-century scientific explanation of nature had two major effects: the rejection of the idea of an animate Earth and an organic concept of nature; and the refutation of the idea that the world is composed of perfect structural symmetries—physical symmetries—for example, that the Earth is a perfect sphere, or that the planets move in orbits that are perfect circles. As discussed in Chapter 6, the first effect led simply to an abandonment of the organic perspective. The result of the second is more subtle; the belief in aesthetically pleasing and theologically satisfying physical symmetries was replaced by a belief in an aesthetically pleasing and theologically satisfying conceptual order. While the belief in gross physical attributes of symmetry, balance, and order was no longer tenable following the new observations of nature, Newton's laws created a conceptual order. Subsequently, theologians used this conceptual order to justify their belief in a perfect world where a perfect order (the laws of nature) ruled our asymmetric and structurally imperfect world.

This point perhaps needs some explanation. An argument based on observation can make use of several kinds of evidence. The evidence may be structural (of form) or conceptual (of either processes or rules—that is, laws—that govern the workings of the universe). Structures, processes, and laws may each provide a kind of balance of nature. The search for this balance had begun with structure, then moved to processes and laws. This adds to the importance of Newton's *Principia*, for during a period in which an argument from structure was becoming more and more difficult to support in regard to the stars and planets, Newton offered evidence that order and proportion exist in universal principles or laws of motion.

For life, a structural balance is represented by a constancy in the number of organisms, and a balance based on processes is exemplified by such universal characteristics as birth and death rates. For example, in the seventeenth century, Sir Matthew Hale wrote of evidence of wisdom and purpose found in the structural balance of nature: "These Motions of Generations and Corruptions, and of the conducible thereunto, are so wisely and admirably ordered and contempered, and so continually managed and ordered by the wise Providence of the Rector of all things" that a balance is maintained, "things are kept in a certain due stay and equability." An equilibrium is evident, "a continual course, neither the excess of Generations does oppress, and over-charge the World, nor the defect thereof, or prevalence of Corruptions doth put a period to the *Species* of things."[12]

The distinction between a structural and a conceptual balance of nature is an important one, although it must be recognized that it is a distinction that we make looking backward and not an explicit one made by either the classical Greek and Roman philosophers or the Renaissance writers who borrowed so many of their ideas and their arguments from the classics. Explanations of a balance of nature based on processes become more and more important as one confronts the questions that particularly disturbed the Christian thinkers of the seventeenth and eighteenth centuries: How can there exist predators, or what they called pernicious and venomous creatures, if there is a perfect world made by a perfect God? The concern extended to geology and cosmology, to the form of the Earth and of the universe, which should be perfect also. Giving up of the belief in structural order, balance, and constancy in the cosmos and in geology was difficult, as illustrated by a classical question: How can a perfect world have mountains, which destroy the perfect proportions of the Earth? The classical answer, according to Marjorie Nicolson, was that given in the seventeenth century by Godfrey Goodman, bishop of Gloucester, who wrote that "the highest mountaines . . . carrie some proportion to the lowest bottome at Sea . . . that God might observe some kind of proportion." This idea that the heights of the mountains were balanced by the depths of the oceans, Nicolson wrote, was "very common in the seventeenth century and continued into the eighteenth."[13]

With this chapter, we have now come full circle in our story, explaining the origin and foundations of the mechanistic view of nature, which has dominated our own time. The modern dilemma can be understood as a conflict among three major explanations of nature: organic, divine order, and mechanical. The organic myth, long dominant in human history, has been abandoned in recent centuries, overwhelmed and replaced by the myths of a machine-nature. Nature has come to appear to us like the devices in the old mill in Alstead, New Hampshire. In the history of Western civilization, this perception of nature is as new as the mill's turbine wheel was a century ago. But like the industry of the machine age, which has so changed and dominated civilization, the machine idea has rapidly risen to dominate our perceptions of nature. But this idea has been reinforced by the much older and more deeply ingrained myth of divine order. Both the myth of divine order and the myth of machine-nature lead to similar conclusions about the character of nature and the possible roles of human beings in nature. From the points of view of both myths, nature undisturbed can function perfectly and beautifully. Both myths allow two possible interpretations of the role of human beings: either to complete the perfection of nature or to interfere in its perfect processes. While our technology has moved us rapidly past Chase's Mill, and while sciences have also moved beyond their insights of the nineteenth century, our perceptions of nature and the science of ecology, which attempts to explain and interpret nature, have lagged behind. Until the past decade ecology has remained a nineteenth-century science and has led us into failures in the management of natural resources and to unsettling contradictions in our beliefs about nature and therefore about ourselves.

III

EVOLVING IMAGES

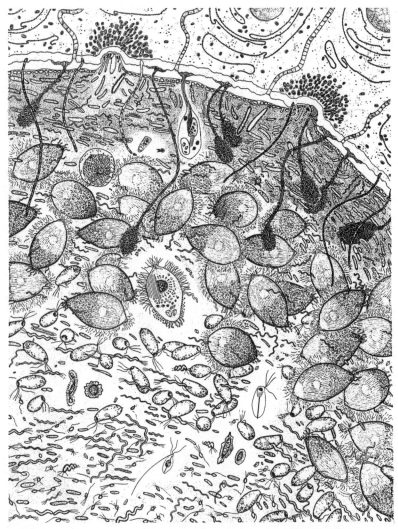

"Microbial Community of a Termite Hindgut," drawing by Christie Lyons, University of Massachusetts, Amherst (courtesy of the artist).

—8———————————

The Forest in the Computer:
New Metaphors for Nature

Nature has . . . some sort of arithmetical-geometrical coordinate system, because nature has all kinds of models. What we experience of
nature is in models, and all of nature's models are so beautiful.
Buckminster Fuller (1966)[1]

If we were to put our ear against the wall of the Sistine Chapel choir
[we would hear the music less accurately than] the entirely new perfor-
mance generated by machinery from the meticulous numerical score
of a digital recording.
Frederick Turner (1984)[2]

Bacteria as Computers

Bacteria, those tiny creatures that rarely enter our thoughts unless they are
making us ill, continually amaze scientists with their importance to all life,
with their capabilities, and with the vast differences between their lives and
ours. A change has taken place in the past decades in our perception of
these microscopic forms of life. On my desk are two books, an encyclopedia published in the early 1950s and a small book translated from the
French and innocuously titled A New Bacteriology. The encyclopedia
describes bacteria much the same way as Louis Pasteur must have viewed
them a century ago, as "minute unicellular organisms, usually classified as
plants . . . [they] range from c. 1/250,000 to 1/250 in. long; reproduce
chiefly by transverse fission."[3] The old description of bacteria seems simple
and straightforward: bacteria are tiny individuals, each cell acting indepen-
dently, obtaining resources, processing chemicals, giving off wastes, like
tiny machines. Sorin Sonea and Maurice Panisset, authors of the book on
bacteriology, see them entirely differently. They write that bacteria "form a
planetary entity of communicating and cooperating microbes, an entity
that, we think, is both genetically and functionally a true superorganism."

Bacterial cells are very different from the cells that compose our bodies. The bacteria, which are prokaryotes, lack a definite cell nucleus; their genetic material is scattered throughout the cell. All other living things, except viruses, have their genetic material neatly packaged in the cell nucleus, and they have other organelles, which are discrete units with specific functions. One type of bacterial cell passes genetic material to another which as Sonea and Panisset explain provides a kind of communication. According to them, bacteria are not so much single-celled individuals as a vast network of cells sharing a gene pool that "may be compared to the central data bank of a large electronic communications network."[4]

"Bacteria work in teams," according to Lynn Margulis. "They contain a *constant*, stable genetic system . . . but they function in the world by acquiring and exchanging a diverse set of variable genetic systems."[5] Bacteria are regarded as resembling nothing more than memory bytes in a computer that operates at the planetary level. Here is a radically different view of life from that which could have been stated before our time, either in machine-age ecology or in the prescience of Cicero and Aristotle. It is a description that could not have been made before the invention of computers, because the metaphors on which it is based did not exist. Sonea and Panisset recognize the originality of their definition of these organisms. "Bacteria are radically different from all other living creatures," they write, but everywhere else bacteria are "still described and discussed in nineteenth century terms."[6] As the contrasting descriptions of bacteria illustrate, technology is changing our perception of nature.

Computers are providing new metaphors not only for bacterial life, but also for our entire perception of life on the Earth, from the way that we regard bacteria to the way that we view ecosystems and our entire planetary life-support system. One key element of the computer metaphor is simultaneity, based on the computer as a network of memory units that can function together simultaneously, so that many tasks can be carried out at the same time or at least so rapidly that they seem to be occurring at the same time. Even older computers could print the results of one program while running another. New computers have true "parallel processing." Do you want to calculate the rate of growth of 100 bacterial populations? In a parallel-processing computer, 100 chips can carry out the calculations for all the populations at one time. In this and other ways, computers are revolutionizing our concept of nature, our perception of our relationship with nature, and our ideas about managing nature.

Mimicking Nature

In 1748, Peter Kalm, a Swedish botanist, arrived in Philadelphia, sent to
the New World by Linnaeus to collect plants that might be used to decorate
the gardens of Europe. One of the most articulate of the early natural-
history explorers of North America, Peter Kalm traveled through much of
what is now the northeast of the United States and the southeast of Canada. Linneanus honored Kalm for his work by naming the mountain laurel
(genus *Kalmia*) for him.

In his travels, Peter Kalm saw the primeval forest, which is so much a
part of our mythology about nature. He recognized that the forests were far
from uniform landscapes, as later naturalists have romanticized them. "I
was told, in several parts of America," he noted in his journal, "that the
storms or hurricanes sometimes pass over only a small part of the woods
and tear down the trees in it." This seemed confirmed to him when he
found "places in the forests where almost all the trees had crashed down,
and lay in one direction."

On his way to Montreal, Peter Kalm passed through virgin forests in
northern Vermont. "Almost every night," he wrote in his journal, "we
heard some trees crack and fall while we lay here in the wood, though the
air was so calm that not a leaf stirred." Knowing no reason for this, he
suggested that the dew loosened the roots of old trees at night or that
immense flocks of passenger pigeons settled on the branches unevenly.
Reading his account, one imagines him confronting the deep woods not
only with curiosity, but also with a sense of mystery and awe at the basic life
processes of birth, growth, and death in those uncivilized vastnesses.[7]

Peter Kalm was interested in explaining the cause of what he observed,
but he could only speculate, which he did, from our modern perspective,
very well. How much better can we deal with observations such as his to
explain cause and effect, or to make predictions about the fate of forests in
the future? Until recently, we could not do very much better. Throughout
most of the twentieth century, our scientific tools took us into the laboratory, where the anatomy of trees and their basic physiology became well
understood. But putting these details of knowledge together to create a
moving-picture show of an entire forest eluded scientists for most of the
twentieth century.

To understand the processes of birth, growth, death, and entire forest
regeneration, one must realize that trees compete at all times for essential
resources—light, water, minerals, and space. In any particular spot in a
forest, the tall trees shade smaller ones, silently suppressing their growth.

In this quiet competition, a tree "wins" by growing faster than and shading its neighbors before they shade it. No one species wins the competition everywhere all the time. As a result of untold years of competition and adaptation, different species have evolved to take advantage of different spatial and temporal conditions, and each species is best adapted to a specific range of environmental conditions. Some species are adapted to the conditions immediately following a catastrophic clearing, like those Peter Kalm observed. In northern New England where Peter Kalm walked, pin cherry is such a species. Its seeds are spread widely by birds and mammals that eat its fruit. The cherry seeds do not sprout in the deep forest shade, but wait until large trees fall. Then from some signal from the environment, all the cherry seeds sprout within a year after the clearing. If soil conditions are right, the seedlings grow and produce a dense stand of cherry trees that are close in age. The young trees grow rapidly, but live a short time. Such rapid growth and short life are typical of trees adapted to the early stages in the development of a forest.

Since the seedlings of pin cherry cannot survive in the shade of their parent trees, a stand of cherries is temporary in any location, slowly giving way to trees whose seedlings can persist in deep shade. In New England, sugar maple, beech, and red spruce are typical shade-tolerant trees. In contrast to the pioneer types, they tend to be slow-growing and long-lived. They are the dominant trees of old undisturbed forests, where Peter Kalm heard the old trees fall in the night. This process of change in the species of trees that dominate the landscape over time as a forest develops is an example of ecological succession, nature's melody of the forest played against the changing chords of storms and fires and short-term climatic changes, all of which are heard against the grander, ponderous themes of glaciation and soil changes. The process of forest succession is real, a pattern that is repeated over time. Once known, it can be remembered like a melody and replayed in our minds as long as the instruments, the species, remain the same. The idea of succession is important to our understanding of nature and our management of natural resources; a problem in our management of forests has arisen because we have incorrectly projected the hypothetical endpoint of succession, believing that nature's melody leads to one final chord that sounds forever.

Not only do the growth, reproduction, and death of trees respond to light intensity, moisture, temperature, and nutrients, but trees, in turn, strongly affect these environmental factors in a locality, and the survival of individual trees depends on their interactions with neighbors and on their species, size, age, or vigor. The interactions are complex, and it is difficult to predict their consequences among even a handful of species. In the past, an understanding of such consequences, when it existed at all, lay only in the minds of a few experienced naturalists.

One such naturalist was Murray Buell, a well-known professor at Rutgers University until his death in the 1970s, and my mentor in ecology. Every Wednesday morning Murray, his wife, Helen, and a friend John Small went for a walk in Hutcheson Forest, the sole remaining primeval stand of oak–hickory forests of the Atlantic coastal states. In the late 1960s, when I was a student of Murray's at Rutgers University, sometimes I went along too, and there were many other occasions when Murray and I would walk through the forests trying to understand the relationships among living things, and between living things and their environment in the woods.

Murray never lost his youthful enthusiasm for and curiosity about nature. One morning, we came upon a walnut tree in Hutcheson Forest, an unusual tree in those woods. "Now, Dan," Murray asked, as he had on many similar occasions, "why do you think that tree is growing here?" We talked for a while, deducing what we could—from the soil and the surrounding species of trees and the shape and form of the individual stems— about the history of the woods, whether it had been cut or plowed, when it had last been cleared, what the requirements for walnut trees might be. Big limbs low to the ground told us that some trees had once grown in an open area. A rough soil surface told us that the soil had never been plowed. By the time we left, I believed we had the answers. Walnut trees, which are uncommon in the area, are only moderately tolerant of shade. The old walnut before us must have sprouted when there was a small clearing in the woods, possibly created by the death and fall of a large old tree. Walnuts are uncommon because New Jersey is too cold for them to grow well, and they can survive only under the best of conditions. We talked about the kind of soil that best suits walnuts, and about other factors that might have limited or promoted this species. But there was no way we could prove to ourselves that we were right. We could not plant another walnut and wait 50 or 100 years to see if it survived and grew, what pests attacked it, and what other trees competed with it. We could not build mechanical trees that would mimic the natural forest and give us an answer about the validity of our insights into natural history.

At the same time I was working at Brookhaven National Laboratory in an experimental forest that was being subjected to radiation as part of a study of the possible environmental effects of nuclear war. Brookhaven is a high-tech place, and its forest was scrutinized with the most advanced devices available, including the first digital-recording system ever used to collect information about a forest. This system recorded observations about the forest in a format that could be read directly by a computer and thus be processed rapidly and efficiently. This system was itself a precursor to a computer, but it was also an early transitional device and in many ways familiarly mechanical. It had been jury-rigged at the laboratory from big surplus telephone-system relays and stepping switches that made loud clicking noises. Standing in front of these devices it was easy to see the parts move and to understand how the mechanisms operated. The data were recorded as a series of holes punched on paper tape, and the trailer in the woods where the whole machine stood was filled with a rat-a-tat-a-tat of the mechanical paper punch, and the floor was covered with the circles of paper from punched holes. At the end of a day the paper tape was taken to a computer, which attempted, sometimes successfully, to read the data.

Computer programming was quite new to biologists, and not many ecologists had tried it. But it occurred to me that Murray and I might have found a way to test what we believed by writing down what we knew about forests in computer code and seeing if our explanations could produce an imaginary "forest" that would grow and change over time, just like a real one. A few years later, I began to work with Jim Wallis, a hydrologist, and Jim Janak, a theoretical physicist, to develop a computer program to mimic forest growth. In computer code, we wrote down what we believed happens between the environment and trees in a forest: how the growth of a tree changes with the amount of light it receives; how this amount of light changes with the size and number of competing trees nearby; how the growth changes with the amount of water in the soil; and so forth. Each idea could be written down mathematically because of the long history of laboratory study of trees that provided mountains of quantitative information about tree growth and reproduction.

The development of the computer model of a forest went through several stages. We talked for days and then set down the ideas about forest growth based on our assumptions and knowledge. This produced a "conceptual" model—a model of ideas, not of quantities—that was translated into a set of mathematical equations, which, in turn, were translated into a computer code. We first wrote a program that grew a single tree, then elaborated the program to grow a group of trees competing with one another under a fixed environment, and finally added more complexity so that the program grew a forest under changing environments.

Since then, the computer program has been shown to mimic forests quite well. It simulates ecological succession accurately and realistically; its projections about the characteristics of a very old undisturbed forest match early surveyors' descriptions of forests in New England, including some observations that were not widely known or widely accepted among modern ecologists. For example, the program predicted that a very old forest in New Hampshire would have many more spruce trees at low elevations than are found today in the White Mountains National Forest, and more than foresters and ecologists believe would grow. However, all of this forest, with the exception of a few very small areas, had been clear-cut at some time since European settlement. It was a common belief that the woodlands that had regrown had recovered to the point that they closely resembled the original forests. But I found reports of measurements made in the uncut forests at the turn of the century that show that spruce had been more common than it is in the present-day younger forests, just as the model predicted.

The program even reproduced qualities about forests that I did not know. David Smith of the Yale Forestry School, the author of a standard book on silviculture, agreed to test the model by asking me to make it grow any kind of forest stand he wished. He suggested that we grow a forest for 50 years at an elevation of 2,500 feet in New Hampshire and then cut all the trees larger than 5 inches in diameter. The computer did this. It projected that the result would not be a catastrophic clearing. Forest growth continued, but only of those species found in mature stands; the imaginary forest was not opened up enough to allow the pioneer trees to grow. Exactly right, Smith said; it was new to me, however.

In the almost two decades since its inception, this model has been tested widely for forests around the world, and is now used by many scientists as part of their work, from Sweden to New Zealand, and from tropical forests to the most northerly forests of Canada. We continue to work with it and improve it, as it continues to relentlessly confront us with the consequences of our assumptions. Over the years, it and we have become more accurate in our projections. [8]

Computer simulation was getting started in many fields in the 1960s, but unlike our forest model many of the approaches were borrowed from engineering, especially engineering methods called systems analysis. These early computer models, unlike our forest model, were based on the assumption that any system under study has a steady-state condition and tends to seek that condition—one of constancy and stability, like that of a well-made mechanical device. In addition, the systems-analysis models assumed that the processes and the steady-state could be described in simple mechanical terms. Thus they were simply reassertions of the older mechanistic view, and they did not mimic nature well.

People generally have a peculiar perception of computers and computer models, believing in the power of computers either too much or too little. We have to accept these models for what they really are. They are, in one sense, an exact and unyielding demonstration of the implications of one's assumptions about how nature works—in my case, the demonstration of the assumptions and perceptions that Murray Buell and I shared when we stood before the old walnut tree in Hutcheson Forest. Assumptions have a tendency to slowly bury themselves in our unconscious, becoming in effect myths; the computer relentlessly confronts us with these assumptions and their implications. When we make nature act like a machine in a computer program, it does so exactly and the results are quite unnatural; when we follow the knowledge and long experience of an ecologist like Murray Buell's, add to it information gained in laboratory studies of photosynthesis and the growth of trees done by many scientists, and then translate these data carefully into computer code, the model works. As G. E. Yule observed 70 years ago, "If you get on the wrong track with the Mathematics for your guide, the only result is that you do not realize where you are and it may be hard to unbeguile you." You have to be on the right track for logic and mathematics to be useful. "To find the right track you must exercise faculties quite other than the logical— Observation, and Fancy, and Imagination: accurate observation, riotous fancy, and precise imagination."[9]

Such models help us avoid two traps of the past that I have emphasized repeatedly in this book: continuing to believe in myths about nature even when they are clearly contradicted by facts, and believing two contradictory ideas about nature at the same time (such as nature is constant and nature is not constant). At the practical level, these models help us synthesize what is too complex for our minds to combine working alone.

The computer model of forests is an illustration of the second way that computers are changing our perception of nature. By allowing us to mimic nature realistically, computers let us return to the intricacies of natural history in our scientific explanations, in our theories, in our tools for making projections, and thus in our management of forests and other resources. In the past two decades, a revolution has taken place in computer simulation, which is now becoming commonplace. Farmers, for example, can use a computer simulation of crop growth that takes into account the current weather patterns and the farmers' past activities and that suggests when they should plant, irrigate, and fertilize. Knowing that bacteria act like data banks and that we can mimic a forest in a computer, we no longer need deny the complexities of nature in our theories and ideas.

Prediction and the Balance of Nature

At dusk one summer in the 1970s, far away from the hum of computers, a pack of wolves began howling near our camp at Washington Harbor on Isle Royale. There is something eerie and fascinating in the calls of the wolves, which begins with the howling of a single adult that is soon joined by its packmates. The sounds build to a crescendo, and at times the wolves call in minor thirds; the result is almost musical, and the calls are always evocative, threatening yet fascinating, primeval, and wild. With the day's field work done, we decided to take advantage of the chance of the moment and follow the calls to try to get a view of the wolves, and as the darkness fell we set off along one of the trails that led back into the forest. We took flashlights along which we used only occasionally; under these conditions their brightly focused beams only blinded us and we made our way much more easily by the dim light of the moon. We hiked a mile or so, up and down, past dense stands of trees familiar to us during the day, across a stream, and finally up a small ridge on which we stood and waited and listened. We knew that we could not predict exactly where the wolves would go or determine very precisely from the calls just where the wolves were. Chance and uncertainty were inherent in our choices and in our understanding of the behavior of the wolves in the wilderness. But that unpredictability added interest to the night. We did not find the wolves, but standing on the ridge in the darkness and listening to the fading sound of the calls, we enjoyed a deep sense of the wild that rewarded us as much as a view of the wolves.

Our failure to find the wolves was the result of two kinds of limitations on our ability to predict where the wolves would go next: our lack of knowledge about the wolves, and just plain luck. Additional knowledge might have helped us in many ways. The call of the wolves penetrated the forest but did not give us a very good idea of the direction of origin of the sound. An instrument that could have improved our ability to detect the location of the sound—to observe nature more accurately—would have increased the likelihood of our predicting the next steps of the wolves and then finding them. A better understanding of wolf behavior, such as how wolves move through the forests, would have also helped. But our ability to reason about the behavior of the wolves and to understand causes and effects was limited. It was possible that more studies of wolves could have led to a computer model of wolf behavior from which we might have made more accurate projections of their location. But no such models existed, and if they had they could have been operated only in a windowless air-conditioned room, of little help to us as we walked in the darkness. As I said, there was also luck, the chance that we and the wolves might have crossed paths without planning on our part. My colleague Peter Jordan, who had worked on the island for years, had had that kind of luck just once, when he met a wolf crossing a trail in the middle of the day. Such luck was not with us that night.

It is an old philosophical question whether luck, as I have just described it, really exists—whether chance or randomness is inherent in nature, or whether there is merely an appearance of chance that results from our incomplete knowledge of causes. Here the key issue is prediction, which is at the heart of science and of the way we can deal wisely with our surroundings. The idea of the predictability of nature will remind some readers of the famous doctrine of the eighteenth-century astronomer and mathematician Laplace: if a mind were as large as God's and were supplied with exact information about the position and velocity of every particle in the universe, then all future states of the universe could be predicted exactly. From Laplace's perspective, the human sense that things happen at random is simply a consequence of our ignorance of the state of the universe and the limitations of our reasoning capacities—the result of uncertainty. Laplace and the wolves confront us with two fundamentally different concepts of the nature of reality: that chance arises simply from ignorance, and that chance arises from truly inherent randomness in nature. To Laplace, our failure to find the wolves at night on Isle Royale was simply the result of our lack of knowledge about them and the rest of the wilderness. Similarly, our inability to predict the life and death of trees in a forest accurately would be solely the result of our imperfect knowledge and limits on our ability to use it. Computer models, by enabling us to make better use of our knowledge, help reduce Laplace's kind of uncertainty. In a nature with inherent randomness, which is referred to as a nature with "risk," the probability of an event may have specific causes and be well determined. When this is so, the chances of things happening can be calculated rather accurately and computers can help us with the calculations.

Most who have thought and written about nature throughout the history of the West have accepted implicitly or explicitly Laplace's point of view, rejecting the possibility of inherent randomness in nature. The classical nature of divine order and the nature of the machine age were not at all like seeking to find a pack of wolves at night on Isle Royale. Classical and machine-age nature was reliable, predictable, and comfortable—although not exciting; everything was in its place, and every future event was exactly calculable. This classical myth created a world of brightness and seeming clarity, which was in fact a faint shadow that had little correspondence to real nature. Beyond, in the wilderness, where the bramble and not the rose grew, where the wolves called in the night, there was the reality of another nature—of movement and sound, an unknown world that only seemed to be unknowable, a nature that to some degree involved chance and thus seemed without cause, unpredictable, and unreliable. But this nature is predictable in its own way, which is intrinsically different from what we used to think and requires a change in our fundamental ideas about nature.

A world that is like a watch not only operates smoothly and is stable in the classical sense, but also is absolutely and completely predictable. When we watch the gears moving inside an old-fashioned grandfather clock, we can see which gear teeth will mesh next, and we can view immediately the realization of this small prediction. The gears are moving according to inexorable laws of physics. This is called a deterministic process; the status of the clock at any time in the future can be predicted exactly from present conditions, as long as the clock keeps operating.

Certainty and predictability are complex ideas in themselves. In the old adage "Nothing is certain but death and taxes," the certainty of each is quite different. Taxes are a deterministic certainty; both the event and its time of occurrence are certain: every April 15, U. S. federal income taxes are due. Death, on the contrary, is a stochastic certainty: the event is certain, but the time of its occurrence is not. Death in this sense involves risk; taxes do not. Philosophers may argue whether each death is ultimately the result of myriad deterministic causes at an ultimate level. But to each of us, at the level that we observe ourselves and our surroundings, and to each of our fellow creatures, at the level that they sense and respond to their surroundings, there is no way to distinguish the timing of that final event from the result of a series of chances. So it was with our attempt to find the wolves at Isle Royale, and their effort to avoid us. The rustling of the wind in a branch might have disturbed either of us and changed our speed or direction. For the trees whose growth I had sought to mimic with a computer model, that same wind might have affected the fertilization of a tree's flower or the direction in which a seed fell to the ground.

The argument between determinism and chance, which has begun to appear in ecology, is familiar to physicists. Whether chance is an essential quality of the universe has been the focus of intense controversies in twentieth-century science, especially among the physicists of the 1920s. This controversy led Albert Einstein to make one of his famous statements, "I shall never believe that God plays dice with the world."[10] Einstein could not accept the idea that the universe functions fundamentally from a set of probabilities. Other physicists had found that events involving fundamental particles can be explained by assuming that there are chance events—events that occur with a certain probability. Werner Heisenberg deduced what has become known as the uncertainty principle: that the position and velocity of a particle cannot be simultaneously determined. Although either can be measured to any degree of precision, the more accurately one is measured the less accurately the other will be known. Although where a particle would be and how fast it would be going could not be predicted with exact certainty, a probability of the occurrence of an event could be written down. The profound philosophical arguments that arose from the development of quantum theory in the 1920s opened up the possibility of a very different perception of the physical universe: the universe as fundamentally stochastic to some degree. With this as a background, it may be easier for us to accept the idea of chance in our perception of biological nature. Because of the ease with which computer programs can be made to mimic chance events, computers reinforce this metaphor and offer in themselves a new basis for the metaphor of nature as a set of probabilities.[11]

The philosophical issues are more difficult for the physicists than for ecologists. In the forests of Isle Royale, infrequent severe storms are an important cause of the death of trees. From a tree's point of view, if one can use that expression, the occurrence of such a storm is unpredictable. The effect of the storm on the tree's survival and on the evolution and adaptation of trees in a forest is a result of events that cannot be distinguished, at the level of perception and response open to trees and other living things, from a truly probabilistic event. One can argue whether the processes that lead to the development of a major storm are at an ultimate level deterministic or stochastic—whether they are like a clock or like dice. But these events occur at a rate and timing which, from the capacities of wolves and trees to detect their surroundings, are indistinguishable from probabilistic events. At the level at which organisms respond to and affect their environment, the world is one of risk, predictable only to probabilities. Nature as perceived by living things is a nature of chance.[12]

Although scientists generally rejected the idea that nature at the level perceived by trees and wolves might play dice, rapid advances in our understanding have been taking place in recent decades—for example, in the late 1970s, findings in geology hinted that randomness might be inherent in nature. New techniques allowed the reconstruction of the Earth's climate for incredibly long periods. It became possible to estimate the total amount of ice that had existed in glaciers, and ice volume is an index of how cold or warm the climate is. These histories of ice volume were subjected to statistical analyses. About one-quarter of the variation in climate for the past 700,000 years could be explained by changes in the direction of tilt of the Earth toward the sun, but the rest could be accounted for only by random variations, referred to as "red noise." Nature seemed to be throwing climatic dice.[13]

The Erratic History of the Whooping Cranes

In regard to living things, the problems posed by the threatened extinction of endangered species required a consideration of risks and probabilities. The whooping crane, the tallest bird in North America, once lived throughout most of the continent. Hunted, subjected to disruption of its habitat by land development, and extremely shy of people, the crane retreated with European colonization of North America. By the mid-nineteenth century, there were perhaps somewhat more than 1,000 remaining. But the population declined rapidly, and by the turn of the twentieth century no more than 100 cranes were left. Although the whooping crane, along with other birds, came under the protection of the Migratory Bird Treaty (1916) between the United States and Canada, the crane population continued to decline and it seemed to be vanishing. Where the remaining cranes nested in the summer or fed in the winter was a mystery.[14]

Things began to look up for the crane in the late 1930s. The last wintering grounds of the bird were discovered in the Blackjack Peninsula of Texas. In 1937, the Aransas National Wildlife Refuge was established there, and an annual count of the entire population which distinguished the number of adults and newborn, was begun. This practice has continued ever since, providing a unique population history. The breeding ground remained a mystery for about 20 more years. In 1955 the last nesting area for this bird was found in Wood Buffalo Park, Northwest Territories, Canada, an area east of the Canadian Rockies in remote wetlands.

The fate of the whooping crane seemed to hang in the balance for many years. The population declined to 10 adults and 4 young in 1938. But then a slow recovery began that has continued for the past 50 years. An interesting aspect of this slow recovery is its erratic pattern; the population rose to 26 individuals in 1940, fell back to 15 in 1941, rose to 34 in 1949, fell back to 21 in 1952, and so on (Figure 10).

With these rises and falls of the whooping crane population over the years, the question naturally arose about the birds' chances of extinction. In the early 1970s, Roy Mendelssohn, Richard S. Miller, and I analyzed the history of the whooping crane population and estimated this risk. The existence of a complete census of adults and young compiled over more than 30 years made this analysis possible. Instead of viewing the population

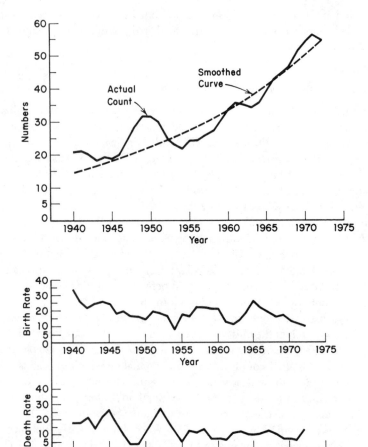

Figure 10. The history of the whooping crane population from its low of 14 individuals in 1938 to more than 50 by the 1970s. The top graph shows a 3-year moving average of the population (the solid line) and a smoothed curve (the dotted line). The lower graphs show birth rates and death rates (source: R. S. Miller, D. B. Botkin, and R. Mendelssohn, "The whooping crane [Grus americana] population of North America," *Biol. Conservation* 6 [1974]: 106–11).

pattern as a classical deterministic growth curve—the exponential or logistic—we viewed it as exhibiting true randomness, known formally as a "linear stochastic birth–death process." With this approach, we could calculate the chance that this erratically upward-trending curve might wander downward to zero—one way to calculate a probability of extinction. Our calculation showed that the chance was amazingly small. Given the population of 51 birds in 1972, the calculated chance that the curve would drift downward to zero by 1992 was only 5 in 1 billion. To my knowledge, this was the first such calculation. This calculation was made with very specific and demanding assumptions, however. The critical assumption was that causes of variation in the previous 30 years would continue into the future and be the only causes of variation. In reality, one good sharpshooter could have eliminated the entire species, or the introduction of a new disease or another new kind of catastrophe in the summering or wintering grounds could have resulted in the birds' extinction. However, contrary to the assumption of the fragility of such small populations, the whooping crane seemed to have almost no chance of extinction unless faced with a new catastrophe, and in fact the species has continued to increase, reaching 170 individuals in the mid 1980s. The kind of analysis done for the crane is different from those done earlier in the century, and illustrates a part of the change in perspective on populations—from a perception of populations as following exact, mechanistic patterns to an acceptance of the essentially stochastic quality of population change over time. Acceptance of this idea allowed the calculation of the chance of extinction. The acceptance of such erratic, random qualities has become more common in the study of populations in the past decade and is an example of one of the transitions that is at the heart of this book, a transition that can lead us to an acceptance of the discordant harmony of nature.

Randomness and Aesthetics of Nature

Nature that is inherently risky may seem less beautiful than nature that is completely deterministic. Superficially, nature characterized by probabilities seems to be less likely to be in balance; random events might throw the otherwise balanced system out of whack for no "purpose" or "reason" except the very probabilities that govern the events. In contrast, nature without chance seems of necessity to be readily predictable. Perhaps there may be some comfort in knowing that, curiously, even completely deterministic populations can appear unpredictable. For example, mathematicians S. A. Woodin and James Yorke showed that there is an equation expressing changes in populations that involves no chance events at all, but for which the future size of the populations cannot be calculated for all times in the future simply from current conditions. Instead, the future size must be calculated step by step from one time period to the next; beyond that, there is an appearance of unpredictability. This is unlike a clockwork mechanism whose position at any time in the future can be predicted exactly from its present position. Robert May, a mathematical ecologist, used this equation as the basis of a discussion of predictability and chaos in populations.[15]

For nature that involves risk, there are three possibilities in regard to prediction, two of which lead to a well-defined kind of predictability: probabilities that are constant over time, such as those determining how dice will fall; probabilities that change over time in response to environmental conditions and are therefore predictable to some range; and probabilities that change in a random fashion and would lead to a chaotic nature from the point of view of living things. When the chances of birth and death remain constant over time, a population of trees, for example, will eventually achieve a constancy of numbers, although the fate of any individual remains subject to chance. After a very long time in such a forest, the relative importance of different species of trees would become fixed even though the location of individuals of any one species could not be predicted exactly. When the probabilities of birth and death change over time, the outcome is more complex. If the changes are direct responses to environmental and biological conditions, then it is possible to project what will happen, but the projections are generally too difficult to make with pencil-and-paper mathematics. For example, the chances that a seed will germinate may increase as the rainfall increases and the sunlight increases and as the abundance of animals that spread the seeds increase.

I said earlier that the chances of finding wolves in the night could have been improved by three things: better observations of the present (the location of the wolves when they first called), better understanding of cause and effect and better ability to use that understanding to make predictions (the factors that led the wolves to call and then move through the forest in a particular direction), and the ability to make predictions that involve chance. Computers help us with all three. Perhaps seeking to find wolves on Isle Royale at night will not seem such a dark search if we know that these devices can be of help to us.

New Ways to Observe Nature

As I mentioned earlier, our search for the wolves might have had greater success if we had had better means of direct observation. Computers are also playing a direct role in changing our ability to observe nature, which, in turn, influences our perception of nature. Computers are at the heart of many of the devices used today for measurement and observation. High in the remote and mist-draped mountains of Taiwan that extend well above

10,000 feet in Lala Shan Nature Preserve, rainfall has been measured since 1987 by computer-based methods, using chips invented in the United States and produced in Japan. Similarly, at many remote locations, data on environmental factors such as rainfall and wind speed and direction are collected and stored on computer chips or in a computer format on tape cassettes. The locations are then visited periodically to collect the information. The potential for the production of electricity from wind energy is being assessed in California using computer-based monitoring.[16] As yet another example, the chemical characteristics of the environment can be analyzed by methods that require as part of their basic workings computers or components derived from the computer industry. The level of pollutants can now be measured in place in the lagoon of Venice by a probe that relies on such computer-based devices. Remote sensing, which will be discussed in later chapters, is possible with the help of computers and computer-derived devices. These are just a few examples of the major changes in observational abilities that are rapidly entering science and management.

New Mythology

Making predictions that involve chance requires not only techniques but also a change in our myths about nature. This is a third way that computers are changing our perception of nature. Until the advent of modern computers, it was not possible to make extensive projections that involve stochastic processes. The acceptance of the idea that we might benefit by viewing nature as characterized by chance and randomness is a deep and unsettling change. On the surface, at the level of visual perception of the environment, the computer model of forest growth is simply an expression of generalizations based on careful observations of nature. But at a deeper level, that program, operating through the rapid processing of numbers within the silence and darkness of microchips, expresses a new perspective toward nature, rapidly moving shadows of the ponderously slow reality outside in the sunlit forest.

There are two key aspects of this deeper perspective. One is the metaphor of many events considered simultaneously in a connected network, which we met before as the definition of bacteria. It allows us, for example, to perceive the forest as made up of many individual trees growing, taking up air, water, and nitrogen, producing seeds, and dying—all these processes occurring simultaneously, interconnected yet independent. The other is the inclusion of chance as a fundamental aspect of life and death. In the computer model of forest growth, whether a tree dies and whether seeds sprout are determined by the computer's equivalent of the roll of dice. The chance of survival depends on two factors, one inherited—a genetic potential expressed in terms of the maximum longevity of the species—and the other environmental—how well the tree grew during the past year. If a tree's growth falls below some crucial minimum in a year, the tree has a much larger chance of dying when the dice are rolled. Reproduction of trees also involves an element of chance. The number of saplings of a species that are added in a year in the model of the forest is determined by the computer version of throwing dice. The computer's ability to handle chance occurrences is one of the reasons why a computer program has been so helpful in considering forest growth. Old-fashioned pencil-and-paper mathematics cannot take us very far in projecting birth and death when these events involve chance occurrences that depend on many factors.[17]

Although this nature of chance may seem less comforting than a clock-work world, it is the way that we find nature with our means of modern observation, and therefore it is the way that we must accept nature and approach the management of resources. Managing from the comfort of a deterministic world when one lives in a world of chance is like following the beam of a flashlight at night on Isle Royale; what appears in the beam is very clear, but one is likely to stumble and fall over the roots and rocks that lie just outside one's vision. Once we accept the idea that we can deal with these complexities of nature, we begin to discover that the world of chance is not so bad, that it is interesting and even intriguing now that we under-stand that chance is not chaos, that seeking the wolves at night involved some probability, predictable itself, in our finding them. Thus we must accept nature for what we are able to observe it to be, not for what we might wish it to be. Accepting this perception of nature, we discover that we have the tools to deal with it. Once we realize we have the tools, this new idea of nature takes on its own appeal, just as the game we played seeking the wolves at night became a pleasure, filling us with a sense of the wild.

Living and Nonliving

In the past, the distinction between life and nonlife seemed simple and clear, but it is becoming obscured by modern technology. This is a fourth way that computers are changing our perception of nature. While comput-ers have made machines seem lifelike, other fields that rely on modern technology are blending the mechanistic and the organic from the opposite direction. Molecular biology and genetic engineering are opening up or-ganic entities to engineering and making life seem machinelike. In this way, genetic engineering also obscures the distinction between life and nonlife because scientists can manipulate life in ways that, even a decade ago, people believed could be done only with nonliving things. We could design a new automobile or transfer an engine from one car to another, but we did not know that we could transfer genes from one life form to another. Today there are discussions about taking the genetic ability from beans that allow them to harbor nitrogen-fixing bacteria and transferring that ability to corn. Thus we can engineer carbon-based, DNA-based life. In the future, we will still be able to separate life from nonlife in a specific way. Life on Earth—as we know it—is self-reproducing and evolving carbon-based, organic-molecule-based systems with genetic codes in DNA molecules. This is a more specific and narrower distinction of our kind of life from other self-reproducing and evolving entities. Thus our technology at the end of the twentieth century is blurring the distinction between living and nonliving.

The strong distinction between life and nonlife is a result of the machine age—the recent industrial and mechanical world. In Western civilization, as late as the eighteenth century, the distinction was not made in the way we understand it. Primitive peoples who believe in animism would not understand that distinction; objects that we, as inheritors of the ideas of the nineteenth-century Industrial Revolution, conceive of as nonliving—rocks, mountains—are believed to be animated in their own way, as was believed in Western civilization before the machine age. Thus the blending of the ideas of life and of nonlife brings us back to a perspective more in harmony with beliefs held throughout most of human history.

Nature as wilderness, the out-there that has played such an important role in western ideas throughout the centuries, seems now fundamentally different from what it seemed before. Wilderness is a nature of chance and complexities that we need no longer fear as unknowable or unpredictable. Strangely, that most novel of our tools, the computer, is helping us grasp what we have feared to seek.

The Earth from the Moon (photograph by Apollo Astronauts, courtesy of the U.S. National Aeronautics and Space Administration).

—9

Within the Moose's Stomach: Nature as the Biosphere

> It is by no means for nothing that [the uninhabited parts of the Earth] come to be. . . . The sea gives off gentle exhalations, and the most pleasant winds when summer is at its height are released and dispersed from the uninhabited and frozen region by the snows that are gradually melting there.
>
> Plutarch (circa A.D. 75)[1]

> The relationship to the living matter of the earth and to its decomposition products must form the central theme. . . . because this relationship is responsible for the most remarkable feature of the atmosphere in contact with the liquid and solid materials at the earth's crust, namely, the fact that the atmospheric gases in contact with water, do not represent a mixture in thermodynamic equilibrium.
>
> G. E. Hutchinson (1954)[2]

An Afternoon on Isle Royale

One summer afternoon on Isle Royale, I came across a moose in a shallow pond that lay back from the shores, sheltered from Lake Superior's chilly winds. I stopped to rest my feet and view the scene, which appeared peaceful, calm, and pleasing. Feeding placidly, the moose seemed alone in the wilderness, breathing oxygen from an inert, lifeless but life-giving air and digging through dank, lifeless mud for a succulent morsel of green water plants. Yet looks are deceptive, and here, after our long journey through time and over the Earth's surface and among its many creatures, it is appropriate to take a lesson from Aristotle and view the "mean and despicable" creatures, for with this inquiry we can, at long last, begin to reinterpret nature for our time.

The moose—with its long spindly legs, which appear too thin for its stocky body, and its sagging belly—seemed an ungainly creature in the wilderness. Who would have designed such a creature? It has none of the attributes of classical beauty: a face without merit; a drooping hang-jaw and protruding lower lips; a hard gummy pallet instead of front upper teeth. The moose has inspired none of the rhapsodies to the grandeur or sublimity of nature, so important to Wordsworth's view of nature. Only a bull moose in the autumn, with its large antlers, presents any semblance of nature's magnificence—viewed, that is, from a distance; close up, the comical reappears.

If I had been hiking with another twentieth-century biologist versed in the Darwinian theory of evolution, he could have explained to me how well adapted a moose is to its environment, despite the superficial ugliness of the adaptations. Its lips, for example, are wonderfully adapted for pulling up underwater plants and tearing leaves from twigs: the lower front teeth push against the upper gums so that only the soft edible leaves are removed, leaving the twigs on the plants. I knew from past experience that the moose's long spindly legs can propel it at a surprising speed over the waters should I disturb it, enabling it to flee or chase me with great agility through the thickets and over dead logs, much faster than I could run.

Watching the peaceful lakeside scene, under the bright blue sky against the tea-colored waters sheltered in the forest, I was reminded of those ancient questions that we have been considering in this book. All seemed constant beneath the sky, unchanging and permanent, without the slightest suggestion of the inevitable death of the moose or of the population explosions and crashes of its ancestors, without a sign of trampled vegetation or of water lilies and yew forced to the brink of extinction on the island by this ungainly herbivore. Although the moose seemed dependent on the wilderness—the air, the water, the soils, and the plants—it seemed to have little influence on its immediate environment or on the rest of nature beyond the island.

In this still-life, there seemed to be only one grazing moose, but in fact the moose was not alone. As an ungulate, a true ruminant with a four-chambered stomach, the moose carries within its intestines an intricate array of symbiotic microbes, just as do its many ruminant relatives, which include the rest of the cervids (the family of northern deer), domestic cattle, and many of the big-game animals of the African plains and savannas. Its stomach teems with microbes—1 billion per cubic centimeter—performing tasks that the moose cannot do for itself. Who would have designed a moose this way—of necessity harboring in its gut vast numbers of creatures on which its life depends, unable to make the enzymes to digest the vegetation that, in the northern wilderness, is its only food?

An ungulate's rumen is so complex that a textbook in animal physiology called it "an ecological system in dynamic equilibrium" with inputs (of food and saliva) and outputs (of those materials that the moose can digest).[3] There are many species of microbes in the rumen. The most important to the moose are bacteria, called anaerobes, that can live only in an oxygenless atmosphere. There are other species of bacteria and other unicellular organisms that feed on the bacteria—predators and prey, all growing, reproducing, feeding, and dying within the gut of this large mammal.

The anaerobic bacteria are truly symbiotic with the moose, making the moose's survival possible and depending on the moose to provide an environment without which they would die. A large fraction of the vegetation swallowed by the moose consists of cellulose and complex carbohydrates, which it cannot digest. The bacteria release enzymes that digest cellulose and other carbohydrates, breaking down these complex compounds into simple sugars that might make a good energy source for the moose, but it does not get a chance to use them. The bacteria take up the sugars and use them as their supply of energy before the lining of the moose's intestines can absorb these compounds. In the oxygenless atmosphere of the rumen, ordinary respiration, which requires oxygen, cannot take place. Instead, the bacteria ferment the sugars and give off fatty acids as the waste products of their metabolism. Of these, acetic acid, the acid in vinegar, is the most important. These acids become, in turn, the moose's food; they are absorbed by the walls of the rumen.

The moose, like all mammals, produces urea in the process of digesting its food. Urea is 47 percent nitrogen, an element essential for all living things and sometimes difficult for the moose to obtain in sufficient quantity, especially in the winter. The excretion of urea is a loss of this valuable resource. Instead of eliminating all the urea, as we do, the moose is able to transfer part of it through the blood to its saliva; when the saliva is swallowed, the urea is returned to the rumen. There, the bacteria are able to convert the nitrogen-rich urea, as well as ammonia, which is produced in other reactions, to proteins. The nitrogen in the urea is important to the bacteria, since it fertilizes their growth. The bacteria also synthesize vitamins that are necessary to the moose. Thus the moose can live on what would otherwise be a very poor diet—low in protein and vitamins, too low for its survival if it were not for the bacteria in its gut.

Of the plant material taken in by the moose, approximately 50 percent is digested by the bacteria; of the rest, about 10 percent is converted by the bacteria to methane, which is belched and released to the air unused by the moose. The remaining vegetation passes down the digestive system, along with a large mass of the bacteria (about 15 percent by weight of the original mass of vegetation taken in by the moose). These bacteria are digested by the moose, serving as high-quality food. The moose is also able to digest about half of the remaining vegetation by its own digestive process.

The moose contributes many things to this symbiosis. It provides the food for the bacteria and maintains an environment with a constant temperature of approximately 102°F. It swallows saliva along with vegetation. The saliva is slightly basic and neutralizes acids produced by the bacteria, helping to maintain an acidity in the rumen within a range that is acceptable, perhaps even optimal, for the bacteria. The bacteria live, grow, and multiply in a protected environment, with a special atmosphere and a steady input of food. The moose removes the fatty acids that are wastes of the bacteria that would otherwise poison the microbes and threaten their survival in the rumen. The rumen is an ecological system overwhelmingly biologically produced and controlled.

In some ways, the moose's rumen is a model in miniature of the biosphere—our planet's entire life-support system. Like the rumen, the biosphere is a system that includes and sustains life. But the rumen is also a system under biological control and is in steady-state within a certain range of conditions—as long as the moose is alive and healthy. In these qualities the stomach of a moose brings us back to the ancient questions about the characteristics of nature without human influence, and the question of whether nature is in a balance. The microbes in the moose's gut live in an environment that seems most bizarre to us and certainly unsuitable for human beings. There is little oxygen and in some parts of the intestine no oxygen at all. Noxious gases, such as methane and ammonia, abound, produced by the microbes and the moose's own digestive processes. The fluids are acidic, and the microbes withdraw nitrogen from the air—nitrogen is the most abundant molecule in air—and convert it to nitrate, nitric acid, ammonia, and other small and unpleasant chemicals.

The microbes that live in the rumen would die in the air outside, the air that was so clear and pleasant to me on that sunlit afternoon by the pond. Oxygen would kill the bacteria rapidly. But in the pond-bottom muds that the moose kicked at and waded through as it fed, there were similar bacteria that also can survive only where there is no oxygen; they live beneath the still waters of the pond where poisonous oxygen cannot penetrate. Nitrogen-fixing bacteria that live in the root nodules of leguminous plants, such as alders on the pond's edge, also cannot survive in an atmosphere rich in oxygen. For them, the nodules provide a home, an *ecos*, protecting them from the oxygen that is so deadly to them.

Ancient Nature

Bacteria are an ancient form of life, the oldest form of life known to us that still exists on the Earth. Just how ancient became known in the 1950s. In 1954, two scientists, S. A. Tyler and Elso Barghoorn, made a microscopic examination of rock called the Gunflint Chert taken from the Canadian Shield several hundred miles north of Isle Royale.[4] The Gunflint Chert was dated using radioisotopic techniques quite new at the time. These measurements indicated that the rock was 2 billion years old. Using tools that were a twentieth-century invention, Tyler and Barghoorn cut extremely thin sections of the chert, thin enough to be transparent to light and to be viewed under a microscope. These thin sections revealed fossils of prokaryotic organisms—bacteria—that appeared to be much the same, perhaps exactly the same species as occur today. Fossil records discovered since 1954 suggest that 2 billion years ago, the Earth was "teeming with prokaryotic microbial life."[5] Indeed, they seem to have been much more abundant and diverse then than they are today. The greatest diversity of prokaryotes occurred about 900 million years ago. As I mentioned in Chapter 8, bacteria differ in fundamental ways from all other life forms. They lack a cell nucleus, which is found in all forms that evolved later (except viruses). Although the prokaryotes have certain primitive features, they are chemically sophisticated and are able to carry out chemical reactions that none of the other, structurally more sophisticated life forms, called eukaryotes, can do.

Curiously, the 2-billion-year-old microbes found in the Gunflint Chert appear to have lived in an atmosphere more like that in the muds beneath the still waters of a pond at Isle Royale or in the stomach of a moose than like that of the present-day Earth. Several kinds of evidence suggest this is true. On the ancient Earth, certain species of bacteria were the only photosynthetic organisms. They, like all other photosynthesizers, took carbon dioxide out of the air and gave off oxygen. Ancient fossils called stromatolites appear to be the remains of such bacteria. The oldest fossils, formed about 3.5 billion years ago, contain these bacteria. The bacteria in stromatolites are single celled, but grow joined together in long filaments that form mats, similar to the mats of blue-green photosynthetic bacteria that can be found today in quiet marine bays, such as Shark's Bay, Australia. The fossil mats have been distorted by time's long travail, which has subjected them to repeated heating and pressure, bending and twisting them to create odd shapes that sparked the curiosity of paleontologists, who described them as appearing like fossil cauliflowers. Within the matrix of the fossilized filaments of the bacteria are pebbles that have a peculiar feature: their surfaces are made of reduced minerals—that is, minerals that are not oxidized and could not have developed in an atmosphere with oxygen.

A pebble is the product of erosion, a bit of rock broken off from a larger surface, perhaps by the action of freezing and thawing water, and then smoothed by wind or water, exposed on all sides to the atmosphere. The outer surfaces of the ancient pebbles within the stromatolites would have been oxidized if the air in which they had formed had been like the present-day atmosphere. The pebbles provide evidence that the atmosphere of the Earth 2 billion years ago lacked oxygen and, at least in this important characteristic, was very different from the modern atmosphere.

Global Nature

When some of the photosynthetic bacteria were buried but did not completely decompose, a slight imbalance resulted in the uptake and release of oxygen, which slowly built up in the atmosphere. Thus early life in the form of these lowly, seemingly insignificant mats began to change the entire planet. Free oxygen in the Earth's atmosphere is the result of 3 billion years of photosynthesis and is therefore a product of life. Like the atmosphere in the rumen in a modern moose's stomach, the Earth's atmosphere has been fundamentally altered by life.

Life appears to affect not only the air we breathe, but also the rocks on which we stand. Perhaps nothing seems less lifelike than a piece of steel or iron, a steel girder or a chunk of iron ore. But the origin of iron ores is intimately connected to life and its history on the Earth. The rocks that form the major economically important deposits of iron were laid down between 2.2 and 1.8 billion years ago, deposited because of the release of oxygen into the oceans by photosynthetic bacteria.[6] A vast amount of unoxidized iron was dissolved in those ancient oceans. Unoxidized iron is much more soluble in water than oxidized iron. Oxygen released into the ocean waters as a waste product by photosynthetic bacteria combined with the dissolved iron, changing it from a more soluble to a less soluble form. No longer dissolved in the water, the iron settled to the bottom of the oceans and became part of deposits that were slowly turned into rock. Over millions of years, these deposits formed thick bands of iron ore that are mined today from Minnesota to Australia. After most of the dissolved iron had been removed from the oceans, the oxygen produced by photosynthesis began to enter the atmosphere, leading to another major change in the biosphere, converting it from a reducing to an oxidizing environment. From the chemistry of rocks such as stromatolites and iron-ore beds, geologists have been able to reconstruct the history of the Earth's atmosphere. The early atmosphere of the Earth, before the emergence of life, was composed primarily of hydrogen, methane, and ammonia. Approximately 3.5 billion years ago, about the age of the earliest fossils, there was a shift to an atmosphere with free nitrogen and carbon dioxide, which was followed by an increase in the concentration of oxygen and a decrease in that of carbon dioxide to approximately present levels. If the Earth had remained lifeless, the concentration of carbon dioxide and nitrogen in the atmosphere would have remained high, as would have the concentration of hydrogen, methane, and ammonia. Although oxygen would have increased as a result of the activity of sunlight, it would not have increased to the same concentration as found today. Carbon dioxide would have been ten times more abundant; free nitrogen, ten times less.[7]

Early life on the Earth altered not only the chemistry of the Earth's atmosphere, but also the heat budget of the Earth and the Earth's surface temperature. The temperature of the surface of the Earth is a result of energy exchange and of physical characteristics of the surface. Energy is received from the sun, and a very small amount is generated from the Earth's core (produced by radioactive processes that heat the center of the Earth). Energy is lost to space by radiation from the Earth's surface. The hotter an object, the more rapidly it radiates energy and the shorter the wavelength of the predominate radiation. A blue flame is hot; a red flame is cooler. The Earth's surface and the surfaces of animals and plants are so cool that energy is radiated predominately in the infrared, which is invisible to us.[8] If an object is cold and gives off less heat than it receives, it will warm up. But as it warms, it also radiates heat more rapidly. As a result, for any constant input of energy, a physical object will eventually reach a temperature that will allow it to radiate energy at the same rate that it receives energy.

The rate at which the Earth's surface radiates heat depends on its average "color" and temperature. A perfect emitter of heat is called an ideal black body, and black surfaces radiate heat much more readily than white surfaces. A white planet would radiate heat very differently from a black planet. Changes in the amount of ice and the distribution of vegetation over the Earth alter the reflecting and emitting characteristics of the planet's surface. Ice reflects 80 to 95 percent of light; a dry grassland, 30 to 40 percent; a coniferous forest 10 to 15 percent.[9] It has been estimated that under present atmospheric conditions, a 1 percent change in the amount of sunlight reflected by the Earth would cause approximately a 3°F change in the average temperature of the Earth's surface.

Changes in the absorption of energy can be due to changes in the cloud cover and in the amount of ice cover on the Earth's land surfaces. Organisms, particularly grasses and trees and algae, can also affect the absorption. Their absorption of light changes with the seasons. Marine algal mats can change from light and highly reflective in one season to almost black and highly emitting in another. Algae can also produce sediments such as calcium carbonate, which, when pure, is chalky white and has a different reflective characteristic than the sediments produced from a lifeless surface. Even a single-cell layer of algae spread over a large area of water could greatly alter the rate of energy exchange and therefore the temperature of the Earth's surface.

These examples suggest that life has greatly altered its environment at a global level over the history of the Earth; this explains in part the "fitness of the environment" that Lawrence Henderson observed in the early years of the twentieth century. The environment appears "fit" for life because life has evolved to take advantage of the environment and, conversely, has greatly changed the environment at a global level. This suggests that living things have a much more important effect on our planet than previously believed.

The Biosphere

Life and the environment affect each other at a global level. Together they form a planetary-scale system, the biosphere, that sustains life. The idea of the biosphere and the growth in understanding it can be traced back to several books published in the first few decades of the twentieth century, including Henderson's *Fitness of the Environment*, and to books published in the 1940s and 1950s by a very small number of scientists, including G. E. Hutchinson in the United States. However, it is only in the past two decades that this idea has gained momentum, helped by the popularization of the photographs of the Earth taken from space by the Apollo astronauts.[10] Just as the images of nearby planets, appearing as objects something like the Earth, with surface features and moons, affected ideas about the universe in the eighteenth and nineteenth centuries, so in the late 1960s photographs from space showing the Earth as a cloudy blue marble floating in inky blackness became profound images for our time. The pictures of our living planet floating alone, a unique cosmic island, evoked in the public consciousness strong feelings about the fragility of all life on our planet, in a way that could not have been possible in times past—not to

Cicero, with his Earth-centered, divinely ordered cosmos; not to Galileo and Newton, with their exact calculations of the continual sweep of planets through the solar system; not to Wordsworth, with his challenges to a powerful nature. Perhaps more than any other single image or any single event these photographs of the Earth have done more to change our consciousness about the character of life, the factors that sustain it, and our role in the biosphere and our power over life. Those images from space have radically altered our myths about nature. The power of this image is demonstrated by its repeated use in recent years in many contexts, from advertisements to discussions of environmental problems. But behind this image, what are the characteristics of the biosphere? It is something like the stomach of a moose.

Life Changes the Earth

The strong effect of life on an entire system is one of the primary qualities shared by the stomach of a moose and the biosphere. In the rumen, the biological effect is obvious; with the biosphere, the biological effect was obscured from the time of the beginning of modern science and the rise of the mechanistic perception of nature, until recently. Evidence of the great influence of life on the Earth can be found not only in the fossil record, but also in the comparison of the Earth with other planets in the solar system. The Earth is a peculiar planet when compared with its nearest neighbors, Venus and Mars. The three planets are similar in many ways. They are within a factor of 2 in their distances from the sun and within a factor of 2 in their diameters. Since they are similar in distance from the sun and in size, one would expect them to be similar in many other ways, including the composition of their atmospheres. However, scientific observations made in the past several decades, both from space probes sent to Mars and Venus and from Earth-based telescopes, reveal that they have atmospheres that are very different from that of the Earth. The atmospheres of Mars and Venus are more like each other than either is like the Earth's. The Venusian and Martian atmospheres are composed mainly of carbon dioxide; nitrogen is the second most important constituent, and oxygen is a rare and minor component. In contrast, the atmosphere of the Earth is 79 percent nitrogen and 21 percent oxygen, while carbon dioxide makes up only 0.03 percent. The atmosphere of Venus is very dense, while that of Mars is very thin.[11] The difference between the atmosphere of the Earth and that of either Venus or Mars in the relative abundance of the primary constituents is due to the effects of life on the Earth's surface.

The Debris in the Bay of Bengal

It is an old argument whether life affects its environment to any significant degree. The resolution of this argument is important to the question: What is the character of nature undisturbed by human beings? Whether living things have important effects on the geological characteristics of the Earth has been argued since the seventeenth century. This possibility was rejected until very recently. The change in conclusions is in part a result of late-twentieth-century observational technology, and in part a result of a change in myths, metaphors, and perceptions, which, in turn, are influenced by technology. To appreciate this change in understanding, it is helpful to consider some of the classic scientific arguments about the influence of life on the environment.

The possible influence of life on air, water, soils, and rocks, on the shape and persistence of the Earth's land forms, on rates of erosion, and on the climate was actively discussed in the eighteenth and nineteenth centuries, when the scientific study of these phenomena was beginning. In the early nineteenth century, when geologists were starting to formulate concepts of the processes of erosion, they began to ask what forces opposed the slow degradation of the land and what created new landforms. A British geologist, Adam Sedgwick, argued that vegetation is the primary force opposing erosion: "By the processes of vegetable life an incalculable mass of solid matter is absorbed, year after year, from the elastic and non-elastic fluids circulating round the earth." This material is "thrown down upon" the Earth's surface, so that "in this *single* operation there is a *vast counterpoise to all* the agents of destruction."[12]

Sir Charles Lyell, one of the fathers of modern geology, dismissed Sedgwick's argument as "splendid eloquence." Lyell's ideas are important to us because of the major role that he played in the establishment of geology as a science. His ideas are a product of the evidence available to him as well as the world views of the time—the metaphors and beliefs about nature that were acceptable and seemed viable. Lyell thought that the idea that life might play an important role in large-scale Earth processes was not worthy of serious consideration, but required attention only because "such an opinion has been recently advanced by an eminent geologist." Otherwise, wrote Lyell, "we should have deemed it unnecessary to dwell on propositions which appear to us so clear and obvious."[13]

As a counter example, Lyell considered the materials washed down annually into the Bay of Bengal, where, as it appeared to him in 1831 "what remains, whether organic or inorganic, will be the measure of the degradation which thousands of torrents in the Himalaya mountains, and many rivers of other parts of India, bring down in a single year." This was an extreme case, with an abundance of vegetation and a high rate of erosion. The forces of physical erosion were so strong, he believed, that the vegetation "can merely be considered as having been in a slight degree *conservative*," merely *retarding* erosion, but not acting as a constructive or an "antagonist power" against the forces of physical erosion. Lyell then generalized from that case to conclude that vegetation can never play an important role in countering erosion.[14]

Lyell also rejected the possibility that organic matter represents a large and increasing fraction of the material on the surface of the Earth. Organic soil, which he called "vegetable mould," was "seldom more than a few feet in thickness" and "often did not exceed a few inches"; thus it represented a small quantity of the Earth's material. Furthermore, this organic deposit did not appear to have increased in past geologic periods. Lyell and his contemporaries had come to recognize that mountains are formed by uplifting generated by forces deep inside the Earth. Mountains and other areas that had been subjected to such uplifting were observed to be generally denuded of soils, implying that they did not retain soils as they rose. Thus, Lyell concluded, soils are not conserved during these processes or over long time periods. Moreover, the rate of growth of vegetation is not correlated with the abundance of organic debris; peat, for example, is common in the far north, where vegetation growth is slow, and uncommon in the tropics, where vegetation growth was believed to be greatest. From these lines of evidence, Lyell concluded that vegetation-derived organic matter in the soil could not be an important cause of the creation of landforms or of the prevention of erosion.

In its totality, life seemed to Lyell to have played a minor role, if any, in geologic processes, including the cycling of the chemical elements necessary for life. Lyell knew that animals and plants withdraw elements from the air, land, and waters, but he argued that their death results in only a small and very slow return of these chemicals to the environment. If this were not true, but

> if the operation of animal and vegetable life could restore to the general surface of the continents a portion of the elements of those disintegrated rocks, of which such enormous masses are swept down annually into the sea, [then] the effects would have become ere now most striking; and would have constituted one of the most leading features in the structure and composition of our continents.[15]

The effects were not visible or striking in Lyell's time with the scientific methods of observation available. Life seemed incapable of countering the major changes in the structure of the Earth's surface, and the role of life in affecting the nonliving environment appeared minor. Instead, Lyell concluded, "igneous causes" must have provided the "real antagonist power" to "counterbalance the leveling action of running water." That is, processes deep in the Earth must offset erosion. Of the materials required for life, "fresh supplies are derived by the atmosphere, and by running water," he wrote, "from the disintegration of rocks and their organic contents, and from the interior of the Earth, from whence all the elements beforementioned, which enter principally into the composition of animals and vegetables, are continually evolved."[16] Life seemed to be dependent on the environment, like the moose alone in the wilderness, but appeared to have little effect on that environment, unlike the community of bacteria teeming symbiotically within the moose's gut.

Lessons from a Dead Mouse in a Jar

In the history of modern science, both before Lyell and since his work, it has been common to dismiss the importance of living things in determining many features of the Earth, including its atmosphere. The total mass of living things is a tiny fraction of the mass of the Earth, a mere 1,000 billion metric tons of the total 6 trillion billion metric tons. If all of life were evenly mixed with the mass of the Earth in a giant blender, the concentration of living things would be two-tenths of 1 part in 1 billion—at the border of detection by the most sophisticated twentieth-century analytic techniques. The total biomass is tiny even in comparison with the mass of the atmosphere, which is estimated to be 5 million billion metric tons, so that if the biota and the atmosphere were evenly mixed, life would represent 2 parts in 10,000 of the mixture. But it is a mistake to attribute importance simply to the amount of material.[17]

That animals and plants have had some impact on the make-up of the atmosphere, in spite of the small fraction of the Earth's materials tied up in living organisms, was recognized first in the eighteenth century by Joseph Priestly. He discovered that green plants grow better in a bell jar in which a mouse has died than in one with ordinary air, while mice, in turn, receive something of value to them from plants, transferred through the atmosphere.[18] He had found that during photosynthesis plants give off oxygen, which is required for animal respiration (and plant respiration as well), and that mice give off carbon dioxide, released by respiration and required for photosynthesis. Priestly's experiments provided an early clue that although life represents a small mass compared with the Earth, life can have an important effect on processes that occur in the biosphere. But the time when the importance of these biological processes for the biosphere would be recognized lay in the future.

In contrast to Lyell's early-nineteenth-century view, late-twentieth-century geologists are beginning to view life as an integral part of geologic processes. Recently, for example, Peter Westbroek of the Netherlands summarized this new perspective. The acceptance of the theory of plate tectonics in the 1960s offered a new image of the Earth's bedrock as a group of huge plates in constant, if very slow, motion and with very slow convection currents of the materials in the rocks. As a result of plate tectonics during the Earth's history, the location and orientation of the continents have changed, resulting in major alterations in the distribution of life, providing opportunities for the evolution of life forms and leading to the extinction of others. Where plates collide, one plunges under the other, bringing its material to the deeper regions of the Earth, where it is heated and subjected to intense pressures and becomes molten. Where plates separate beneath ocean waters, fresh molten material is released from the deeper Earth. Over extremely long periods, material is recycled, carried down from the biosphere by the continental plates and then returned to the biosphere at the sites of sea-floor spreading. This new understanding is built not only on the discovery and acceptance of the idea of plate tectonics, but also on modern chemical methods that have allowed chemists to understand better the origin and causes of the composition of the Earth's rocks.

Life and the rock cycle seem intimately connected to each other. The rock cycle has been greatly changed by life, as the origin of iron ore illustrates. In addition, biological evolution has "favored the emergence of powerful biological 'mining' mechanisms" by which living systems obtain the chemicals they need from rocks, water, and air. For example, organic acids produced in forest soils leach chemical elements from rocks. The process of biological evolution has also led to biochemical mechanisms that remove toxins from the biosphere. Mercury, which is toxic to all living things, occurs in some soils. Bacteria take up mercury from the soil and produce methyl mercury, which is a gas that is readily lost from the soils. As a result of these processes, "supplies of raw materials," made available by geologic processes, are "efficiently exploited" by life, while "toxic substances are removed."[19]

The Biosphere and the Balance of Nature

During the past decade, more and more scientists have acknowledged the significant impact of life on the Earth. This raises the possibility of another role of life—that life, in its entirety, might increase the stability of the biosphere, or, to put it in older terms, affect the balance of nature at the global level. The environment of the moose's stomach is maintained under very exacting conditions; the temperature, for example, remains within a very small range of variation. In the biosphere, conditions for the persistence of life are more flexible. There is a range of permissible conditions for life as we know it. For most life, temperatures must be approximately between 32°F and 122°F. The acidity of water must be close to neutral but can vary from slightly acidic to slightly basic. The elements essential to living organisms must be available, and in ratios that are acceptable to the needs of individuals. For life to continue, these factors must remain within certain ranges, but they need not be at single values continuously. Is the biosphere, then, at an exact steady-state? a precise balance of nature?

There are three schools of thought about a balance of nature at the global level. One assumes that the biosphere is in a steady-state, exactly as nature at a local level had been assumed to be in steady-state in nineteenth- and twentieth-century management of biological resources. Speaking about the "biosphere" at "steady-state" is a twentieth-century way of saying that nature in the largest sense has a balance, a constancy of form and structure that, if undisturbed by human influence, will remain indefinitely. This idea is consistent with a machine metaphor and the idea of divine order. The second school of thought believes that life acts as the Earth's thermostat, requiring and creating constant conditions, like physiological feedback mechanisms in a moose that maintain its body temperature near 102°F. This is also consistent with a machine metaphor, but can be extended to have aspects that are organic. According to the third school, the biosphere is always changing and it is this very quality at the planetary level that has allowed life to persist.

Most current analyses of the biosphere are based on the first school of thought. Mathematical models and computer simulations of chemical cycles treat the biosphere as though it were a steady-state system operating at normal or optimum conditions except where disturbed by human influence.[20] James Lovelock and Lynn Margulis are proponents of the second school of thought. Lovelock has made an important and major contribution to the thinking of our time about the biosphere by proposing the "Gaia hypothesis." *Gaia* is the Greek Goddess Earth, and Lovelock uses the word as "a shorthand" for a hypothesis that "the biosphere is a self-regulating entity with the capacity to keep our planet healthy by controlling the chemical and physical environment." More specifically, he lists several of "Gaia's principal characteristics," which include "vital organs at the core" and a "tendency to keep constant conditions for all terrestrial life."[21]

The first section of this book provided evidence that constancy and steady-state did not exist for nature at all levels smaller than the biosphere and that we had to abandon the machine metaphor for the entire range of ecological phenomena from individual populations to entire forests, to abandon the idea that they were like watches, car engines, or steam engines. With what can we replace that metaphor? Lewis Thomas asked the question "What is [the Earth] *most* like?" and answered "it is *most* like a single cell."[22] How far can we push a new organic metaphor? How much is the biosphere like the internal organs of a large mammal? The metaphor holds for the influence of life on its environment and for the complex interplay between environment and life. But a fundamental difference between the environment within the moose's gut and the environment outside it is the matter of steady-state, of constancy, of a balance of nature. Within the moose, all is in balance as long as the supply of food is constant and the moose is alive and healthy; that is, the moose is stable within certain limits.

In the nineteenth century, Lyell considered the possibility of a global balance of nature in terms of uptake and loss in the cycling of the chemical elements through living things. Lyell thought that a balance was possible in theory and could in theory be affected by life, so that the supply of necessary "hydrogen, carbon, oxygen, azote [nitrogen] and other elements" might be obtained from the "putrescence of organic substances" and the release of the elements to the atmosphere. This would imply that "vegetable mould would, after a series of years, neither gain nor lose a single particle by the action of organic beings." Although Lyell concluded that this was "not far from the truth," he believed that most organic matter washed down from the land to the sea became "imbedded in subaqueous deposits" and would "remain throughout whole geological epochs before they again become subservient to the purpose of life."[23] The persistence of life seemed to Lyell to be made possible only by a continual release of the essential chemicals from the Earth's interior, which he assumed could not be affected by life, and not by the recycling of the elements by the biota. Lyell believed that life depends on the Earth, but life could not create a balance or constancy in the supply of the elements on which its survival depends.

Biospheric Biography

Since the origin of life, a number of major events in biological evolution, in addition to the release of oxygen, have changed the rest of the biosphere—the atmosphere, oceans, soils, and rocks. These are one-way events; once they have taken place, the biosphere cannot move backward from them to previous conditions (Table). In this way, the biosphere has a history—a unidirectional change over time. Among these events were the origin of life itself, the evolution of oxygen-breathing organisms, of cells with true nuclei (eukaryotic cells, the cells of animals and plants) and of calcium-containing skeletons; the colonization of the land by plants and animals; and the evolution of flowering plants and of *Homo sapiens*.

Organisms that could carry out photosynthesis were not the first to evolve on the Earth. They were preceded by forms that could obtain energy from compounds in the primitive oxygenless atmosphere and waters. Free oxygen in the atmosphere was highly toxic to those organisms. Their descendants are forced to live in obscure corners of the modern Earth, in

---

Causes of Biospheric Changes in Earth History

Biological innovations perturbing the biosphere
  Origin of life
  Origin of photosynthesis
  Origin of aerobic photosynthesis
  Origin of aerobic respiration
  Origins of other biogeochemically important metabolisms
  Origin of eukaryotic organisms
  Origin of calcium-containing skeletons
  Origin and expansion of bioturbating organisms
  The colonization of land by plants and animals
  The evolution of angiosperms
  The evolution of humans

Abiotic perturbations
  Extraterrestrial perturbations
    Changes in solar luminosity
    Impact on the Earth of such bodies as asteroids
      and comets
  Crustal changes
    Major tectonic change at the Archean/Proterozoic
      transition (the growth of large continents)
    Variation through time in volcanism
    Plate tectonic changes altering continental
      geographies, topography, and ocean circulation
    Climatic change, principally glaciations
    Sea level changes

From Community on Planetary Biology, *Remote Sensing of the Biosphere* (Washington: National Academy Press, 1986), p. 43.

the stomachs of ruminants, the muds beneath still pond waters, the root nodules of alders and other legumes, the guts of termites. However, oxygen is a high-energy element; when it combines with unoxidized compounds, a lot of stored energy is released. Organisms that could utilize oxygen to "burn" their biological fuel could use energy rapidly. This ability has had many advantages. An oxygen-using individual can move faster for a longer time, and its internal structure and biochemistry can be more complex. The kinds of life most familiar to us, including animals and flowering plants, require a high rate of energy use and could not have evolved in an oxygenless world. Free oxygen produced by life presented both a problem and an opportunity. It was lethal to many existing forms of life, but led to the evolution of species that could make use of this energy-releasing quality. Given the presence of oxygen-using organisms, a whole new evolutionary "game" was possible.

Each of these major events has three stages. First, there is a kind of biological breakthrough in evolution; new opportunities are opened up by the evolution of a group of species, which evolve rapidly, "taking advantage," so to speak, of the new opportunities. Next, the new forms of life cause some kind of change in the biosphere. Finally, other life forms evolve to "take advantage" of the altered environmental conditions; evolution takes place within the new environmental conditions of the biosphere, which provide a new set of problems and opportunities.[24]

Biological evolution has led to global changes in the environment, which, in turn, have led to new opportunities for biological evolution. In this way, a long-term process of change has occurred throughout the history of life on the Earth, which is an unfolding, one-way story. A machine is not a good metaphor for this system. You can stop a steam engine and start it again at a later time. You can move the wheels and levers and gears backward to some point and then restart the engine. But you cannot turn the biosphere backward from one of its major evolutionary steps to a previous one. Instead, the new emerging history of the biosphere is reminiscent, metaphorically, of the organic idea of the Earth described in Chapter 6. Like an idealized organism, the biosphere has had an origin and has passed through major stages. Like an idealized organism, the biosphere has had a history and what it will be tomorrow depends not only on what it is today, but also on what it was yesterday. Like an organism, the biosphere proceeds through its existence in a one-way direction, passing from stage to stage, each of which cannot be revisited.

The biosphere has been characterized by change at every time scale. The geologic processes of burial and return of chemical elements are among the slowest of these changes, on the order of hundreds of millions of years. At shorter time scales, climate has always been fluctuating. It is worth repeating that variations in climate are known for a large range of time scales, from 1 billion years to days. During ice ages, major changes occur in the patterns of the circulation of ocean currents and in the transfer of heat from the equator to the poles. As the climate has fluctuated, major changes have occurred in the distribution of life and the abundances of species. It would be highly unlikely if such fluctuations did not result in variations in the cycling of chemical elements necessary for life. Recent measurements of air trapped for thousands of years in pockets in glaciers indicate that the concentration of carbon dioxide in the atmosphere has varied considerably since the end of the most recent ice age, decreasing at the height of glaciation to about one-half of its value at the start of the industrial era. Thus in terms of climate, the cycling of chemical elements, the distribution of species and ecological communities, and the rate of extinction of species, we must reject the possibility of constancy in the biosphere. If the biosphere has not been in a precise steady-state, then life has not been a precise stabilizing device for the biosphere.

The remaining basic issue has to do with whether life has functioned to promote "the tendency to optimize conditions for all terrestrial life." The question itself can be best understood in terms of the relative roles of life and the nonliving aspects of the environment in determining the conditions on the Earth. If life functions to dampen changes that would have occurred had life not evolved and if such changes would have led to an environment outside the range that can support life, then it could be said that life has had a tendency to promote its own persistence. The geologic evidence as described by Westbroek suggests that life has functioned in this fashion, against a background of large-scale changes in the environment. Whether the tendency is toward an optimum in any sense, however, cannot be answered at this time.

The image that emerges is of the biosphere made up of four dynamic parts—rocks, oceans, air, and life—each with its own characteristic ranges of movement and rates of change, rocks changing in composition most slowly, the oceans much more rapidly, and the atmosphere more rapidly still. Each part affects the others, and the inherent differences in their movement and rates of change can create complex patterns in time and space. Modulating all these changes is life. Life has greatly increased the rates of many chemical reactions and the transport of chemical elements from one part of the biosphere to another and has led to new patterns in the cycling of chemicals.

In spite of this new knowledge, the mechanistic ideas persist in attempts to explain and understand the biosphere. Such mechanistic explanations occur in the analyses of whether life tends to create negative-feedback mechanisms that maintain the environment in specific states that are in some way or other "optimal" for the continuation of life. The blending of new metaphors, the extent to which the biosphere is like a computer or like a rose, and the influx of some of the older machine-age ideas into these newer ones is a task for scientists to debate during the next decades, whether they recognize the underlying metaphors or not. The fact that the issues have come to this stage is in itself a fundamental change in the perception of nature. The biosphere is very different from a machine. The Earth is not alive, but the biosphere is a life-supporting and life-containing system with organic qualities, more like a moose than a water-powered mill. The biosphere is not a mystical organismic entity contraposed to rationality, but a system open to scientific analysis and to a new kind of understanding because of new knowledge and new metaphors. In its dynamic qualities, its one-way history, and its complexity, a new Earth is revealed. Like a pond on a quiet afternoon at Isle Royale, the reality of nature is revealed not by what is seen in the stillness, but by what is perceived within.

A Kirtland's warbler in its jack pine habitat of Michigan (photograph courtesy of the
Department of Natural Resources, State of Michigan).

–10

Fire in the Forest:
Managing Living Resources

People are here (and in many other places) in regard to wood, bent only upon their own present advantage, utterly regardless of posterity . . . [they take] little account of Natural History, that science being here (as in other parts of the world) looked upon as a mere trifle, and the pastime of fools.

Peter Kalm (1750)[1]

Monuments of Living Antiquity

Soon after they were discovered in the Sierras of California near Yosemite Valley in 1852, the giant sequoias came to be regarded as great natural monuments, curiosities of nature to be dismantled and displayed, and as a kind of natural sculpture.[2] Along with Yosemite Valley itself and with the geysers of Yellowstone, the giant trees were viewed in the mid-nineteenth century as an American answer to the paintings and sculpture and other trappings of culture of Europe, an American contribution to the world, and symbols of antiquity connecting the past and the present. No "fragment of human work, broken pillar or sand-worn image half lifted over pathetic desert—none of these link the past and today with anything like the power of these monuments of living antiquity," wrote the American explorer and surveyor Clarence King after viewing these trees in 1864. When the famous journalist Horace Greeley saw sequoias in 1859, he wrote that they "were of very substantial size when David danced before the ark, when Solomon laid the foundation of the Temple, when Theseus ruled in Athens, when Aeneas fled from the burning wreck of vanquished Troy."[3]

   With this perception, it is no wonder that once Yosemite, with its famous Mariposa Grove of sequoias, became a national park in 1890, the sequoia "monuments of living antiquity" were managed as though, like sculpture, they would persist indefinitely as long as they and their environment were preserved without change and disturbance.[4] Until the second half of the twentieth century, Mariposa Grove was managed to protect the forests from all disturbances. While it may have seemed natural to assume that trees several thousand years old survived in and required undisturbed environments, by the 1960s, after decades of protection, the sequoias were not regenerating in the protected, undisturbed stands. Trees produced seeds, but seeds did not sprout. Naturalists noticed that the seedlings did sprout where dirt roads had been cleared through the forest so that sunlight penetrated to the soil surface and the soil was scraped clear of its litter. A comparison of photographs taken between 1859 and 1932 showed that the undisturbed forests were no longer as open as they had been, but were becoming crowded with white fir, a species whose seeds can germinate and whose seedlings survive in the dense shade of the sequoia groves. In 1964, Richard Hartesveldt, a scientist studying the impact of tourists on the sequoia groves, realized that giant sequoias might rely on fires to regenerate.[5] An extraordinary thing was discovered: even the largest and one of the longest lived of all organisms requires disturbance to persist.

In 1968, the National Park Service established a new policy that allowed controlled burns in national parks; in 1970, the first controlled fire was lit in sequoia groves.[6] The fires had to be managed very carefully because a huge amount of fuel in the form of dead branches, twigs, bark, leaf litter, and so forth had built up within the forests during the decades of fire suppression. Managed improperly, or started by lightning or otherwise inadvertently, a fire might become unnaturally intense and either spread too far too quickly or have undesirable effects within the forests.

The century from the 1860s to the 1960s, during which sequoia reproduction declined in natural stands because of fire suppression, is a mere flick of a page on the calendar in the life of these trees, and so the artificial management of the sequoias for this length of time hardly makes a difference in the long run. This is not the way we have been threatening this species. We have threatened it by clear-cutting large stands and destroying its habitat, leaving the sequoia, which has highly specific habitat requirements, with only a small remnant of its former dominion. But the acceptance of controlled burning and of the necessity for disturbance even in sequoia forests is an example of a transformation in attitude that must occur so that we can make wise use of natural resources.[7]

Managing for Change

The management of the sequoia is reminiscent of the problem of the Kirtland's warbler. The change in management policy to allow some fires to burn or to set controlled fires to protect the habitat of the warbler illustrated the beginning of a change in underlying assumptions about nature. The old ideas were no longer tenable, and controlled burning was one of the first examples of movement in a new direction. The attempt to move away from the "Bambi" and "Smokey the Bear" image of forest fires to a perspective that fires are a natural and desirable part of the patterns found in most forests, shrublands, and grasslands began, to the best of my knowledge, in earnest in the United States in the early 1940s. The change has come slowly, and episodes of large fires in famous parks repeatedly set the process back, as occurred in 1988 with the fires in Yellowstone National Park, but controlled burning is becoming widely accepted as part of the management of forests and shrublands.

The sequoia, the Kirtland's warbler, and similar cases posed a serious dilemma for the social and political movement known as environmentalism, a dilemma stated and explained in the first part of this book: much of the environmental ideology was based on the belief that nature undisturbed was constant and that this constant condition was most desirable, while in fact nature itself is highly variable, subject to change and requiring change in some cases. A question now arises: If we have a new perspective, has it helped us manage our environment better? If it has not helped, perhaps it is equally flawed. This brings us back to the second and third of the three ancient questions that people have discussed about nature throughout Western history: What is the influence of human beings on nature? What is humanity's role in nature?

We are living at a time of transition from the machine-age metaphor for nature to a new perspective that blends the older organic metaphor with a new technological metaphor. Our management of the environment has only begun to make the transition.[8] The difference between the old and the new approaches to management of biological resources can be put simply. In the old management, one managed for constancy and in terms of uncertainty (a lack of precise knowledge about the condition of the resource and its environment). In the new management, one accepts the need to manage in terms of uncertainty, as well as in terms of change, risk (the inherent unpredictability of events, such as the risk of death and extinction), and complexity. Complexity includes a number of qualities: the ecosystem context (a complex system of interrelationships, mutual causalities, and so forth), simultaneity of many events and conditions, and the possibility that there can be a variety of uses in different places at any one time so that there is complexity in the patterns of the landscapes and seascapes.

The underlying goal of both the old and the new approaches is the ideal of sustainability, but they differ in their interpretation of this ideal. Under the old management, a sustainable harvest could be obtained forever at the same rate in every time period. Under the new management, a sustainable harvest is one whose long-term time-averaged yield does not decline, but the rate of harvest may vary from time period to time period and may have to vary in the short run in order to lead to long-term sustainability. Under the new management, sustainability can be expressed in terms of a specific planning period, a planning time horizon, although in the ideal case this would be, from a human perspective, no different from a plan that would appear to last forever.

Under the old management, management for conservation and management for utilization (such as harvesting fish and cutting forests for timber) appeared to be different and, in general, incompatible goals. From an old preservationist perspective, nature undisturbed achieved a constancy that was desirable and was disrupted in an undesirable way only by human actions. From an old utilization perspective, the forest was there to cut, take apart, replace, and put back together as one chose. If nature was like a watch, then one had to choose between the stereotyped preservationist's approach—appreciate the beauty of the watch, and use it to tell time—and the stereotyped engineer's approach—attempt to take the watch apart and improve it, or use the parts for something else. Under the new management, our role in conservation is active; for example, harvesting may serve the interests of conservation as well as of utilization, and the goals of utilization and conservation can be part of one approach. This statement, however, must be considered with great care. It has become common to speak of "sustainable development," but as the British economist David Pearce has pointed out, this phrase is an oxymoron if strictly interpreted.[9] The rate of use of a resource cannot be increased forever, so in realistic terms a sustainable development must lead through a period of increasing rates of use of a resource to a range of levels that is not exceeded.

An important warning is necessary in regard to the new management. It is worth repeating that admitting that change is necessary seems to open a Pandora's box of problems for environmentalists. The fear is simple: Once we have admitted that some kinds of changes are good, how then can we argue against any changes—against any alteration of the environment? There are several answers to this question. First, as we have seen with the story of the elephants at Tsavo, the failure to accept change leads to destructive, undesirable results. It is only by understanding how nature works and accepting this understanding that our management of nature can really succeed.

Second, to accept certain kinds of change is not to accept all kinds of change. Moreover, we must focus our attention on the rates at which changes occur, understanding that certain rates of change are natural, desirable, and acceptable, while others are not. As long as we refuse to admit that any change is natural, we cannot make this distinction and deal with its implications. With the sequoia, for example, neither complete suppression of fire nor fires that burn every year are desirable; neither fires that are too intense nor those that are too weak are desirable. There is a rate and intensity of fires to which the sequoia have adapted over the millennia and which provides a basis for management. Somewhere in between is a rate of disturbance that would keep the forest in an actively growing state, and thus fires, when they did occur, would have a relatively small destructive impact and a relatively large beneficial effect, promoting recovery and regeneration. Dealing with natural resources is reminiscent of the passage in *Through the Looking-Glass* in which Alice discovers that she can reach a looking-glass house only by walking away from it; every time she tries to walk toward it, she winds up somewhere else. Several examples of this kind were given in Chapter 4: to maintain the forests in the dunes of Australia, the rain forests of the coast of New Zealand, or forests along the coast of Alaska, change is necessary; the soil must be disturbed and turned over to bring to the surface the chemicals required for life.

Third, there are novel aspects about some of the changes that we have brought about, some of which are desirable, but many of which are not. For example, plowing is a novel alteration of soils, as is the introduction of many new chemicals into the environment; since they are novel, they should be used extremely carefully. Another guideline for management is: minimize the use of new technologies when these lead to novel alterations of the environment.

Our approach to management of the environment has been dominated by the machine image of nature, which has been reinforced by the idea of divine origin. But we are now free to let go of that idea because we have new ideas and images that are equally powerful and equally well founded in science and mathematics. We must release ourselves from the grip of this image because it is contrary to the facts about nature and leads us down a path to misguided, destructive, and costly management policies.

Sea Otters, Sea Urchins, and Abalone

The recognition of the inherent erratic and variable character of population abundance is another part of the transition that is taking place in our perception of nature. We are in a transition in the management of biological resources, at the same time looking backward and looking forward. This transitional situation is apparent along the California coast near Hearst's Castle, where one can catch an occasional glimpse, in the wave-tossed kelp and the spray exploding against the shore, of a sea otter floating on its back and looking like a child's cuddly stuffed toy. The otter, which appears simply playful and innocent, has been a focus of an intense controversy over its management. The controversy brings out several central points about the new management as well as illustrates the dilemmas of the transitional situation in which we find ourselves. Recent management of the sea otter has focused on reducing the risk of its extinction, and this policy, by promoting an increase in the populations of otters, has created a controversy. The risk of extinction can be reduced by several means. Under the old management approach, the goal was simply to increase the total numbers. But there are other ways to distribute and reduce the total risk, including the establishment of several populations in different locations that are more or less isolated from one another and relatively protected from the risk of disease or local environmental catastrophes, such as an oil spill. It is a better bet that sea otters will persist because there are at present two populations, one in Alaska and one in California, than if the total population were concentrated in either location. The greater the number of separate, more or less isolated, populations, the greater the chance of survival of this species. From this perspective, recent management has attempted to create a second California population centered along one of the islands in the Santa Barbara Channel, which has led to conflict between fishermen and conservationists.

Managing for Complexity

Sea otters illustrate the need to manage not only with risk in mind, but also with complexity in mind, which in this case means management within what is known as an ecosystem context. Sea otters feed on shellfish, including sea urchins and abalone, both of which are commercially valuable. Sea urchins feed on kelp, the large brown algae that form undersea "forests." The kelp beds are important habitats and spawning areas for many species. Sea urchins do not eat entire kelp; they graze along the bottom of the beds, feeding on the holdfasts, the bases of the kelp that attach them to the bottom. When a holdfast is eaten through, the kelp floats free and dies.

A study of sea otter populations was conducted on two Aleutian Islands of Alaska: Amchitka Island, where the otters were abundant, and Shemya Island, where there were no otters. The high density of sea otters on Amchitka Island was accompanied by abundant kelp beds and few sea urchins, while Shemya Island, lacking sea otters, had abundant sea urchins but little kelp. In an experiment, the removal of sea urchins led to an increase in kelp.[10] These studies suggested that sea otters affected the abundance of kelp, but that the effect was indirect. Sea otters do not eat kelp, nor do they protect individual kelp plants from attack by sea urchins. Sea otters eat sea urchins, which reduces the number of sea urchins feeding on the kelp and thus leads to a larger abundance of kelp. Where kelp is abundant, there are many other species using the kelp forests as habitat. Thus the sea otters affect the abundance of kelp and many other species indirectly.

The current controversy over the sea otters concerns this larger role it plays within its marine ecosystem. Conservationists have argued that the sea otters are necessary for the persistence of many oceanic species that use the kelp forests as breeding grounds or as habitat during parts of their life cycle. These species include a number of economically important ones. But fisherman argue that the sea otters take enormous numbers of abalone and that there are now so many sea otters that the abalone is in danger of declining below a level that would allow the abalone fishermen to make a living. They contend that there are now plenty of sea otters and that the numbers and the locations of the sea otters must be restricted to allow the abalone to remain a viable commercial resource, that the conservation of the otter has led to policies that are destroying the fishery.

Managing for Risk

Under the old management, the goals of the preservationists and of the fishermen would have been seen to be in opposition, with a place for only one or the other. Under the new management, the issue becomes a set of quantitative and specific questions that require scientific study (as well as mediation and discussion among the various parties). One starts with the question: How many sea otters are enough? To answer this, one has to know about the risks of extinction and the factors in nature that tend to reduce this risk.

It is helpful to know how the sea otters became endangered. Around the turn of the century, sea otters were believed to be extinct, the victims of overzealous hunting for their fur, which had been considered to be among the finest in the world. Hunting of sea otters began at the end of the eighteenth century, when the otters were distributed throughout a large area of the northern Pacific Ocean coasts—from northern Japan, northeastward along Russia and Alaska, and southward along the coast of North America to Morro Hermoso in Baja California.[11] According to the standard story, a group of shipwrecked Russian sailors survived a winter eating sea otters and keeping warm in sea otter pelts. The furs that they brought back led to the development of the sea otter fur trade and to intense hunting of this species. Although by the end of the nineteenth century, so few sea otters were left that the hunting ceased and the species was thought to have become extinct, two small colonies were later discovered—one in the Aleutian Islands of Alaska and the other along the California coast from Monterey Bay south to Point Conception.

Legal protection of the sea otter by the United States government began in 1911. Today, the sea otter is protected by two federal laws: the Marine Mammal Protection Act of 1972 and the U.S. Endangered Species Act of 1973. The Marine Mammal Protection Act has some curious phrases. As was explained in Chapter 2, this law states that the primary objective of the management of marine mammals should be "to maintain the health and stability of the marine ecosystems" and that "whenever consistent with the primary objective," the goal should be to obtain "an optimum sustainable population." The act goes on to explain that the curious phrase "optimum sustainable population" is the "number of animals which will result in the maximum productivity of the population of the species," but that in seeking this goal one must keep in mind "the optimum carrying capacity of the habitat and the health of the ecosystem of which they form a constituent element."[12] The idea of an optimum sustainable population can be traced back to the logistic growth curve and to the ideas of sustainable yields and maximum sustainable yields as they were used in fisheries and wildlife management.

The management of the sea otter, as set down in the Marine Mammal Protection Act, looked forward in its discussion of a marine ecosystem, but looked backward in its phrasing of an optimum sustainable population. The wording in the law allowed two definitions of an optimum-sustainable population: either that population size which has the greatest production (the logistic maximum-sustainable-yield population size, or one-half the carrying capacity) or the logistic growth curve's carrying capacity level. The actual management of the sea otter has retained the ecosystem concept and moved past the simpler idea of a single, fixed optimum-sustainable population to a de facto focus on reducing environmental and genetic risks and on maintaining the species above critically small numbers concentrated in too few populations. Whether the attempt to establish a separate population of sea otters in a new habitat will be successful, and whether this new population will have an undesirably large impact on abalone, remain unclear at this time. But the change from a focus simply on the total number of otters to a concern with the geographical distribution of the otters and the relationships between the otters and the rest of their marine ecosystem, is part of the new management approach. The sea otters, floating peacefully on their backs and eating abalone and sea urchins, epitomize the present transition in our approach to the management of living resources.

Minimum Population Size

The attempt to conserve endangered species brings up the question of the minimum-viable-population—the smallest number of individuals that can be expected to persist for a reasonably long time. What events might have caused the extinction of either of the two isolated populations of sea otters that remained at the end of the nineteenth century when the commercial hunters thought that the otters had become extinct? One can imagine that an episode of severe winter storms, or the outbreak of a disease, might have caused a small otter population to become extinct. In a small population it is also possible that by chance certain undesirable genetic traits would be found in most of the population. Imagine a few sea otters that by chance had a majority of individuals with thinner than normal fur; this trait could then become fixed in the population over several generations, and the resulting population would be susceptible to an episode of extremely stormy weather.

What is a number that is reasonably safe from risk? Scientists are just beginning to understand how to determine what is a safe population size. The minimum acceptable population size depends on the planning time period. There is a different minimum viable population size for short term than for long term. The earliest work has focused on problems arising from undesirable genetic traits that become fixed in a small population. Studies of domestic cattle suggest that for the short term, a population can avoid such genetic problems if it remained above about 50 individuals and that over the long term, to avoid genetic problems, the minimum population size should be 500 or more.[13] There is much more work to do to understand what size population is safe against small, random fluctuations in the environment. This topic is subject to active study today and the recommended numbers are likely to change in the near future, but it is an example of the change in approach, which in this case accepts the ideas of risk and complexity as an essential part of management.

The Ecosystem Context

The sea otters and the whooping cranes provide another lesson in management of natural resources, a lesson that one can learn by comparing the whooping crane with its only avian rival for size in North America, the California condor. While the whooping crane is America's tallest bird, the condor has the greatest wingspread, almost 5 feet. Rare and declining through the nineteenth century and into the mid-twentieth century, the condor population dwindled to just more than twenty individuals by the 1970s, without undergoing the recovery that took place with the crane. Simply being rare did not seem to imply the same fate for the two species. What was the difference between them? It seems to lie primarily in the condition of the habitats of the birds and in the supply of their life-sustaining resources. The crane feeds on small animals in wetlands, and such food sources have been plentiful in its summer and wintering grounds. The crane's food supply and the ecosystems on which this food supply depends have remained intact and self-sustaining. In contrast, the condor's food supply and nesting areas and other features of its habitat have disappeared or been radically altered. The condor feeds on carrion, primarily of large mammals, and it once survived on wild game in the open savannas of the Sierra foothills and the coastal ranges of southern and central California. But much of that game has been eliminated, and, with fire suppression in the twentieth century, much of the condor's habitat has changed from open areas within which carrion could be seen from afar to dense shrublands in which dead animals are harder to find. Some experts have even suggested that the shrublands have made landings and take-offs for the condors difficult and have prevented them from taking food in much of their home range.

From the comparison of the crane and the condor, we learn that the condition of the habitat is more important than simple population numbers. It is better to have a good habitat sustaining a small population than a large population in a poor habitat. Conservation of endangered species is, in this way, understood to depend on the idea of an ecosystem rather than on simple analyses of populations. This is a movement toward managing with complexity as a basic consideration.

Clear-cutting: Harvesting with Complexity

To this point, I have discussed a new perspective on the management of ecosystems or individual endangered species that we want to conserve, but do not want to harvest. Now it is important to consider species that we do want to use or harvest, and the harvesting of forests provides a set of good examples, of which the controversy over clear-cutting is pertinent. Clear-cutting, a common practice, means cutting down all the trees in an area at the same time and either replanting the forest or abandoning it to regenerate itself (or simply abandoning it completely). Is this a good or a bad practice? Environmentalists have tended to view it as a universally bad practice, and a newly clear-cut area is often visually unpleasant in comparison with the grand forest that once grew there. As long as we viewed nature as a simple, wind-up unique machine there seemed to be only one answer to any question, and if clear-cutting was bad in one place it must be bad everywhere.

But now that we understand that disturbance is necessary for many kinds of forests and that it is the frequency, kind, and degree of change that is important, not change itself, we can realize that we must examine each kind of situation on its own merits. In some cases, clear-cutting has desirable results; in other cases, it does not. Whether clear-cutting is desirable depends on the kind of species we would like to be dominant in the forest in the future, the kind of forest, the kind of habitat (its bedrock, soil type and depth, and slope and direction of slope), the rate of recurrence of the clear-cutting, and the logging practices. It is now well known that construction of logging roads and use of wheeled and tracked vehicles in the woods cause soil loss and promote erosion. New logging methods move logs with cables or other devices (balloons and helicopters have been tried); these methods are less destructive and are preferable.

In a classic experiment at the Hubbard Brook Experimental Forest in New Hampshire, an entire forested watershed of approximately 50 acres was clear-cut, and an herbicide was applied to the ground to prevent regeneration. For more than 20 years, the flow of water from this watershed and the eroded materials and dissolved chemical elements carried by the water have been studied. In a later experiment, a commercial logging company was brought in to log narrow strips set out horizontally on a hillside, with every third strip cut in one year, and the remaining strips left for later clear-cutting. This practice had many benefits: erosion was retarded, because the intact forests acted as buffers against erosion; mature seed-bearing trees were near to each clear-cut because each cut was of moderate size. Clear-cutting changes chemical cycling in forests, leading to loss of chemical elements necessary for life from the soil. When a forest is clear-cut, trees are no longer available to take up nutrients. The ground, opened to the sun and rain, becomes warmer, and the process of decay is speeded up; chemical elements such as nitrogen are converted more rapidly to forms that are water soluble and can be readily leached in water runoff during rains.[14] Experiments like those at Hubbard Brook show that clear-cutting can degrade soils on steep slopes in areas of moderate to heavy rainfall. However, where there is little slope and light rainfall and where the desirable species require open areas for growth, clear-cutting may be the preferred harvesting strategy. In the forests of eastern North America, a number of species that require open areas to regenerate, such as white and yellow birch, are useful commercial timber trees, and a forest stand of birches is a pleasant and desired part of the New England landscape. In a flat area with a well-drained soil that is reasonably fertile and not too shallow, the early successional species regenerate naturally, and clear-cutting stands of certain sizes may lead to a landscape that is both economically productive and aesthetically pleasing. If the clear-cut areas are too small, not enough light reaches the ground to stimulate the sprouting of the birches. If the area is too large, it is opened up to more intensive erosion, and reseeding may be low if not enough seed trees are left nearby.

From these examples we see that whether clear-cutting should be used depends on many factors. Understanding that complex patterns in space are natural, we can accept a landscape that supports a variety of uses and recognize that we appreciate diversity in the landscape, and we can maintain at the same time several kinds of areas, including nature preserves in which there is no direct active interference by people, other nature preserves whose goal is to save a particular species, such as the Kirtland's warbler, and within which many direct actions are taken, and land that is subject to a variety of other uses, including commercial harvests. With the new knowledge that we are gaining and with the new perspective on nature that is developing, we can begin to use natural resources more wisely than we have in the past.

This is not to say, naively, that there are no threats to such resources as forests. Of course there are. The primary threat is widespread cutting without regard for regeneration. Large areas that were once white pine stands in Michigan have never recovered from their first logging, which began in the late 1840s and continued until about 1920. It is estimated that 19 million acres of white pine were cut. Only a few remnants of the original forests remain; one of them is at Hartwick Pine State Park in central Michigan, where one small stand that originally occupied approximately 90 acres was abandoned uncut in 1873 at the time of an economic crash. It was uneconomical to log that small stand after the economy recovered, and the area remained intact and was set aside as a park. About half of the original stand was blown down in a storm, and now only about 50 acres remain as a virgin white pine forest.

While some of the cutover areas have regrown to forests, large tracts in Michigan called "stump barrens" have never regenerated, but are occupied by reindeer moss and other lichens, bracken fern, grasses, and shrubs. In the mid-1970s, I visited many of these areas and tried to determine why forests had not regenerated. An old red oak in one of the stump barrens near the town of Pellston, Michigan, provided a small clue. Gray old stumps and partially decayed gray logs lay on the ground among the grasses and lichens, but under the shade of that old oak were a half-dozen saplings of white pine, distinctive because they were alone in the field. Perhaps the oak protected the saplings, but from what? The field lay at the base of a hill created thousands of years ago as the glaciers retreated and deposited sands along an ancient lake shore. The base of that hill was subjected to downhill drainage of cold air, which occurred when cold air in the autumn, winter, and spring, being denser than warmer air, moved down the slope making the base of the hill colder at night than the top. Near the border of a tree species's range, early spring frosts or late fall frosts can kill young trees; frosts are more likely near the ground because the surface loses heat by direct radiation. It is warmer at night under the branches of a large tree, just as it is cooler during the day in the shade of a tree. These factors would have been accentuated at the base of the hill. It appears that white pine reached its northern limit during a very warm period, about 4,000 years ago, the warmest period since the end of the last ice age until the present. The climate of the late nineteenth and early twentieth centuries was cooler than that earlier climate. But forests have considerable inertia. Mature trees may have shielded seedlings and saplings of the white pines from frost. Once the mature trees were removed, such protection would have been lost. This is not to say that the forests had always been white pine stands for the past 4,000 years. As the climate warmed and cooled, the northern limit of the white pine would have responded with a change in distribution. But this would have occurred very gradually in comparison with the logging of the immense area, which took place in less than 100 years. The rapidity of the logging over a vast area greatly reduced the possibilities for the white pine and other tree species to respond to the changes.

The failure of the forests to regenerate may be also the result of the unnaturally intense fires that followed the logging. The loggers took only the main trunks of the trees and left the rest—limbs, twigs, leaves, stumps—in the forest. There was little concern about fire, and when fires accidentally started the unnaturally large amount of firewood fuel on the ground may have produced fires intense enough to destroy the organic matter in the soil. The inability of the forests to recover may also result from a lack of seed-bearing trees, too few of which remained after the intense fires. The explanations I have just given are based on informal observations, not rigorous scientific experiment. But whatever the exact explanation, which is not yet known, the fact is that much of this region has failed to recover. Rapid clear-cutting over such a large scale in such a short time, with little care taken for the treatment of the soil and the intensity of fires (not simply the existence of fires), led to undesirable results; in this situation, clear-cutting should not have been carried out as it was. But modified clear-cutting—smaller cuts scattered among intact stands, with care for the soil and the avoidance of erosion—could have been part of an ecologically sensitive approach.[15]

The City, Civilization, and Nature

One autumn afternoon when on a visit to Venice, I was taken on a pleasant boat trip by members of the World Wildlife Fund to see the work they were doing on the conservation of the lagoon. We traveled to the north of the lagoon, to the marshes out of sight of the Grand Canal and Santa Maria della Salute, the scene with which I began this book. There in the salt marshes, nature seemed to rule. Along the shore, in that hazy sunlight so often portrayed by artists who have interpreted Venice over the centuries, shore birds lingered and breezes brushed the salt grass. In the declining sunlight, we could look away from the city and believe that civilization was far distant, even though we knew that the shape of the shoreline, the chemistry of the waters, and the quality of the air were strongly influenced by the city and civilization.

While I have chosen to illustrate the central qualities of a new management of the environment through examples that have to do with the forest and the ocean—the nature of the "out-there" seemingly away from our homes and our cities, away from the apparent center of our civilization—the approaches to management I have discussed apply broadly to the total environment, including the environment of our cities and the city as an environment. As the great thinkers about cities and civilization, such as Lewis Mumford, have made us realize, the city has been both the center of civilization in the past and a part of, not separate from, its surroundings.[16] For civilization to survive, we cannot believe that the management of nature means only the management of wilderness preserves.

Most of us live in cities and cities are nature for us. But in most urban areas, unlike Venice, architecture and nature seem separate, and we tend not to perceive so readily the close relationship between the city and its environment. As urban areas continue to spread over the landscape with the growth of human populations, however, it becomes imperative that we understand that cities must be managed as local environments, both for their own continuation and because of their effects on regional and global environments. Venice epitomizes the urban dilemma. Of all cities, Venice is perhaps most visibly set within and dependent on a fragile, changing, and human-influenced environment. Venice attracts us because of the blend of its architecture (the technological) with the surrounding lagoon (naturalistic, providing an appearance of the natural). Each, the intentional artifice and the intended natural, strongly influences the other. The lagoon has been much altered by human technologies over the centuries, beginning with the millions of saplings driven into the shifting muds to provide a foundation for the architecture itself and continuing with alterations of watercourses that led into the lagoon and of the lagoon itself. These human actions have had both positive and negative results. In the twentieth century, removal of ground water on the nearby mainland for use by modern industry increased the rate at which the city was sinking, making the architecture increasingly vulnerable to the *aqua alta*, the flood waters that occur with high tides during winter storms. Air pollution from the city of Mestre, on the mainland, erodes the statues in St. Mark's Square and at La Salute. Sewage from the city flows into the lagoon, making the waters dangerous to fall into and making the city completely dependent on the flushing action of the tides and storms, which moves the polluted waters out into the Adriatic. Solutions to Venice's environmental problems, like the solutions to managing the habitats of the Kirtland's warbler, the giant sequoia, and the sea otter, involve the acceptance of nature's ambiguities and variability, the necessity for new knowledge, and the recognition that our engineering must enter into the modification of the environment as a constructive power. In 1988 such an approach was attempted in Venice as newly designed floodgates were being put into place at the outer edge of the lagoon. The gates lie underwater, allowing the movement of the tides to flush the city's waters, until a storm comes. Then they are inflated, rise to block the high waters, modulate the action of the storms, and prevent damage to the city's buildings. We will have to wait to see if this specific technology is successful, but the approach takes into account risk, uncertainty, variability, and complexity. The conservation of Venice requires facts, knowledge, and a change in myth and metaphor about nature. Others whose expertise about cities is greater than mine will know how to translate the new management perspective downtown. Without that translation, without the recognition that the city is of and within the environment, the wilderness of the wolf and the moose, the nature that most of us think of as natural, cannot survive, and our own survival on the planet will come into question. The management of nature, although most easily illustrated by a tree and an otter, is not restricted to those elements from which most of us are separated. The management of nature lies just outside the door, and affects not only ourselves and our neighbors, but also nature in its largest sense.

–IV–

RESOLUTIONS FOR
OUR TIME

The observatory on Mauna Loa from which measurements of the carbon dioxide concentration of the atmosphere have been made since 1957 (photograph by E. Botkin).

–11

The Winds of Mauna Loa:
How to Approach
Managing The Biosphere

> From the region of an endless summer the eye takes in the domain of
> an endless winter, where almost perpetual snow crowns the summits
> of Mauna Kea and Mauna Loa.
>
> Isabella Bird (1873)[1]

Taking The Earth's Pulse

On an October morning in 1982, I traveled to the upper slopes of Mauna
Loa, Hawaii, driving on a dirt road that climbed more than 10,000 feet
above sea level. The trip was much like that described a century earlier by
Isabella Bird—from endless summer along the coast, from dense shade of
the lush green tropical forest landscape heavily modified by human action;
through dry woodlands of 'ohi'a trees opening to the sun at mid-elevations;
and into endless sun-drenched winter seemingly untouched by human
hands, a sparse, moonlike landscape of solidified streams of fresh black lava
covering swaths of older brown lava. On this morning, I was struck once
again by the brilliant colors, as I had been on every trip from temperate
zones to subtropics and tropics. Isabella Bird saw it 100 years ago, when she
wrote that the coast near Hilo had "glades and dells of dazzling green,
bright with cataracts," above which the "snow-capped mountains
gleamed." "Creation," she wrote, "surely cannot exhibit a more brilliant
green than that which clothes windward Hawaii."[2] On the way up, occasional bracken ferns struggling to grow in crevices of older lava were life's
last outposts; once they were left behind, life seemed absent, the rich green
of tropical vegetation only a distant haze below the thermocline, the ham-
mer and shovel of our own civilization visible only in the dirt road that led
upward. Mauna Loa seemed a place relegated to the physical Earth, untouched in one's vision by any life, a place of nature undisturbed. But in

171

this brightness our vision betrays us, for life touches these slopes in the chemistry of the winds.

On this barren slope at 11,500 feet stands a small collection of buildings: observatories painted a light blue, in striking contrast to the rock and sky, from which a network of black electric cables and tubes swarms outward to small towers. I came to visit a famous observatory, now operated by the National Oceanographic and Atmospheric Administration, which looks not at the stars, but at the Earth. Since 1957, the concentration of trace gases in the atmosphere, including carbon dioxide, had been measured at this laboratory.

From its location at 11,500 feet above sea level, the Mauna Loa observatory stands above local effects of life on the big island, protected by atmospheric conditions from the tropical forests and the tourists. More than 2,000 miles downwind from the nearest continent, Mauna Loa is also distant enough to be protected from major concentrations of continental land plants and animals and major industrial centers and from their combined short-term local variations in release of gases to the atmosphere. For these reasons, the upper slopes of Mauna Loa form an ideal place to measure the atmosphere.

From a thin tower, the high-altitude air is pumped down and through a tube into one of the buildings, where instruments scan the moving air with infrared light and measure its absorption by carbon dioxide. Alongside are tanks of carefully calibrated gases to ensure that measurements made years apart are consistent with one another. These measurements are a key to life's activity. Like the mouse in Joseph Priestly's jar, all oxygen-breathing organisms give off carbon dioxide as they respire. All photosynthetic organisms remove carbon dioxide from the air, converting the carbon to sugar and giving off oxygen as a waste product. Life's activity is summed up by the breathing in and breathing out of carbon dioxide in the atmosphere; on Mauna Loa, the totality of the inhalations and exhalations of all the organisms in the Northern Hemisphere are recorded faithfully and have become famous as a monitoring of life on the Earth for a generation.

Over the years, the measurements at Mauna Loa have shown two clear patterns (Figure 11): an annual oscillation, with a decline in summer followed by an increase in winter, a periodic pattern as regular as the vibrations of a plucked guitar string; and, imposed on this rising and falling, a steady annual increase like a rising tone.[3] The summer decline is the result of photosynthesis on the land in the Northern Hemisphere: the summation of the growing of the 'ohi'a trees on Mauna Loa's slopes, the spruce and fir at Isle Royale, the oaks and hickories in Hutcheson Forest on the Atlantic coast, the acacia and baobabs on Tsavo's desolate plains, and

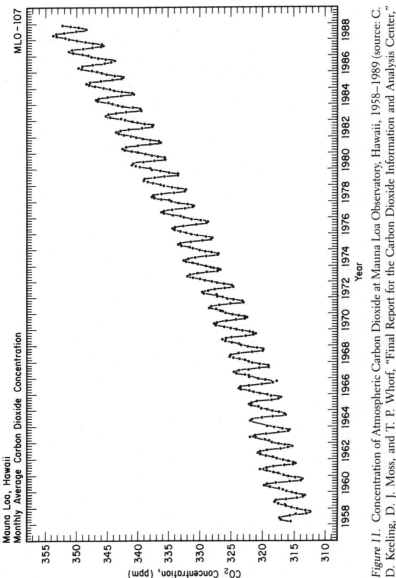

Figure 11. Concentration of Atmospheric Carbon Dioxide at Mauna Loa Observatory, Hawaii, 1958–1989 (source: C. D. Keeling, D. J. Moss, and T. P. Whorf, "Final Report for the Carbon Dioxide Information and Analysis Center," Martin-Marietta Energy Systems, Inc., Oak Ridge, Tennessee). Measurements are from a cooperative program of the National Oceanographic and Atmospheric Administration and the Scripps Institution of Oceanography.

all the other thousands of species of land plants in the hemisphere. Photo-synthesis in the oceans contributes little to these seasonal patterns because most algae are short-lived and lack ways to store organic compounds for long periods. The increase during the winter is the result of respiration without photosynthesis: the breaths of the moose struggling in the snows on Isle Royale, the elephants, with their silent steps, on the Tsavo plains; the arctic lynx and rabbit, whose populations are varying wildly year to year; and the billions of people. Life on the land in its totality touches the slopes of Mauna Loa invisibly, its effects brushed against the black rocks by the winds. Our civilization is part of this invisible touch, reaching the slopes as the continual increase in the concentration of carbon dioxide in the atmo-sphere, which is a result of the burning of fossil fuels and the clearing of land—the destruction of forests and soils and the conversion of their stored organic carbon to carbon dioxide.

From the vantage point of Mauna Loa, we stand and observe our planet the way that Priestly watched the mouse in the bell jar; we discover that we influence the Earth much as microbes affect a moose's stomach. That people can affect the entire Earth in such an invisible way is a relatively new idea, possible only after the technological and scientific revolutions of the past two centuries. As recently as 1967, such human influence seemed preposterous even to most of those who had thought deeply about nature. For example, Clarence Glacken dismissed the argument that large, unin-habited areas of the Earth, whether forests or oceans, might serve a useful purpose, as suggested by some philosophers: "It is the kind of argument which a defender of the design [argument for the universe] must be pre-pared to make."[4] But 20 years later, during the transition that marks the end of the machine age, a headline in a local newspaper—"Restoring Tropical Forests May Ease Warming Trend"—suggested that replanting forests in the tropics might help to stave off a global climatic change.[5] In a few decades, we have jumped from dismissing the possibility that any life might affect the Earth at a global level to considering a newspaper proposal that we make use of this effect to modify the climate.

Right or wrong, that proposal is a late-twentieth-century novelty, whose antecedents were first published half a century ago in the more obscure scientific literature. The possibility that modern civilization might be changing the Earth's climate was suggested in 1938 by G. S. Callendar, who found that measurements of carbon dioxide concentration in the atmosphere taken in the twentieth century were higher than those made in the nineteenth century.[6] Callendar suggested that the difference could be accounted for by the amount of carbon dioxide added to the atmosphere from the burning of coal, oil, and natural gas since the beginning of the

Industrial Revolution. He also suggested that the increase might lead to a global warming. Could it be that the machine age was changing the biosphere? Callendar was attacked by his scientific colleagues for this suggestion, some dismissing the notion simply on the grounds that nineteenth-century scientists could not have done as good a job as scientists in the 1930s, and therefore the measurements were inaccurate. But Callendar's speculation has been confirmed in the measurements at Mauna Loa that show a steady increase in carbon dioxide in the atmosphere.

Callendar began a set of controversies that are still unresolved today. Why would a newspaper article suggest that planting trees might reduce climatic changes? The energy received from the sun and emitted to space by the Earth's surface is affected by the chemical composition of the atmosphere. Certain compounds absorb infrared wavelengths more strongly than other compounds, but are transparent to visible light, and in this way warm the Earth through the greenhouse effect. The greenhouse effect is just that—the effect that glass has in a greenhouse. Glass is transparent to visible light, but is much less transparent to infrared radiation, the wavelength at which heat is transmitted by radiation from objects at temperatures that are found on the Earth's surface. Thus greenhouse glass lets in sunlight energy, which heats the surfaces inside the greenhouse. These surfaces reradiate energy, but at longer infrared wavelengths, to which the glass is opaque. When this infrared light reaches the glass, it is absorbed and reflected, and the greenhouse warms up. That is one reason why a greenhouse is warmer than the outdoors and warmer than a room whose windows do not allow visible light through. (Another reason is that a greenhouse prevents heat loss to the flowing air.) The glass in the greenhouse is a one-way window open to visible light and closed to infrared. Carbon dioxide, water vapor, and some other trace gases such as methane in the atmosphere act in the same way, while condensed water droplets in clouds are opaque to both infrared and visible light and thus cool the Earth.

Each chemical compound absorbs and transmits a unique combination of wavelengths. If the water content of the atmosphere or the carbon dioxide content of the atmosphere changes, so does the reabsorption of the energy released from the surface. During the ancient history of the Earth, the removal of carbon dioxide from the Earth's atmosphere by the earliest photosynthetic organisms was like opening a window in a greenhouse; the Earth's surface must have cooled. As life evolved on the Earth and increased in abundance, it changed the chemistry of the Earth and the characteristics of its surface, particularly the reflection and absorption of radiant energy. Astronomers tell us that there is evidence that the sun became hotter during the early history of the Earth, so these two processes may have tended to counteract each other: as the sun heated up, the amount of carbon dioxide in the atmosphere declined; as a result, the Earth warmed less than a lifeless planet would have. The surface of Venus is much hotter than it would be if the planet supported life because of the high concentration of carbon dioxide in the Venusian atmosphere.

Any major change in the abundance and distribution of life on the Earth's surface will change the reflection and absorption of light and infrared radiant energy and therefore the surface temperature of the Earth. Some human activities, particularly those that are the result of a technological civilization, can affect climate by introducing into the atmosphere pollutants, such as dust, smoke, or small compounds, such as carbon dioxide, that absorb infrared light.

Although the greenhouse effect of carbon dioxide was first proposed in the 1930s, only recently has it been realized that other small, trace compounds that are in the atmosphere because of life—methane, oxides of nitrogen, and the like—might have had extremely potent effects on climate. These small biologically produced gases share some important characteristics. They absorb infrared light at wavelengths that atmospheric physicists refer to as being in the "atmospheric window." This window includes those wavelengths in the infrared that are not absorbed by water vapor, and therefore the atmosphere is transparent to these wavelengths. Through this window a great fraction of the heat from the Earth is released into space. This loss of heat energy is essential for life.

Because the small biologically produced compounds such as carbon dioxide and methane absorb infrared light in that portion of its spectrum that the atmosphere is otherwise transparent, very small changes in the amounts of these compounds in the atmosphere could have very large effects on the temperature of the Earth. It has been estimated, for example, that a doubling of the amount of methane in the atmosphere—which in the mid-1980s made up only 1.7 parts per million of the atmosphere—might increase the average temperature of the Earth by nearly 2°F.[7] Since scientists have estimated that the difference between a twentieth-century climate and that of an ice age represents a lowering of the Earth's average temperature by 7 to 13°F, a 2°F shift would, one expects, result in a large change in the Earth's surface characteristics.

But the story is even more complicated and more intricately related to life. An increase in the average concentration of methane in the atmosphere could take place either because more methane was produced or because the rate of degradation of this compound decreased. And only one chemical pathway removes methane from the atmosphere; it involves methane's combination with the hydroxide ion, the OH⁻ in H_2O, and the concentration of this ion depends on the acidity of the atmosphere, which is affected by both human and nonhuman life.

If the average temperature of the Earth is to remain constant, there must be a balance between the energy received from the sun and the energy lost to space. If the rate of loss decreases while the amount of sunlight that reaches the Earth remains constant, the temperature of the Earth must increase; as the temperature increases, the rate of energy loss by radiation would increase. In this way, a new steady-state temperature would be attained that would be higher than the previous one.

The article in the newspaper proposed planting trees to "ease a warming trend" based on the belief that the trees can scavenge the atmosphere of unwanted carbon dioxide. If we carried out this proposal, we would not be planting trees because we wanted them for themselves, but because of a service they provide. This in itself is one way that our perspective on life and on nature has changed from the view of trees as of value individually or as fixed groups in stands, to a perception of all vegetation as serving a public function through a dynamic process.

What will happen as the upward trend in carbon dioxide that is measured on Mauna Loa continues? In the past—before the invention of modern instruments that could measure small concentrations of chemicals in the environment, remote sensing by satellite, and computers—there was little that people could do to assess the current situation or to make projections about future conditions. In recent years, large, fast computers have made possible the development of global climate models. They are still crude; in them, the atmosphere is divided into very large sections on the order of 5° latitude and longitude on a side. In these models, many events and processes are considered together in order to project change. The processes that lead to exchange of energy in the atmosphere are simplified, but even with simplification the number of calculations that must be made are so great that the models require large amounts of computer time. The models give a crude first estimation of climatic dynamics, and they are undoubtedly inaccurate in some aspects, but they are a step in the direction of understanding an important component of the biosphere.

Present climate models predict that if we double the concentration of carbon dioxide in the atmosphere as we burn fossil fuels—an increase that is expected to take place in approximately the next century—then the average temperature of the Earth's surface will increase by about 4 to 8°F. But the effect is much more pronounced at higher latitudes than at lower ones, more pronounced in the Boundary Waters and Isle Royale than in Tsavo. In Minnesota and Michigan the temperature might climb by between 6 and 12°F.[8]

What would these changes mean for life? The soils of the Boundary Waters and Isle Royale would become warmer and drier. Recently, I had the opportunity to bring the computer model of forest growth that I had developed to bear on the issue of the effects of climatic change. We obtained projections into the twenty-first century from several climate models for monthly temperature and rainfall at several locations in the Midwest, one of which was Virginia, Minnesota, not far across Lake Superior from Isle Royale and the nearest weather station to the Boundary Waters Canoe Area. The forest model projected that if the expected climatic warming were to take place, the spruce and fir forests of the Boundary Waters and Isle Royale would be replaced by sugar maple and red maple, which grow to some extent in these areas but are more characteristic of areas to the south. The effects would depend on soil type and soil water conditions. In the Boundary Waters Canoe Area, wetter habitats where balsam fir dominates, and dry areas where white birch or quaking aspen are dominant would be converted to forests of sugar maple; white cedar bogs would become treeless bogs. To the south in southern Michigan, the projected effects are even more dramatic: forests that are transitional between northern hardwoods, of which sugar maple is typical, and oak forests to the south would be converted to oak woodlands or savannas or even to treeless prairies, which are now located much farther west. Thus the boreal forest would be replaced by northern hardwoods; the habitat of the moose would change dramatically, the waters that now reflect a gliding canoe would mirror a different image. Even more striking, the projections suggest that these effects might be readily noticeable in as little as 30 years from now, to be seen by the next human generation.

Not only would recreation and wildlife be changed, but commercial wood production would be affected. Again, the impact would depend heavily on soil type and soil water conditions. Dry sandy soils in the southwestern part of the region might be converted to prairie and savanna in which no significant wood production takes place. Soils with abundant water might continue to support trees, but the forests would have less organic matter and would produce less timber.

The climatic change would lead to major dislocations in the forest industry in the Great Lakes states. This industry is currently adapted for a certain complement of species, primarily softwoods used in the production of paper pulp and construction materials. The species that would become most economically important under a doubling of the carbon dioxide concentration would be hardwoods such as oaks and maples, which are useful for furniture and decorative purposes. They have much longer rotation times (harvesting would be done less frequently) than the softwoods. Thus there would be a major shift in the character of the forest industry whose costs should be evaluated; the shift would require different equipment and lead to sales to new markets.

What are we to do in response to the increase in carbon dioxide level? Suppose we did set out to manage the biosphere by planting trees to remove the "excess" carbon dioxide that had been added each year by the burning of fossil fuels. The total amount added in this way each year that the trees would have to take up is about 4 billion tons of carbon. A square mile of tropical rain forest has been estimated, optimistically, to produce annually an amount of organic matter containing about 2,600 tons of carbon.[9] At that rate, about 1.5 million square miles of tropical forest could take up all the excess carbon. This is an area about three times as large as Peru and about 9 percent of the total area estimated to be in tropical rain forests in. 1973. But this is the minimum amount of forest area needed, assuming that it could remain steadily productive, continually pulling carbon dioxide out of the atmosphere. For the area set aside to remain highly productive, the forests would have to be maintained indefinitely in mid-successional stages. A recently clear-cut area would not have this high rate of production, nor would a very old forest. Considering what we know about the variability of climate, leading to good and bad years, to the changes induced by fire, storms, and disease, a much larger area would have to be set aside. The exact extent we can only guess at, but it would probably be 3 to 10 times the minimum.

We might take a more democratic approach and try to replant woody plants locally everywhere, not just in the tropics, to disperse the responsibility for removing carbon dioxide from the atmosphere to all the nations of the world, not just those in the tropics. It is estimated that, on the average, the production of new organic matter by natural vegetation results in the annual removal and storage of about 830 tons of carbon in each square mile, less than that in the highly productive tropics. On the basis of this average, a total of 4.3 million square miles of forests is the minimum needed to take up the annual increase in carbon dioxide in the atmosphere. The total continental landmass, excluding bare rock, ice, and sand, is estimated to be 49 million square miles. If we were to set aside land and allow vegetation to grow solely to take up the carbon that our other activities were adding to the atmosphere, then we would have to allocate about 10 percent of the continental land mass that is not bare rock, sand, or ice. If we set aside enough land to reduce the rate of carbon dioxide buildup in the atmosphere by 20 percent, then 2 percent of the continental land mass would have to be set aside for this purpose. And none of the organic matter produced each year could be allowed to burn or decompose.[10] This is possible theoretically, but it would require a huge and worldwide cooperative effort.

We have fewer options to deal with human-induced global-climate change than with the management of local renewable resources. Our options appear reduced to projecting changes and trying to adjust to them—for example, using our ability to make projections to have enough time to choose what trees we plant and harvest in locations that would seem most likely to be affected.

Remembering that autumn morning on the slopes of Mauna Loa, I cannot help but think about where we have come in our perceptions of nature and our role in nature. In understanding and awareness, we stand in much the same relation to global environmental problems as did George Perkins Marsh a century ago in his understanding and awareness of local environmental problems. One hundred years ago, deforestation and de-struction of soils were taking place in sparsely settled areas of Michigan and Minnesota that would have seemed just over the horizon of daily activities to most citizens of the United States—out of sight, out of reach, and therefore not a problem that would have seemed to require drastic, immedi-ate attention. At that time few measurements of nature could be made and few ways to chart trends into the future were available. So it is with us and global-climate change, as well as with the other well-known global environ-mental problems—for example, the ozone layer, acid rain, pollution of coastal waters.

In our first attempts to deal with these global issues, we have not com-pletely shed the legacies of the machine age. The first attempts to analyze how carbon cycles in the biosphere, which were published in the scientific journals in the late 1940s, had the same steady-state assumptions as machine-age population dynamics. These assumptions are clearly evident in diagrams and in the mathematical models of the carbon cycle—the route supposedly taken by the element as it moved into and out of living things, and into and out of the atmosphere, the oceans, and rock sedi-ments. The biosphere was assumed to be in a steady-state in regard to carbon, except for human interference. As with other features of life on our planet, recent information shows—to the contrary—that the level of car-bon dioxide in the atmosphere has varied over thousands of years, reduced to a minimum at the height of the last continental glaciation and increas-ing since.

Accustomed as we have become to instant responses, fast foods, and 3-minute television editorials, we would like instant answers to the question of what to do about the human-induced climatic change, assuming that it will come about. From the slopes of Mauna Loa, events seem to move at a slower pace, and it is clear that we must be patient until we achieve greater understanding. But most important, we must complete the transition in our perception of nature, the transition that is the theme of this book. Only then can we proceed to do our best to analyze the biosphere and to project the changes that will occur. Modern computer models, which are being developed more and more from this new perspective, are a first step along this pathway. Although we may want instant answers, we cannot get them. We need to support the development of fundamental sciences that help us understand the workings of the biosphere; along the way, we will undoubtedly go through many roller-coaster rides of reinterpretation of the dangers that might lie ahead. There are fewer satisfying answers that we can give at this time concerning global environmental issues than local ones. With more understanding, we will have a better idea of whether the purported climatic change is likely to cause great difficulties, and we will have a better means to determine how we can adjust. With better knowledge of how life and chemistry affect the climate, we may find new options to ameliorate the undesirable effects.

The Kinds of Global Environmental Issues

The carbon dioxide problem forces us to take a new perspective on the meaning of our role in nature. We find once again that nature changes at many scales of time and space, that we cannot expect nature to remain in a constant condition and thus provide us with a simple solution to the questions of what is "natural" and what is desirable. At the global level, most changes take place over intervals that seem long in comparison with our lifetimes, and thus we have been able to ignore them. But the speed with which our technology is changing the biosphere allows us to ignore global environmental changes only at our peril.

I have used the threat of global-climate change as an example of the issues we face if we try to deal with global environmental problems. From this example, some generalizations can be made.[11] The key ideas at the global level are the same as those at the local: we should avoid making novel kinds of changes and imposing rates of change at each level of the biosphere that exceed the ability of life to respond to them. At the global level, our opportunities for action are clearly much more restricted than at the local level; the biosphere has a great momentum, and we understand almost nothing about its functioning.

The first task that confronts us is to clarify our goals, all the more important because we see now that nature does not provide us with a simple answer in a single context. In our laws and policies, we have tended to set down regulations for the cleanliness of air and water, in large part because of their importance to life. But we must recognize that the real focus of our efforts is the maintenance of life. We are often directed away from this focus by the way that policies and laws are formulated; clean-air and clean-water standards designed originally to protect life become, under policies and practices of large bureaucracies, ends in themselves. But we should remember in this regard that life is the focus. As Thomas E. Lovejoy has written,

> In the last analysis, even when we have learned to manage other aspects of the global environment, even if population reaches a stable level, even if we reach a time when environmental crises have become history, even if most wastes have gone except the most long lived, even if global cycles have settled back into more normal modes, then the best measure of how we have managed the global environment will be how much biological diversity has survived.[12]

We must distinguish between merely the persistence of some kinds of life and the maintenance of a biosphere that is desirable to human beings. The constraints on the conditions for the latter are much more stringent than those for the former. Accepting the second idea, we must make a further distinction: whether we want the world environment to remain constant or nearly constant with respect to some time that we consider desirable, or whether any condition that continues to support a large number of people with a reasonable level of well-being is acceptable. To sustain the biosphere to meet conditions for the well-being of people, we will have to slow down the rates of changes that we are creating in the biosphere. Temperature and rainfall patterns have to remain within ranges that are much more narrow than those that have existed during the past 2 million years. However, this may not be possible or desirable from a very long-term perspective on the survival of life on the Earth. (One could argue for the beneficial effects of continental glaciation, such as restoring the fertility of the soils.)

We face three kinds of global environmental problems as the result of human activities: catastrophic, acute, and chronic. The catastrophic includes nuclear war and nuclear winter. Acute global problems are sudden and short-term, lasting perhaps a year, such as the emission of a toxin that is carried from its place of origin or the accidental release of an undesirable strain of bacteria. Chronic global environmental problems take place over a long time in terms of human planning and are typically the result of a slow environmental change. Acid rain, the depletion of the ozone layer, and the greenhouse effect are major examples of chronic global problems. Most of our current global environmental problems are chronic.

We can set our goals for the biosphere into two stages, a transition stage, and a long-term stage. The transition stage is how to get from where we are now to where we would like to be. The long-term stage would be a biosphere that we considered "healthy." A healthy biosphere would vary within a set of conditions acceptable to us or necessary for the persistence of life. The rate and magnitude of variation would be small enough so that: the rate of extinctions would return to its precivilization level, soil erosion would be reduced to a range of levels so that soils could be replenished by human actions within our capabilities, fresh water would again become a sustainable resource, pollutants that do not decay (such as arsenic) would be eliminated or reduced to vanishing levels and the concentration of other pollutants would be lowered. The abundance of natural resources would vary within acceptable limits, subject to management actions within our capabilities (both technical and economic), and we would have constrained our energy uses to a sustainable level, increasing the utilization of renewable sources. The human population would cease to increase overall, but would vary from place to place (increasing in one while decreasing in another), and even undergo some total decreases over time; it would remain below an upper bound that is our best estimate of the human carrying capacity of the Earth. These we can take as long-term goals toward which we would strive.

The view from Mauna Loa shows us an Earth whose entire atmosphere we are capable of changing and which we have begun to change. Nature in the largest sense is a system that has varied over time and space at many scales. We are left with the realization that we have the power to change the biosphere, and we are forced to make choices; nature in the large does not provide a single simple goal. There are many themes in nature's symphony, each with its own pace and rhythm. We are forced to choose among these, which we have barely begun to hear and understand.

Landsat satellite image of northern Italy, from the lagoon of Venice (lower right) to the Alps. Smoke from industries on the mainland can be seen passing over Venice. A cloud obscures the bottom of the image (courtesy of the Map and Imagery Library, University of California, Santa Barbara).

_12

The Moon in the Nautilus Shell: Nature in the Twenty-first Century

> As the plan holds, life is poured copiously throughout a Universe, engendering the things and weaving variety into their being.
>
> Plotinus (third century A.D.)[1]

> [The newly designed sunlight-power car is a] meaningful syntheses of biology and technology, bringing man toward an accommodation with dwindling resources.
>
> Paul MacCready (1987)[2]

Dawn Flight

Leonardo da Vinci Airport lies on the mainland north of Venice along the shore of the lagoon, where it is most conveniently reached from the city by water. I had arranged to leave Venice on an early morning flight, and departed from St. Mark's Square before dawn by water taxi. Before daylight, the city was as much sound as light, as we traveled slowly along small side canals where, in the dark, the wavelets of the lagoon and the wake of the boat brushed against the buildings, the sound of city and sea brought together. As the dawn broke, we were free of the main islands, speeding into the open waters of the lagoon, where the fresh wind spoke not of the city but of shore birds and salt grasses. The airplane took off in full daylight, and from within one of the magnificent creations of the twentieth century, the jet aircraft, we viewed the classic city of history, the city within the lagoon, for one last time. Quickly below us passed St. Mark's Square; the church of Santa Maria della Salute, supported by its 1 million saplings driven long ago into the shifting muds of the lagoon; and the Grand Canal with the Rialto Bridge, site of so many famous paintings of Venice in the hazy light of the Adriatic coast. Wave patterns showed that the water was in motion, and the wake of boats traveling from the city to the mainland showed that they too moved, but all else, in the few seconds it took the city to pass below, appeared stationary. A quick impression, and the scene was gone. From this vantage, all seemed clear, constant, and beautiful; the polluted waters and the decaying statues crumbling in the acidic air were invisible. Nature and the city appeared briefly as one. As in a painting, the view from 1,000 feet was of a graceful still-life without a hint of the changes that had occurred over the centuries, wrought by man and by nature. Below was a city founded when people had believed that the Earth was a fellow creature and nature was the product of a divine order. Before the rise of modern science, in the age of Venice as a great city of history, nature was viewed as a whole: the universe, the physical Earth, and life were one, or each appeared to be merely different expressions of the same truths, of the same balance, order, and harmony.

The roar of the engines caught my attention, and I thought about the many systems that made this wonderful machine glide smoothly over the Earth with great reliability, stability, and precision. A steady roar reassured me that the engines were spinning at a constant speed under the control of intricate monitoring systems. Up front, the pilots relied on solid-state radio-navigation and communication systems, each tuned to a specific frequency, and on guidance systems made possible by gyroscopes spinning steadily. Now I was within a machine with all the qualities of order, harmony, and balance that had once been attributed to the nature I saw below.

Nature and technology have always been part of my own experience. Each of the places I have been and described in this book were reached by modern machine, and the equipment that we camped with and hiked with and measured nature with were all products of late twentieth century technology. Piloting a small airplane over the landscape and walking through the wilderness had each in their own ways brought me in touch with nature, and I have been uncomfortable over the years with the division between the views of my engineer friends and my conservationist friends, when they seem to see these two parts of my life in opposition. From an aircraft, from within a machine, we are in touch with nature; we see the view below, and we experience the winds and weather. The machine shows us nature in ways we could not see it otherwise. No wonder that modern scientific perspectives on the environment have emphasized the mechanical image; sciences depend on machines for observation.

As the airplane departed from the Adriatic, my mind meandered from thoughts of the shallow European sea to those of the far-off Pacific Ocean and one of its humblest and most obscure creatures, the chambered nautilus (*Nautilus pomplilus Linnaeus*), which lives far from Venice in the southwestern Pacific. Although the shell of the chambered nautilus decorates many a coffee table, alive it is a cryptic creature with nocturnal habits, living in the depths of the ocean as much as 1,000 feet below the surface and rarely seen alive by human beings.[3] The nautilus lives only in the outermost chamber of its shell, periodically pulling itself forward to the outside of its shell and depositing a wall behind it. As it grows, the nautilus requires a larger protective shield, and the chambers increase in size and the shell develops in a most interesting way, coiling into the convoluted shape of a logarithmic spiral, following a simple but elegant mathematical formula. As its shell grows, the chambered nautilus records two different rhythms of the solar system. Along the opening of the outer chamber of the shell, small deposits of calcium carbonate are laid down in groups of three to five, which are separated from adjacent groups by a ridge known as the growth line. There is an average of thirty growth lines per chamber, one for each day in the lunar cycle, suggesting that a new chamber is put down each lunar month and a new growth line each day. This implies that the chambered nautilus contains in its shell two clocks: one timed to the sun, and the other to the moon. These are relative clocks, marking the number of days within a lunar month.

The chambered nautilus is an ancient form of life whose oldest fossil ancestors have been dated at 420 million years before the present, and fossils have been found representing most of the geologic periods from that time to the present. Strangely, the number of growth lines per chamber has increased over time. The oldest fossil shells have only nine growth lines per chamber, compared with the thirty of modern shells, suggesting that the lunar month has grown longer and that the moon used to revolve faster around the Earth than it does now. This, in turn, implies that the moon must have been closer to the Earth, since the closer a satellite is to a planet, the faster it must revolve to remain in orbit. The clocks in the nautilus shell indicate that the revolution of the moon 420 million years ago took only 9 days.[4] The timing of the chambered nautilus's clocks, corroborated by other evidence, has been of sufficient accuracy to allow two geophysicists, P. G. K. Kahn and S. M. Pompea, to infer that there have been three major stages in the Earth–moon history. In the first period, liquid water was not present on the surface of the Earth, and the distance between the Earth and the moon increased very slowly. Astronomers tell us that the recession of the moon from the Earth would have been caused by a loss of energy from friction, of which the friction of the tides against the land would have created the most rapid loss. In the second stage, the oceans appeared to cover all or so much of the Earth that there was still relatively little loss of energy from the friction of the tides, and the moon continued to recede slowly. Finally, when the continents emerged about 600 million years ago and the water began to pound against the shores, the frictional loss of energy from tidal action increased, and the moon receded more rapidly.[5] This is indirect evidence of when the continents emerged from the oceans. The lines on fossil nautilus shells tell us about the history of the motions of the Earth and the moon, about the history of the Earth, and about the origin of the oceans and continents, which are so important in the history of life on the Earth. Thus in the chambered nautilus, the solar system, the physical Earth, and life on Earth are linked. Similarly, our perception of nature is returning to a unity, but with a great difference from the past prescientific ideas. The moon in the nautilus shell is not a fable; it is an insight based on sophisticated modern methods of scientific observation, open to tests of validity and accuracy and to disproof. As with the scientific analysis of the fossil nautilus shells, science is taking our ideas to a new stage, where the separations between the organic and the machine and between the cosmos and the Earth—distinctions that have dominated ideas since the rise of modern science—are disintegrating.

In the Mirror of Nature, We See Ourselves

The answers to the old questions—What is the character of nature undisturbed? What is the influence of nature on human beings? What is the influence of human beings on nature?—can no longer be viewed as distinct from one another. Life and the environment are one thing, not two, and people, as all life, are immersed in the one system. When we influence nature, we influence ourselves; when we change nature, we change ourselves. A concern with nature is not merely a scientific curiosity, but a subject that pervades philosophy, theology, aesthetics, and psychology. There are deep reasons that we desire a balance and harmony in the structure of the biological world and that we seek to find that structural balance, just as our ancestors desired and sought that kind of balance in the physical world.

Clearly, to abandon a belief in the constancy of undisturbed nature is psychologically uncomfortable. As long as we could believe that nature undisturbed was constant, we were provided with a simple standard against which to judge our actions, a reflection from a windless pond in which our place was both apparent and fixed, providing us with a sense of continuity and permanence that was comforting. Abandoning these beliefs leaves us in an extreme existential position: we are like small boats without anchors in a sea of time; how we long for safe harbor on a shore.

The change in perception of nature and the new answers to the ancient questions about nature arise from new observations and new ways of thinking that even now seem radical. The transition that is taking place affects us today and will continue to affect us deeply, in ways that may not be obvious, for decades. These changes strike at the very root of how we see ourselves. We have clouded our perception of nature with false images, and as long as we continue to do that we will cloud our perception of ourselves, cripple our ability to manage natural resources, and choose the wrong approaches to dealing with global environmental concerns. The way to achieve a harmony with nature is first to break free of old metaphors and embrace new ones so that we can lift the veils that prevent us from accepting what we observe, and then to make use of technology to study life and life-supporting systems as they are. A harmony between ourselves and nature depends on—indeed, requires—modern technological tools to teach us about the Earth and to help us manage wisely what we realize we have inadvertently begun to unravel.

Once we realize that we are part of a living system, global in scale, produced and in some ways controlled by life, and once we accept the intrinsic qualities of organic systems—with their ambiguities, variabilities, and complexities—we can feel a part of the world in a way that our nineteenth-century ancestors could not, but our ancestors before them did. We can leave behind the metaphors of the machine, which are so uncomfortable psychologically because they separate us from nature and are so unlifelike and therefore so different from ourselves, and we can arrive, with the best information available for us in our time, at a new organic view of the Earth, a view in which we are a part of a living and changing system whose changes we can accept, use, and control, to make the Earth a comfortable home, for each of us individually and for all of us collectively in our civilizations.

The machine-age view provided simple and immediate answers to the classic questions about the relationship between human beings and nature. Nature knew best; nature undisturbed was constant. Individuals, depending on which of the interpretations of nature they chose, had a certain fixed relationship to their surroundings. From the new perspective, nature does not provide simple answers. People are forced to choose the kind of environment they want, and a "desirable" environment may be one that people have altered, at least in some vicinities some of the time.

An awareness of the power of civilization to change and destroy the biological world has grown since the nineteenth century. We recognize that civilization has had a tremendous impact on nature, and it is tempting to agree with George Perkins Marsh that the absence of structural balance in the biological world is always, or almost always, the result of human activity, that "man is everywhere a disturbing agent. Wherever he plants his foot, the harmonies of nature are turned to discords."[6] But we understand, in spite of our wishes, that nature moves and changes and involves risks and uncertainties and that our judgments of our own actions must be made against this moving image.

There are ranges within which life can persist, and changes that living systems must undergo in order to persist. We can change structural aspects of life within the acceptable ranges. Those changes that are necessary to the continuation of life we must allow to occur, or substitute for them at huge cost the qualities that otherwise would have been achieved. We can engineer nature at nature's rates and in nature's ways; we must be wary when we engineer nature at an unnatural rate and in novel ways. To conserve well is to engineer within the rules of natural changes, patterns, and ambiguities; to engineer well is to conserve, to maintain the dynamics of the living systems. The answer to the question about the human role in nature depends on time, culture, technologies, and peoples. There is no simple, universal (external to all peoples, cultures, times) answer. However, the answer to this question for our time is very much influenced by the fact that we are changing nature at all levels—from the local to the global—that we have the power to mold nature into what we want it to be or to destroy it completely, and that we know we have that power. This leads us to a very different kind of answer from those of the Greek and Roman philosophers, their intellectual descendants in the Middle Ages and Renaissance, or the people of the early and mid-industrial–mechanical age.

Now that we understand that we are changing the environment at a global level, we must accept the responsibility for the actions we have taken and the changes these actions have wrought. It is prudent to minimize these effects and to slow down the rates of change as much as possible. This requires not only information and understanding, but also a political will and social and economic means and policies to accomplish what we need and desire, issues to which little attention has so far been paid. It is uncomfortable to us that the new perspective does not give the same simple answers to all questions, but requires that our management be specific and that answers to questions be dependent on the particular qualities of our goals and the actions open to us. Knowing what to do in each case requires considerable information, surveys, monitoring, knowledge, and understanding, which we as a society have been most reluctant to seek. Perhaps we have been too much like those people Peter Kalm met in eighteenth-century America, who believed that the study of nature was "a mere trifle, and the pastime of fools."[7]

A new awareness of biological nature is coming and is inevitable, and it can easily be misused. If we persist in arguing that what is natural is constant and what is constant is good, then those of us who value wilderness for its intrinsic characteristics or believe that the biosphere must be maintained within certain bounds will have lost our ability to live in harmony with nature as it really is. If we do not understand the true nature of populations, biological communities, and ecosystems, how can we expect to husband them wisely? When we had less power, we could live with myths. But today, as Joseph Campbell recognized, "Science itself is now the only field through which the dimension of mythology can be again revealed."[8]

The task that I am encouraging the reader to join in continues that begun by George Perkins Marsh, a task that acknowledges the great destructive powers of human civilization but is optimistic that we may begin to choose as a prudent person would in our dealings with nature. The message of this book is consistent with the ethical outlook of Paul Sears, who wrote that "nature is not to be conquered save on her own terms."[9] I have tried simply to give a modern view of "her" terms. It is also consistent with the land ethic of Aldo Leopold: "Conservation is a state of harmony between men and land."[10] We have not abandoned that belief or Leopold's ethic, but have redefined "harmony." To achieve that new harmony, we must understand the character of nature undisturbed, that discordant harmony which has been the topic of this book.

The proper response to the problems we have created for the environment with our technology is not to abandon civilization or modern technology, as some have argued and as seems so comfortable and desirable a course of action to those who have suffered most the destructive effects of human actions against the natural world, or to cling to the belief that everything natural (that is, nonhuman) is desirable and good. Having altered nature with our technology, we must depend on technology to see us through to solutions. The task before us is to understand the biological world to the point that we can learn how to live within the discordant harmonies of our biological surroundings, so that they function not only to promote the continuation of life but also to benefit ourselves: our aesthetics, morality, philosophies, and material needs. We need not only new knowledge, but also new metaphors, which are arising from an amalgamation of the organic metaphor with a new technological metaphor, evolving from the old machine idea that we have been accustomed to using for the past 200 years.

In this book, we have journeyed through nature and natural history as we understand it today, and we find that at the end we have come, in a sense, full circle; our ideas have evolved from organic to mechanical and now return to a new linkage, connecting life and technology in metaphor and in fact. And as the plane banked and climbed toward the Alps, the central issue of our relationship between ourselves and nature seemed to come into focus. Could that most magnificent machine of the twentieth century, the airplane, serve as the proper model for the system of nature visible below? Machines can help us see nature, but they alone are not the proper model, the right metaphor for nature. We have things backward. We use an engineering metaphor and imagine that the Earth is a machine when it is not, but we do not take an engineering approach to nature; we do not borrow the cleverness and the skills of the engineer, which is what we must do. We talk about the spaceship Earth, but who is monitoring the dials and turning the knobs? No one; there are no dials to watch, only occasional alarms made by people peering out the window, who call to us that they see species disappearing, an ozone hole in the upper atmosphere, the climate change, the coasts of all the world polluted. But because we have never created the system of monitoring our environment or devised the understanding of nature's strange ecological systems, we are still like the passengers in the cabin who think they smell smoke or, misunderstanding how a plane flies, mistake light turbulence for trouble. We need to instrument the cockpit of the biosphere and to let up the window shade so that we begin to observe nature as it is, not as we imagine it to be.

Postscript:
A Guide to Action

People ask me what the changes I have written about in this book imply for the actions we should take in the future. For that reason, it seems appropriate to include as a postscript a brief discussion to illustrate that the change in perception about nature does lead to different actions. This book is not meant to be a treatise on specific methodologies, and the postscript is not meant to be a complete or definitive treatment of all the issues, but merely an illustration of some of the practical implications of the new perspective that I have called for in this book. I have chosen a few examples to represent a variety of issues.

Nature in the twenty-first century will be a nature that we make; the question is the degree to which this molding will be intentional or unintentional, desirable or undesirable. What is the likely outcome of our modern role in nature? We can envision several specific futures. The worst, nature after a nuclear war, might be a nature like that of 2 billion years ago, a biosphere of only bacteria, which we would not want for ourselves.

A more likely future lies on the path that we have followed, in which we continue to treat natural history as a hobby not to be taken seriously and to deal with environmental problems after they have arisen using whatever tools and knowledge we happen to have with us at the moment, assuming that nature can be taken apart and repaired and put back together again, following a machine analogy.

A third future is one that we might achieve if we were to begin a massive effort today to make up for what we have not done in the past: to obtain the information, knowledge, and understanding to manage nature wisely and prudently. To this end, we must set aside enough lands so that we have baselines from which to measure our actions and to conserve as much of the remaining biological diversity as possible. We must train professionals and allocate large amounts of funds for the right kinds of research and management.

Even if we adopt the third approach, the changes that are taking place now and will continue to take place as the result of our past actions will lead to major dislocations in nature. If the present projections of the global climatic models are realistic, the climate will change so rapidly, especially in northern latitudes, as to pose serious problems for the persistence of large areas of forests as well as for the present distribution of agricultural lands. Projections suggest that forests may begin to experience significant changes in species composition within the next 20 or 30 years. The rate of climatic change will exceed the natural rate of seed migration, and forests may not be able to regenerate. A seedling of a species suited to the climate at the time of its planting may find itself in a climate too warm for the seeds it produces by the time it reaches maturity several decades in the future. The severity of the problem is unknown at this time, but might exceed our ability to plant and maintain forests. In this case, clearly, considerable research is necessary if we are to conserve the forests of the higher latitudes.

Global warming represents one of the extreme problems that may confront us during the next decades. As many ecologists have warned in the past decade, acid rain; pollution of the oceans, fresh waters, air, and soils with toxic substances; reduction of ground waters; deforestation; and destruction of habitats, including those of most coastal areas will continue to threaten not only us, but all other organisms in spite of our best efforts. We can expect only limited improvements in the next decades in many areas. These large-scale problems make the approaches to conservation discussed in this book necessary.

Wilderness in the Twenty-first Century

Since there is no longer any part of the Earth that is untouched by our actions in some way, either directly or indirectly, there are no wildernesses in the sense of places completely unaffected by people. But there are three kinds of natural areas that we must maintain in the future, two of which we can regard as wilderness and designate legally as protected wilderness areas: no-action wilderness, preagricultural wilderness, and conservation areas. The first is an area untouched by direct human actions, no matter what happens. This kind of wilderness is necessary for observation as a baseline from which scientists can measure the effects of human actions elsewhere; it is an essential calibration of the dials we should set up to monitor the state of nature. Such areas are also important because they will help in the maintenance of biological diversity. Some of them may be pleasant for recreation, but some may not be, and some may become a nature never seen before. As in Hutcheson Memorial Forest, this kind of wilderness might be occupied by introduced species and native species in novel combinations.

The second kind, preagricultural wilderness, is an area that has the appearance of landscape or seascape that most closely matches the ideal of wilderness as it has been thought about in recent decades. In North and South America, Australia, New Zealand, and other places in which the time of arrival of modern technological man is readily dated, the idea is to create natural areas that appear as they did when first viewed by the European explorers. In the Americas, this would be the landscape of the seventeenth century. It is necessary to choose a time period that has the desired appearance; if we do not, then we face the situation that I discussed for the Boundary Waters Canoe Area, which, from the end of the last ice age until the time of European colonization, passed from ice and tundra to spruce and jack pine forest. If natural means simply before human intervention, then all these habitats could be claimed as natural, contrary to what people really mean and really want. What people want in the Boundary Waters Canoe Area is the wilderness as seen by the voyageurs and a landscape that gives the feeling of being untouched by people.

The conservation area, the third type of natural region, is set aside to conserve biological diversity, either for a specific species—for example, the Kirtland's warbler—or for a kind of ecological community. Because we have so altered the landscape and have allowed inadvertently only small patches of former habitats to remain, most of these areas require active intervention on our part if they are to persist. For example, to manage the habitat of the Kirtland's warbler in a way that allows the species to survive, we must pay attention to the frequency of fires and increase or reduce the rate so that it best suits the needs of that species. When and if climate changes through our actions, we might have to relocate the natural area for the warbler and learn how to persuade it to move as well.

It is important that we understand the distinctions among these three kinds of natural areas, each of which represents a different aspect of the older meanings attached to wilderness. Each is quite different from the others, and it is generally not going to be possible to manage the same area to be all three at once: truly undisturbed; appearing as in a presettlement landscape; and functioning to conserve endangered species or biological diversity. Under the old perspective on nature, one could assume that all three goals would be accomplished in any area simply by removing all human actions. Each kind of natural area must be a certain, and generally as yet undetermined, size to be viable. For example, Kirtland's warbler conservation areas must be large enough to support the breeding territories of hundreds of males.

The smaller the size of a conservation area, the more diverse and more intense must be our actions. The amount of intervention required increases as the size of any specific preserve decreases.[1] The smallest area is simply a zoo within which we provide all the necessities and remove all the wastes for the forms of life that we maintain there. At the opposite extreme is nature before technological civilization, where vast areas unaffected by human beings existed. The amount of effort required to maintain a preserve of any size depends also on the characteristics of the species found there, including life history characteristics such as size and longevity. As a general rule, large and longer-lived organisms require large habitats. Tsavo, which is the biggest national park mentioned in this book, was not extensive enough to function as an independent preserve for the African elephant without active intervention by people. Of the examples discussed in this book, the Boundary Waters Canoe Area is perhaps the area that could persist with the least direct human action. The largest mammal within the Boundary Waters is the moose, which is much smaller and shorter-lived than the elephant. (A moose weighs about 1,000 pounds and lives for about 17 years; elephants weigh as much as 6 tons and can live for 60 years.) The number of actions required of us will increase as our global impacts create more indirect effects on natural areas, and therefore our actions will have to increase in the future. This is especially true if global warming takes place in the next century.

To maintain wilderness areas in the future will require that we develop means to make these lands secure from undesirable uses. As resources become limited and the human population continues to grow, there will be increasing pressure on natural areas for the extracting of timber, harvesting of wildlife, and mining of minerals. As an example, the poaching of elephants, a crisis whose countermeasures required so much effort when Tsavo National Park was established, remains a serious problem. Elephant populations are undergoing a severe decline because poaching has continued widely, and it is unclear whether the African elephant will be able to survive in the wild in the twenty-first century unless new approaches are found for their security. Elsewhere, as resources such as firewood and valuable furniture timber become scare, there will be more and more pressure for people to simply take them from an area even if it was set aside as a preserve. How to ensure that large natural areas are physically secure is an issue that has received very little attention and is not a simple problem. A nature preserve surrounded by police with weapons seems to violate the idea of the preserve and to require funds that would seem impossible to obtain.

Obtaining Necessary Information

Knowledge about nature is essential if we are to achieve a new harmony between ourselves and our environment. We believe we are changing nature, but we cannot know that we are and cannot know how much we are changing it unless we have baseline surveys of the present status of those aspects of interest to us and unless we continue to monitor their status over time. In most areas, we lack even the most basic information about the condition of nature. We do not have many primary numbers: the number of species, the abundances of populations, and the amount of organic matter by geographical region and for the whole Earth. We need the ecological equivalents of the United States Geological Survey, institutions whose purpose is to describe and monitor the status of ecological systems, just as the Geological Survey creates maps of the geologic terrain. As long as we thought that nature undisturbed sought the condition that was right and desirable, we could believe that we did not need such knowledge. Since the ship of nature was self-guiding, we did not have to read the dials. Under the new perspective, we must have specific knowledge because policies must be specific. Devising a program that can provide baseline surveys and monitoring is not an amateur activity and will require considerable sums of money and the development and extension of technologies so that measurements can be made efficiently and with reasonable costs. Many aspects of modern technology will be important in providing this new knowledge, just as they have been important in modifying our perceptions of nature. Remote sensing, computers, and modern methods of chemical measurements have an important role.

Not only is monitoring of the state of nature required, but scientific research must be an integral part of the management of nature. We lack not only information about the state of nature, but also an adequate understanding of how ecological systems function, and we must continue to improve this understanding. Under the old perspective, such an understanding was not necessary in detail, because we believed that nature simply knew best and our understanding was irrelevant to management. We thought that we needed only an appreciation of nature, not an understanding of it. In the past, scientific research about nature was often regarded as an activity that interfered with recreation and conservation. The research that we did at Isle Royale was considered at times by the park's management to be a nuisance that interfered with the real function of the park, which was believed to be simply to provide recreation for visitors. Some conservation organizations have considered scientific research as inhumane and unnecessary. We no longer have the luxury to believe that we can live in harmony with the environment without knowledge and understanding of natural systems.

Limits to Our Actions

The problem of erosion illustrates the new management perspective for human effects on land use. One of the major undesirable results of the misuse of forests has been the increase in erosion, but the processes that control erosion are more complex than were believed only a few decades ago. It used to be thought that a high rate of erosion occurred primarily as the result of human actions. For example, in his landmark book, *Deserts on the March*, Paul Sears discussed erosion from the perspective of the 1930s. Each living thing receives a "loan" from the Earth of chemical elements such as phosphorus, and it pays for the loan with a return of those elements with its death. "No plant or animal . . . can establish permanent right of possession," for these resources.

> Left to herself, nature manages these loans and redemptions in not unkindly fashion. She maintains a balance which will permit the briefest time to elapse between burial and renewal. The turnover of material for new generations to use is steady and regular. Wind and water, those twin sextons, do their work as gently as may be.[2]

These statements were true for the dust bowl and many other areas of the Earth. The warnings were important at that time as part of increasing public awareness of what people were doing to the environment. Today, when we are confronted by high rates of erosion in many areas around the world where our power to act is limited, it is important that we refine these ideas and seek to understand where we may be effective in controlling erosion and where we may not. Sears wrote that erosion is "a normal enough process, and certainly inevitable," but that the "danger of the present situation is not that any new force is at work, but rather that the rate of its action has been speeded up far beyond the capacity of nature to replace the eroded soil."[3]

A great advance in our understanding of erosion has come about in part as a result of the acceptance of the theory of plate tectonics. It is now understood that three characteristics of an area lead to a naturally high rate of erosion. According to Andrew J. Pearce, erosion is severe where the three factors occur together: intense plate-tectonic activity, soft bedrock, and high rainfall.[4] In these regions, there is little that people can do to decrease the overall rate of erosion and sedimentation, although in any one place, people can protect their own plots and decrease soil loss in a small area. Elsewhere, where the background rate of erosion is low, human actions such as the removal of vegetation can greatly increase the rate of erosion. This new knowledge about erosional processes offers a new perspective on the effects of human beings on nature. There is not a single answer for all situations, but there are processes that, if we understand them, predict where erosion will be high and where it will not. The comforting result is that we learn that we are not always to blame for high erosion rates. We learn when we can be effective in controlling erosion and when we cannot, when our actions will be productive and when they will not be. The uncomforting result is that in some areas nothing can be done to slow down the overall rate of erosion and sedimentation. The change in our understanding and management of erosion illustrates how our approach to land use is changing and should continue to change in the future.

Managing Commercially Important Renewable Resources

Managing fisheries exemplifies the challenge of managing a population that varies over time, and about which we always know too little. This presents an economic problem because fishermen would like to have a reliable, high, profitable, and constant harvest every year. However, fish populations vary in an apparently random fashion. Under the old management, the approach was to manage for a maximum sustainable yield or an optimum sustainable yield as calculated from the logistic growth equation. Under the old perspective, the optimum harvest simply took into account the uncertainty in measurements, but did not consider complexity or inherent random variations in populations.

What are the options open to us when fish populations are subject to random variations that cannot be accounted for by the logistic, and the carrying capacity and the current population size cannot be estimated very accurately? One is to focus on estimates of the abundances of those age classes that are not yet large enough to harvest, but will be ready for harvest in the next year or two. In this case, the emphasis is on age structure (a first step consideration of the complexity of real populations) within the context of environmental change and large scale patterns in time and space.

Satellite monitoring of the oceans suggests that variations in some fish production may be related to the patterns of movement of giant "warm-core rings," large circular "eddies" of warm water in the oceans. Like storms in the atmosphere, they move across the oceans with a general trend in direction, but with considerable random variation. When one of them passes over a fish breeding ground at a crucial time of year, the size of that year's cohort of fish may be smaller than normal. Several years later, when these fish reach harvestable size, the catch may decline from earlier levels. Satellite monitoring of the oceans may allow prediction of the relative expected fish catch. Fishermen could use these projections in their planning. As we gain better understanding of how the atmosphere and oceans interact to produce climate and ocean currents, we can develop models to improve our prediction of variations in ocean currents, which will also give us more lead time to deal with harvest policies for fisheries. Even given such improved forecasting techniques, there will always be considerable variation from year to year, some of it unpredictable. This approach illustrates a change in management of economically useful biological resources.

Prudent and wise management of nature requires a large effort. There is a great need for educational programs on the management of the environment, but such curricula currently have very little support and little academic status, and there are few appropriate interdisciplinary educational programs. An increase in funding for education in the management of the environment is essential.

The augmentation of scientific programs is necessary. It is imperative to develop what I have referred to elsewhere as the new science of the biosphere as well as other ecological sciences.[5] This requires interdisciplinary efforts at a level not approached at present. With life as the primary concern, the biological sciences must play a major role, but in recent years large interdisciplinary projects, especially those that deal with the biosphere, have reduced the emphasis on the biological aspects of issues, focusing instead on the physics and chemistry of the atmosphere and oceans. A shift in the balance in the allocation of resources is needed. In recent years, the scientific study of large-scale processes has been driven by technology—by the tools available and by those who would like to see particular tools used—rather than by the concepts and issues. This is another way that the new perspective called for in this book becomes important: concepts must direct the choice of technologies and their use.

If nature in the twenty-first century will be a nature that we make, then the guide to action is our knowledge of living systems and our willingness to observe them for what they are, our committment to conserve natural areas, to recognize the limits of our actions, and to understand the roles of metaphor and myths in our perceptions of our surroundings.

Notes

Chapter 1

1. The number of pilings used as a foundation for the church of Santa Maria della Salute is given in *Venezia, città nobilissima del Sansovino* (Venice, 1663), cited in A. Storti, *Venice: A Practical Guide* (Venice: Storti, 1981), p. 5.

2. Accounts differ on the actual date of the founding of Venice. Some authorities give a date as late as A.D. 811, but John Julian Norwich attributes the first settlers of Venice to the attack by Goths on Aquileia in A.D. 402 (*A History of Venice* [New York: Knopf, 1982], p. 4). He notes that Venetian histories give Friday, March 25, 421, as the date when the city of Venice was "formally brought into being," but he states that this standard story is not validated and perhaps marks the date of the establishment of a Paduan trading post on one of the islands in the lagoon. In 466, a meeting at Grado, 60 miles south of Venice, established a government for the islands, but the site of the modern city was apparently not yet under a formal government. By the mid-sixth century, Venice seems to have been established; in 568, the Lombards invaded Italy and whole communities fled to Venice (before this, individuals or families fled to the lagoon). As a sidenote to illustrate the obscurity of the actual founding of Venice, Norwich states that the "first" doge of Venice never existed, even though a painting of this purported doge hangs in Venice.

3. Some of the proceedings from this conference are published in "Man's Role in Changing the Global Environment, Proceedings of an International Conference, Venice, Italy, 21–26 October, 1985," *The Science of the Total Environment*, ed. A. A. Orio and D. B. Botkin, 55(1986): 1–399, and 56(1986): 1–415.

4. The term "spaceship Earth" has been attributed to Buckminster Fuller and to Kenneth Boulding; it is said that Adlai Stevenson was the first to popularize it.

5. L. J. Henderson, *The Fitness of the Environment* (New York: Macmillan, 1913; Boston: Beacon Press, 1966).

6. H. J. Morowitz, *Energy Flow in Biology* (Woodbridge, Conn.: Oxbow Press, 1979).
7. E. O. Wilson, ed. *Biodiversity* (Washington, D.C.: National Academy Press, 1988).
8. C. J. Glacken, *Traces on the Rhodian Shore: Nature and Culture in Western Thought from Ancient Times to the End of the Eighteenth Century* (Berkeley: University of California Press, 1967).
9. G. P. Marsh, *Man and Nature*, ed. D. Lowenthal (1864; Cambridge, Mass.: Harvard University Press, 1967), pp. 29–30.
10. D. Lowenthal, *George Perkins Marsh, Versatile Vermonter* (New York: Columbia University Press, 1958).
11. D. B. Botkin and M. J. Sobel, "Stability in Time-Varying Ecosystems," *American Naturalist* 109(1975): 625–46.
More discussion of the importance of change in ecological systems can be found in D. B. Botkin, S. Golubeck, B. Maguire, B. Moore III, H. J. Morowitz, and L. B. Slobodkin, "Closed Regenerative Life Support Systems for Space Travel: Their Development Poses Fundamental Questions for Ecological Science," *Life Sciences and Space Research XVII*, ed. R. Holmquist (Elmsford, N.Y.: Pergamon Press); D. B. Botkin, "A Grandfather Clock Down the Staircase: Stability and Disturbance in Natural Ecosystems," *Forests: Fresh Perspectives from Ecosystem Analysis*, ed. R. H. Waring, Proceedings of the Fortieth Annual Biology Colloquium (Corvallis: Oregon State University Press, 1980).
12. M. H. Nicolson, *Mountain Gloom and Mountain Glory: The Development of the Aesthetics of the Infinite* (Ithaca, N.Y.: Cornell University Press, 1959).

Chapter 2

1. A. J. Nicolson, "The Balance of Animal Populations," *Journal of Animal Ecology* 2(1933):133.
2. Charles Elton, *Animal Ecology and Evolution*, (New York: Oxford University Press, 1930).
3. The word *nature* has been used to mean (1) the natural world on the Earth as it exists without human beings or civilization--that is, the environment, including mountains, plains, rivers, lakes, oceans, air, rocks, and all nonhuman, nondomesticated living things; and (2) the universe, with all its phenomena, including objects and forces (*The Random House Dictionary of the English Language*, 2nd ed. [New York: Random House, 1988]). Throughout this book, unless otherwise noted, the word *nature* stands for the first definition. The first and second definitions are not so clearly distinguished in modern discussions of the classical Greek and Roman philosophers; nature is seen as encompassing both concepts: nature as the universe, and nature as the Earth.
In the science of ecology and in most discussions of natural history, the term *environment* generally means the nonliving aspects of nature, but in popular writ-

ing it is sometimes synonymous with the first definition of nature. In the science of ecology, the word *ecosystem* is the closest term to the first definition of nature. Ecologists do not speak of the universe as nature except in specific contexts, as in dealing with ecological life-support systems that might be used in space travel.

4. This paragraph is based on Daphne Sheldrick, *The Tsavo Story* (London: Collins and Harvill Press, 1973). The quote is on page 113.

5. Ibid., p. 113.

6. Ibid., pp. 186–87.

7. Ibid., p. 283.

8. Ibid., pp. 277–78.

9. Ibid., p. 190.

10. Information about fisheries catch is from D. B. Botkin and E. A. Keller, *Environmental Studies: Earth as a Living Planet* (Columbus: Merrill Pub. Co., 1987), p. 220 and Table 8.2.

11. Pierre-François Verhulst was born in Brussels on October 28, 1804 and died on February 15, 1849. G. E. Hutchinson has written a brief and interesting biography of him. Verhulst taught at the University of Ghent and became interested in mathematical problems related to the repayment of public debt by state lotteries. Hutchinson suggests that this was the "beginning of his interest in social and demographic problems." He went to Italy during the Belgian revolution of 1830 and "became unsuccessfully involved in politics and also published one original historical study. By 1834 he had returned to science and began giving instruction in mathematics at the *École militaire*, where he later became a professor." Hutchinson notes that "though his contemporaries ignored the logistic, his interest in population studies led him into sociological problems . . . and the Belgian government appointed him to commissions on the relief of poverty and on state insurance policy" (*An Introduction to Population Ecology* [New Haven, Conn.: Yale University Press, 1978], p. 20).

12. Public Law 92–522, H.R. 10420, 92nd Cong., October 21, 1972.

13. D. B. Botkin and M. J. Sobel, "Optimum Sustainable Marine Mammal Populations," (report prepared for the Marine Mammal Commission 1977).

14. C. J. Glacken, *Traces on the Rhodian Shore: Nature and Culture in Western Thought from Ancient Times to the End of the Eighteenth Century* (Berkeley: University of California Press, 1967).

15. R. F. Nash, *Wilderness and the American Mind* (New Haven: Yale Univ. Press, 1967).

16. Plotinus, *The Enneads*, trans. S. MacKenna, revised by B. S. Page, 3rd edition (London: Faber and Faber Ltd., 1956).

Chapter 3

1. R. H. MacArthur, *Geographical Ecology* (New York: Harper & Row, 1972).

2. W. S. Cooper, "The Climax Forest of Isle Royale, Lake Superior, And Its Development," *Botanical Gazette* 55(1913): 1–44, 115–40, 189–234.

3. The complex hunting behavior of wolves is described by L. D. Mech, *The Wolves of Isle Royale*, U. S. National Park Service Fauna Series no. 7. (Washington, D.C.: Government Printing Office, 1966) and *The Wolf: The Ecology and Behavior of an Endangered Species* (Garden City, N.Y.: Natural History Press, 1970).

4. D. B. Botkin, P. A. Jordan, A. S. Dominski, H. D. Lowendorf, and G. E. Hutchinson, "Sodium Dynamics in a Northern Terrestrial Ecosystem," *Proceedings of the National Academy of Sciences* (1973): 2745–48. At the time of this writing, the wolves of Isle Royale have undergone a drastic decline, suffering, I am told, from a viral disease introduced on the island by domestic dogs of tourists. In such ways even what appears to be an excellent example of wilderness is now indirectly touched by our hands.

5. The books referred to here are: C. R. Darwin, *The Origin of the Species by Means of Natural Selection or the Preservation of Favored Races in the Struggle for Life*, (London: Murray, 1859); G. P. Marsh, *Man and Nature*, ed. D. Lowenthal (1864; Cambridge, Mass.: Harvard University Press, 1967); and E. Haeckel, *Generelle Morphologie der Organismen: Allgemeine Gründzuge der organischen Formen-wissenschaft, mechanisch begründet durch die von Charles Darwin reformirte Desendenz-Theorie.* 2 vols. (Berlin: Reimer, 1866).

The word *ecology* is derived from the Greek word *oikos*, meaning "a dwelling place." Haeckel originally coined the term as *Oekologie*, but the spelling was Anglicized at the Madison, Wisconsin, Botanical Congress of 1893 into its present spelling, according to R. P. McIntosh. Ernst Heinrich Haeckel was a German biologist who lived from 1834 to 1919. Within his field, he was known for his studies of marine organisms, but was also well known, according to McIntosh, as a leading proponent of Darwinian ideas in Germany ("Ecology Since 1900," pp. 353–72 in B. J. Taylor and T. J. White, *Issues and Ideas in America*, ed. [Norman: University of Oklahoma Press, 1976.]).

6. Excellent examples of machines as objects of art are shown in: R. G. Wilson, D. H. Pilgrim, and D. Tashjian, *The Machine Age in America: 1918–1941* (New York: Abrams, 1986).

7. For more information on the history of ecology, see McIntosh, "Ecology Since 1900" and *The Background of Ecology: Concept and Theory* (New York: Cambridge University Press, 1985); D. Worster, *Nature's Economy: The Roots of Ecology* (San Francisco: Sierra Club Books, 1977).

8. S. A. Forbes, "The Lake as a Microcosm," *Illinois Natural History Survey Bulletin* 15(1925): 549. Also of interest are additional comments by Forbes: "Although every species has to fight its way inch by inch from the egg to maturity, yet no species is exterminated, but each is maintained at a regular average number which we shall find good reason to believe is the greatest for which there is, year after year, a sufficient supply of food" (Ibid., p. 549). This becomes of interest in regard to assumptions about the expected yield of animals such as fish or wild game under management regimes.

The use of the term "balance of nature" by ecologists is discussed in F. N.

Egerton, "Changing Concepts of the Balance of Nature," *Quarterly Review of Biology* 48(1973): 322–350.

9. B. J. Le Beoeuf, "The Elephant Seal," in *Problems in the Management of Locally Abundant Wild Mammals*, ed. P. A. Jewel, S. J. Holt and D. Hart (New York: Academic Press, 1981).

10. F. N. Egerton, "Aristotle's Population Biology," *Arethusa* 8(1975): 307–30.

11. A. J. Lotka, *Elements of Physical Biology* (1925), reprinted as *Elements of Mathematical Biology* (New York: Dover, 1956). Influential works by the others referred to in this section are: G. F. Gause, *The Struggle for Existence* (Baltimore: Williams and Wilkins, 1934); V. I. Vernadsky, *La Biosphère* (Paris: Félix Alcan, 1929); and V. Volterra, "Variazioni e fluttuazioni del numero d'individui in specie animali conviventi," *Mem. R. Acad. Naz. dei Lincei*, 6th Ser., 2 (1926):31–113.

12. Gause, *The Struggle For Existence*, p. 25. That the comments came from Volterra's son-in-law is stated by G.E. Hutchinson in *An Introduction to Population Ecology* (New Haven: Yale University Press, 1978), p. 120.

13. This simple experiment demonstrates that under certain circumstances a predator can cause the extinction of its prey, after which the predator also suffers extinction. If this occurred consistently in nature, there would be few living predators and prey. The contrary is true; a great many organisms, including ourselves, are predators or prey or both, and certain predator and prey pairs are known from the fossil record to have persisted for a very long time. Gause's experiment raised a number of questions, one of which is: If a predator can completely eliminate its prey in a laboratory experiment, how can predator and prey coexist in nature? Gause found one answer to this question in a second experiment, in which he provided the paramecia with a refuge that consisted of sediment containing food. A paramecium covered by sediment was protected from attack by its predator. Some paramecia spent some of the time in the refuge and were missed by the predator. With the refuge, the outcome was quite different. The predator declined and became extinct, after which the prey continued to increase, undergoing an exponential rise until the end of the experiment. The refuge provided protection for the prey, but did not lead to the coexistence of predator and prey. The second experiment suggests that complexity in the environment may increase the chance of persistence of the prey.

A Lotka-Volterra predator regulates its prey. Without the predator, the prey would increase exponentially, a situation that, as we have seen, cannot be sustained in the real world indefinitely and that leads inevitably to a population crash, when the population exceeds its own resources. The predator, in turn, depends on the prey. Without the prey, the predator declines exponentially, eventually becoming extinct. Whether the predator and prey persist depends on the relative values of the intrinsic net rate of increase of each (the rate of increase in the absence of the other species), and the relative impact of predator on prey and prey on predator.

14. Gause, *The Struggle for Existence*, p. 140.

15. K. E. F. Watt, "Use of Mathematics in Population Ecology," *Annual Review of Entomology* 7(1962): 243–52.

16. This discussion is based on D. B. Botkin and M. J. Sobel, "Stability in Time-Varying Ecosystems," *American Naturalist* 109(1975): 625–46.

17. H. G. Andrewartha and L. C. Birch, *The Distribution and Abundance of Animals* (Chicago: University of Chicago Press, 1954).

18. D. Lack, *The Natural Regulation of Animal Numbers* (London: Oxford University Press, 1954).

19. C. S. Elton, *Voles, Mice, and Lemmings* (Oxford: Clarendon Press, 1942). These records owe their origin to Charles II of England, who, in 1679, granted ownership and exclusive trading rights to all the land, including "countries, coasts, and confines of the seas, bays, lakes, rivers, creeks, and sounds," along Hudson Bay in Canada to a firm later known as the Hudson's Bay Company.

20. Most long-term records for animal populations come from commercial harvesting—as for example, the records of haddock from Icelandic fishing grounds and whales in the Pacific. These records also show variation, rather than constancy, over time. But they are even more likely to be confounded by the effects of variations in effort—the number of boats and the market for the fish—than the Hudson's Bay Company's records of animals caught in traps. This is shown dramatically in the catches for both haddock and whales from 1915 to 1919 and 1939 to 1945, when fishing was halted by world wars.

21. Lack, *The Natural Regulation of Animal Numbers*, p. 1.

Chapter 4

1. Thomas Pownall, *A Topographical Description of the Dominion of the United States* Lois Mulkean, ed. (1784; Pittsburgh: Univ. of Pittsburgh, 1949).

2. P. Kalm, *Travels in North America: The America of 1750*, 2 vols., trans. A. B. Benson (New York: Dover, 1966).

3. Ibid., p. 175.

4. J. T. Cunningham, "Woodland Treasure," *Audubon* July-August 1954.

5. L. Barnett, "The Woods Of Home," *Life*, November 8, 1954.

6. Among the earliest uses of the term "succession" are: H. D. Thoreau, "The Succession of Forest Trees; An Address Read to the Middlesex Agricultural Society in Concord, Sept., 1860," extracted from the 8th Annual Report of the Massachusetts Board of Agriculture (1860); G. P. Marsh, *Man and Nature*, D. Lowenthal (1864; Cambridge, Mass.: Harvard Univ. Press, 1967).

7. M. F. Buell, H. F. Buell, and J. A. Small, "Fire in the History of Mettler's Woods," *Torreya* 81(1954): 253–55.

8. There has been considerable discussion of the role of American Indians in the burning of forests, especially in the Atlantic coastal states. In a classic and often cited paper, G. M. Day suggests that fires were common and set on purpose to clear the forest in order to make traveling and hunting easier and to drive game ("The Indian as an Ecological Factor in the Northeastern Forest," *Ecology* 34[1953]: 329–46). A number of historical sources mention large fires and suggest that they were

set on purpose. For example, Adriaen Van der Donck, a Dutch settler, wrote in 1655 that "a yearly custom" of the Indians was an autumn burning of the woods and that this burning was done "to render hunting easier . . . to thin out and clear the woods of all dead substances and grass, which grow better the ensuing spring . . . to circumscribe and enclose the game within the lines of fire, when it is more easily taken" ("A Description of the New Netherlands," in *Collections of the New York Historical Society* (second series), ed. T. F. O'Donnell [Syracuse, N. Y.: Syracuse University Press, 1968] 1:125–242). E. W. B. Russell provides one of the most thorough analyses of the role of American Indians in setting fires and concludes that "the frequent use of fires by Indians to burn the forests was probably at most a local occurrence," but "their use of fire for many purposes did, however, increase the frequency of fires above the low levels caused by lightning." She argues that the activity of the Indians did not lead to wholesale burning of the entire forests of New Jersey every year ("Indian-Set Fires in Northeastern USA," *Ecology* 64[1983]: 78–88). However, the alteration of the forests that I have described required a much less frequent recurrence in any one area. A frequency of once a decade, consistent with the evidence of fire scars on the trees in Hutcheson Memorial Forest, would be sufficient to favor oaks over maples without preventing oak reproduction.

9. The interpretation of forests as part of a changing landscape described here is mine; some ecologists still oppose it and hold on to the older idea. For example, Russell states that "the similarity of contemporary forests in North America to those that predated European colonization indicates the resilience, and thus the static stability of the forest types" ("Vegetation Change in Northern New Jersey from Precolonization to the Present: A Palynological Interpretation," *Bulletin of the Torrey Botanical Club* 107[1980]:432) using a term from one of my papers (D. B. Botkin and M. J. Sobel, "Stability in Time-Varying Ecosystems," *American Naturalist* 109[1975]: 625–46).

She states that three periods are observable in the pollen records: precolonial, when forests dominated: 1740 to 1850, when there was extensive land clearing by European colonists, and reforestation after 1850, when much of the land was allowed to return to forests. According to her analysis, chestnut and oaks dominated the precolonial upland forests. Thus Russell concludes "The common denominator in the original as well as in the present forests is oak. . . . Differences are primarily in the less dominant taxa" (p. 444). In part, the point that I am making is revealed in the changes in the less dominant taxa, since they represent the beginnings of a change delayed by the longevity of oaks. Oak as a genus could dominate the pollen found in lakes because oaks are abundant on the settled and manipulated landscape of which Hutcheson Memorial Forest is only a tiny fraction.

Although pollen deposits provide a wonderful kind of information not available any other way, they offer only a crude index of abundance. Species differ greatly in their production of pollen, and since the size of the grains differs among species, the distance that pollen travels varies with species. The percentage of pollen from oaks might vary by 10 or 20 percent, and oaks would still appear as the dominant species. The abundance of oaks could vary as much, and the percentage of pollen falling into the ponds under study could still appear relatively constant. Moreover, the area from which pollen reaches the ponds includes land that has been directly altered by human activities since presettlement times, whereas Hutcheson Memorial Forest is a tiny remnant that was not cut. Finally, the changes that were beginning to appear in Hutcheson Forest, such as the shift in the understory saplings toward maples (too young to produce pollen) and the gradual influx of exotic species, would not show up in the pollen records of the ponds that Russell studied. Chestnut has been essentially eliminated except as root sprouts. Native maples have increased in abundance for too short a time, and introduced species have grown in the state for too short a time and are too small a factor in the overall heavily manipulated landscape to show up as a large percentage of the pollen found in lakes. The pollen deposits are simply not sensitive to the changes that I have described.

Russell's comments are therefore valuable to compare with mine to see the importance of point of view and interpretation of data in what is usually regarded as a subject of "objective" facts. To put this another way, while pollen deposits provide us with a wonderful window from which to view the ancient past—in the case of the history of Hutcheson Memorial Forest, a tiny spot of natural forest on a large and settled landscape—the information in pollen percentages collected from muds in a distant lake is filtered many times, by the mathematical calculations of percentages, by the differential flux of pollen through lake water, by the variations in the aerodynamic characteristics of the pollen of several species as the grains are wafted by the winds, by the differences among species in their production of their male element in reproduction. Without pursuing the details of the scientific analysis further, we can say that it is difficult to discover what has happened to less than 100 acres in less than 200 years from the pollen deposits.

10. Marsh, *Man and Nature*, p. 29 and p. 35.

11. R. H. Whittaker, *Communities and Ecosystems* (London: Macmillan, 1970), p. 73.

12. E. P. Odum, "The Strategy of Ecosystem Development," *Science* 164(1969): 262.

13. W. S. Cooper, "The Climax Forest of Isle Royale, Lake Superior, and Its Development," *Botanical Gazette* 55(1913): 1–44, 115–40, 189–235. There is no single, universal division of vegetation communities, but the number of different communities on the landscape is large. The United States, for example, has been divided into 114 vegetation communities occupying the lower 48 states (A. W. Küchler, *Potential Natural Vegetation of the Conterminous United States*, American Geographical Society Special Publication, no. 36 [New York: American Geographical Society, 1964]).

14. Cooper described as an ideal representation of this final equilibrium the forest on Smithwick Island, a small islet just off Isle Royale. The first impression one gets of this forest, he wrote, is "of great density, the thick foliage extending to the ground at the edge of the forest, allowing no view of the interior. The sky line is

ragged, made up of an irregular combination of sharp points and rounded curves"—
the mixture of deciduous or coniferous tree shapes, and the tops of very old spruces
rising above the other trees. "Upon entering the forest, we seem in many places, to
be in the midst of a dense growth of nearly pure balsam. The individuals of this
species are of all sizes, and there is a pronounced tendency among them to grow in
close groups." (Ibid., pp. 13–14).

15. The discovery that there have been major ice ages can be traced back to the
observations of the farmers and herders of the Swiss Alps. As a glacier expands, it
pushes ahead of itself a great mound of boulders, rock and soil, including particles
of all sizes, from clays to sands. Some of this debris is pushed to the sides and to the
front ends of the ice.

At the leading edge of the glacier, the melting ice creates a rapidly flowing
stream, colored military gray by the many small claylike particles known as "glacial
flour" that are suspended in the rushing waters. As a glacier melts and recedes, the
flow of water becomes more intense, and the glacial streams move fast enough to
carry larger particles of sand and gravel. They are deposited in beds according to
their size, the heavier gravel dropping from the stream when the waters first begin to
slow down, the sands depositing in slightly quieter waters, and so forth. The study
of the history of the continental glaciations has continued throughout the twentieth
century, with geologists, climatologists, geographers, and biologists seeking the
details of the duration and extent of these ice sheets.

16. K. W. Butzer, *Environment and Archeology* (Chicago and New York: Aldine
Atherton, 1971).

17. The species of hominids can be traced to the Tertiary period before the
Pleistocene. The oldest known direct ancestors of *Homo sapiens*, the genus
Ramapithecus, have now been traced back 14 million years. However, the earliest
known toolmakers are the *Australopithecus*, who are known to have made tools 2 to
3 million years ago. *Homo sapiens* is now believed to have arisen between 500,000
and 100,000 years ago (J. Jelínek, *The Evolution of Man* [New York: Hamlyn,
1975]).

18. M. L. Heinselman, "Fire in the Virgin Forests of the Boundary Waters
Canoe Area, Minnesota," *Journal of Quaternary Research* 3(1973): 329–82. The
Boundary Waters Canoe Area has also been relatively undisturbed. It has been
subject to some human influences, though, both before and after European colonization, especially the suppression of fires from 1900 until quite recently, and
logging and trapping before its establishment as a protected wilderness.

19. R. F. Flint, *Glacial and Quaternary Geology* (New York: John Wiley, 1971).

20. M. B. Davis, "Pleistocene Biogeography of Temperate Deciduous Forests,"
GeoScience and Man 13(1976): 13–26. In the discussion that follows, the information about rates of movement of trees also comes from this reference.

21. Davis, "Pleistocene Biogeography of Temperate Deciduous Forests." Where
they overlap, beech occurs on slightly warmer, better drained soils; and the hemlock, on cooler, moister valleys, stream sides, and ridges. Neither hemlock nor
beech occurs on Isle Royale, although both species grow farther east in forests that

are otherwise typical of the warmer areas of the island, forests that on Isle Royale contain yellow birch and sugar maple and that in New York, New England, and Pennsylvania contain yellow birch, sugar maple, hemlock, and beech. Given enough time, these species might also reach Isle Royale; they would grow there if they were planted.

22. Rinderpest is a disease produced by virus of the genus *Morbillivirus*; the symptoms are lesions of the skin, diarrhea, and high fever. The word comes from the German *rinder*, which means "cattle." A. R. E. Sinclair, *The African Buffalo* (Chicago: University of Chicago Press, 1977).

23. D. A. Livingstone, "Late Quaternary Climatic Change in Africa," *Annual Review of Ecology and Systematics* 6(1975): 275.

24. D. Walker, "The Changing Vegetation of the Montane Tropics," *Search* 1(1970):217–21; R. L. Kendall, "An Ecological History of the Lake Victoria Basin," *Ecological Monographs* 39(1969):121–76.

25. The New Guinea sediment cores were obtained from fire sites stretched out over almost a 60-mile distance between Laiagam and Mount Itagen Town (approximately latitude 5° longitude 145°). The information discussed here is from Walker, "The Changing Vegetation of the Montane Tropics."

26. D. Walker, "Changing Vegetation of the Montane Tropics."
The evidence of past glaciers in New Guinea is similar to that in East Africa. There are large moraines ending at elevations of 9,000 to 11,000 feet on Mount Carstensz and Mount Wilhelm in New Guinea. Dating of the organic debris on the top of the moraines sets a minimum age and suggests that the ice retreated before 13,000 years ago. But there were several advances afterward, one after 11,600 and another sometime before 3,000 years ago. In more recent periods, between 2,500 and 1,300 years ago, there were three glacial advances.

27. A. P. Kershaw, "A Late Pleistocene and Holocene Pollen Diagram from Lynch's Crater, Northeastern Queensland, Australia," *New Phytologist* 77(1976): 469–98. The history of forests near Lynch's Crater in Australia is clouded by the possible influence of human beings. The change from vegetation characteristic of high rainfall areas to that of lower rainfall regions could also result from an increase in the frequency of fire. The drier-site vegetation can survive more frequent fires than the rain-forest vegetation. It is unlikely that the rate of natural (lightning caused) fire would have varied sufficiently to produce the modification in the vegetation. But the change in fire frequency could have resulted from an increase in the number of fires set by human beings. The earliest radiocarbon date for *Homo sapiens* in Australia is 38,000 years ago, coincident with the beginning of the long but definite change in the vegetation. Thus we cannot be certain whether the temporal patterns in vegetation near Lynch's Crater, whatever the cause, were primarily the result of human activities or the result of climatic change.

28. J. M. Bowler, G. S. Hope, J. N. Jennings, G. Singh, and D. Walker, "Late Quaternary Climates of Australia and New Guinea," *Quaternary Research* 6(1976):359–94.

29. Walker, "The Changing Vegetation of the Montane Tropics," *Search*, p. 217 and p. 220.

Notes

213

30. J. Walker, C. H. Thompson, I. F. Fergus, and B. R. Tunstall, "Plant Succession and Soil Development in Coastal Sand Dunes of Subtropical Eastern Australia," in *Forest Succession: Concepts and Applications,* ed. D. C. West, H. H. Shugart, and D. B. Botkin (New York: Springer-Verlag, 1981).

31. W. A. Reiners, I. A. Worley, and D. B. Lawrence, "Plant Diversity in a Chronosequence at Glacier Bay, Alaska," *Ecology* 52(1971):55–69.

32. J. Byelich, et al., "Kirtland's Warbler Recovery Plan," U.S. Dept. of Interior and Fish and Wildlife Service, 1985, p. 1.

33. M. L. Heinselman, "Fire and Succession in the Conifer Forests of Northern North America," in West, Shugart, and Botkin, *Forest Succession.*

34. Information about the Kirtland's warbler and its habitat is from: H. Mayfield, *The Kirtland's Warbler* (Bloomfield Hills, Mich.: Cranbrook Institute of Science, 1960), pp. 24–25; and Byelich et al., "Kirtland's Warbler Recovery Plan," p. 12.

35. Norman A. Wood, quoted in Mayfield, *Kirtland's Warbler,* p. 23.

36. Byelich, et al., "Kirtland's Warbler Recovery Plan," p. 22.

37. L. Line, "The Bird Worth a Forest Fire," *Audubon* (1964): pp. 371–75.

Chapter 5

1. L. J. Henderson, *The Fitness of the Environment* (New York: Macmillan, 1913; Boston, Beacon Press, 1966).

2. Ibid., pp. 108–9. Among the key passages in Henderson's book concerning the remarkable properties of water are the following: "water shares the characteristic of very high specific heat with a very small number of substances, among which hydrogen and ammonia are probably the only important chemical individuals" (ibid., p. 84); "water possesses certain nearly unique qualifications which are largely responsible for making the earth habitable. . . . The most obvious effect of the high specific heat of water is the tendency of the ocean and of all lakes and streams to maintain a nearly constant temperature. . . . A second effect . . . is the moderation of both summer and winter temperatures of the earth" (pp. 85–86). He also lists as important the high latent heat of melting and evaporation of water (the amount of heat required to convert a unit of ice to water and a unit of water to water vapor). These tend to stabilize the temperatures of the planet, for "so long as water and ice exist in contact, the system constitutes a thermostat. . . . Heating serves merely to melt the ice, cooling to freeze the water" (p. 93). In addition, water has an unusually high freezing point, which Henderson calls "one of the most important facts with which we are concerned, for while a very large number of chemical processes take place quite freely at 0°, the conditions are very different at the freezing point of ammonia, for instance," which is much lower and reactions therefore take place much more slowly (pp. 93–94). The latent heat of evaporation "is by far the highest known," which is "one of the most important regulatory factors at present known to meteorologists" (p. 98).

3. In regard to a teleological view of nature and the universe, there is the recent idea of an "anthropic principle," that the fundamental laws of the universe are

214 Notes

"tuned" to permit the evolution of life and consciousness. For example, see J. D. Barrow, and F. J. Tipler, *The Anthropic Cosmological Principle*, (New York: Oxford University Press, 1986). This idea is discussed by scientists interested in the origin of life and in the exploration of space, as indicated by G. Wald, "Fitness in the Universe: Choices and Necessities," in *Cosmochemical Evolution and the Origins of Life*, eds. J. Oró, S. L. Miller,C. Ponnamperuma, and R. S. Young (Dordrecht: Reidel, 1974). The editors of this book have been active in the study of the origin of life and in biological issues that make use of satellite technology. Other relevant references include: B. J. Carr, and M. J.Rees, "The Anthropic Principle and the Structure of the Physical World," *Nature* 278(1979): 605–12; G. Gale, "The Anthropic Principle," *Scientific American*245(1981): 154–71; B. Carter, "Large Number Coincidences and the Anthropic Principle in Cosmology," in *Confrontation of Cosmological Theories with Observational Data*, ed. M. S. Longair (Dordrecht: Reidel, 1974). I thank J. B. Callicott for these references.

4. A. Leopold, "Deer Irruptions," reprinted in *Wisconsin Conservation Department Publication* 321(1943):3–11. This is the source usually quoted as initiating the mountain lion–Kaibab deer story. See also A. Leopold, L. K. Sowls, and D. L. Spencer, "A Survey of Over-populated Deer Ranges in the United States," *Journal of Wildlife Management* 11(1947): 162–77. Accounts based on Leopold's can be found in: W. S. Allee, A. E. Emerson, O. Park, T. Park and K. P. Schmidt, *Principles of Animal Ecology* (Philadelphia: Saunders, 1949); D. Lack, *The Natural Regulation of Animal Numbers* (London: Oxford University Press, 1954); H. G. Andrewartha, and L. C. Birch, *The Distribution and Abundance of Animals* (Chicago: University of Chicago Press, 1954); and E. P. Odum, *Fundamentals of Ecology* (Philadelphia: Saunders, 1971).

5. D. I. Rasmussen, "Biotic Communities of Kaibab Plateau, Arizona," *Ecological Monographs* 3(1941): 229–75.

6. Leopold, Sowls, and Spencer, "Survey of Over-populated Deer Ranges in the United States." The following information is based on the excellent article by G. Caughley, "Eruption of Ungulate Populations, with Emphasis on Himalayan Thar in New Zealand," *Ecology* 51(1970):53–72.

7. A. Leopold, *A Sand County Almanac and Sketches Here and There* (New York: Oxford University Press, 1949), pp. 130–32. Those familiar with Aldo Leopold's work know that the point of view toward predators expressed in this book was a major change from the viewpoint that Leopold had held earlier in his career, when, during his years with the United States Forest Service, he was a public advocate of predator eradication from the southwestern ranges. According to J. B. Callicott, who is an expert on Leopold's career, it was very difficult for Leopold to admit that he was mistaken, and his article "Thinking Like a Mountain" was written as a kind of confession of past misdeeds. This is discussed in D. Ribbens, "The Making of *A Sand County Almanac*," in J. B. Callicott, *Companion to A Sand County Almanac*, (Madison: University of Wisconsin Press, 1987). The discussion, begun by Caughley, suggesting that there may be little evidence that the mountain lions actually had a beneficial effect may seem ironic, since it would

seem to deny the point of view with which Leopold ended his career and which he arrived at only after a long and apparently introspective consideration. But the main thrust of my discussion is that we must seek a view that is consistent with our observations, a point of view clearly shared by Leopold. The fundamental purpose of my discussion is to help us achieve a better way to live with our environment, which was Leopold's desire as well. That mountain lions may not regulate the abundance of their prey is not an argument in favor of hunting lions. The conservation of endangered species and of biological diversity has, in recent years, expanded greatly to a much larger scientific and philosophical basis, as will be discussed later. Since science is a process and knowledge continually changes, so our interpretations and our understanding of how to achieve that goal must change.

8. This discussion is based on the excellent analysis by Caughley "Eruption of Ungulate Populations."

9. Rasmussen, "Biotic Communities of Kaibab Plateau, Arizona."

10. Quoted in L. P. Coonen and C. M. Porter, "Thomas Jefferson and American Biology," *BioScience* 26(1976): p. 747.

11. W. Derham, *Physico-Theology: or, A Demonstration of the Being and Attributes of God, from His Work of Creation*, (London: A. Strahan, et al., 1798). The original edition included the statement that this work was "the substance of sixteen sermons, preached in St. Mary-le-Bow Church, London; at the Honourable Mr. Boyle's lectures, in the years 1711 and 1712."

12. These issues are thoroughly discussed by C. J. Glacken in his excellent book *Traces on the Rhodian Shore: Nature and Culture in Western Thought from Ancient Times to the end of the Eighteenth Century* (Berkeley: University of California Press, 1967). Another classic and important book on this topic is A. O. Lovejoy, *The Great Chain of Being* (Cambridge, Mass.: Harvard University Press, 1942). Other interesting analyses can be found in F. N. Egerton, "Changing concepts of the balance of nature," *Quarterly Review of Biology* 48(1973):322–50. The discussion that follows merely outlines the history of these ideas; a reader interested in this history should refer to these references especially.

13. Derham, *Physico-Theology*, Vol I. p. 257.

14. Ibid., pp. 257–59.

15. Quoted in F. N. Egerton, "Changing Concepts of the Balance of Nature," *Quarterly Review of Biology* 48(1973): p. 338.

16. Glacken, *Traces on the Rhodian Shore*, p. 36.

17. Ibid., p. 62.

18. Herodotus, *The History of Herodotus*, trans. George Rawlinson, ed. E. H. Blakeney (New York: Dutton, 1964), p. 148. See Glacken, 1967 *opus cited* for further discussion of the Greek and Roman ideas about the character of nature.

19. Cicero, *The Nature of the Gods*, trans. H. C. P. McGregor (Aylesbury: Penguin, 1972). The quotations that follow are from pp. 172–73.

20. Quoted in A. O. Lovejoy, *Great Chain of Being*, p. 50.

21. A. Pope, *An Essay on Man*, 1734, quoted in Lovejoy, *The Great Chain of Being*, p. 60.

22. G. L. Leclerc, *Natural History, General and Particular*, vol. 3, trans. W. Smellie (London: C. Wood, 1812). The quotations that follow are from pp. 455–57.
23. Cicero, p. 176.
24. Cicero, p. 177.
25. Lucretius, *De Rerum Natura*, Book 5, lines 200–237, trans. R. Humphries (Bloomington: Indiana University Press, 1968), pp. 164–65.

Chapter 6

1. Lucretius (Titus Lucretius Carus), *De Rerum Natura*, trans. R. Humphries (Bloomington: Indiana University Press, 1968).
2. M. H. Nicolson, *Mountain Gloom and Mountain Glory: The Development of the Aesthetics of the Infinite* (Ithaca, N.Y.: Cornell University Press, 1959), pp. 160–61.
3. A. Kircher, *Mundus Subterraneus* (1665), parts of which were published as *The Vulcanoes or Burning and Fire-Vomiting Mountains, Famous in the World: With Their Remarkables*, (no trans. given) (London:John Allen, 1669), p. 35 and Preface (n.p.).
4. Ibid., Quotations in this paragraph are from p. 56, p. 43, and p. 3.
5. Ibid., Quotes in this paragraph are from p. 55, and p. 58.
6. The idea that change is intrinsic in nature can be found in the poetry of Patrick Carey, especially "Fallax et Instabilis," a poem of the "Caroline" period: " 'Tis a strange thing," he wrote, "Nothing but change I see" with the sea never in rest and "mountains do sink down." Quoted in Nicolson, *Mountain Gloom and Mountain Glory*, p. 155.
It is also worth pointing out that Alfred North Whitehead distinguished an organic theory from a materialistic (read "mechanistic") theory in a more abstract way: "On the materialistic theory, there is material—such as matter or electricity—which endures. On the organic theory, the only endurances are structures of activity, and the structures are evolved. "Enduring things are thus the outcome of a temporal process; whereas eternal things are the elements required for the very being of the process" *Science and the Modern World* ([1925: New York: Mentor Books, 1959], pp. 101–2).
7. I would like to acknowledge my debt to Nicolson, for her excellent discussion in *Mountain Gloom and Mountain Glory* of the history of the aesthetics of nature and the change in the perceptions of nature from the Renaissance to the Romantics, and for her general insights tying this discussion to the classical Greeks and Romans. My discussions extend hers, and hers provide a key background for this chapter.
8. Quoted in Nicolson, *Mountain Gloom and Mountain Glory*, pp. 198 and 200.
9. Ibid., pp. 199–200.

10. From *Nicolai Stenonis de Solido intra Solidum naturaliter contento dissertationis prodromus*, (Florence, 1669). English translation published as *The Prodromus to a Dissertation concerning Solids Naturally Contained within Solids* (London; Henry Oldenburg, 1671). Quoted in Nicolson, *Mountain Gloom and Mountain Glory*, p. 156.

11. Lucretius, *De Rerum Natura*, trans. R. Humphries (Bloomington: University of Indiana Press, 1968), Book V: quotations are selected from lines 784–836.

12. Ibid., Quotations selected from Book V, lines 247–260.

13. Nicolson, *Mountain Gloom and Mountain Glory*, pp. 160–61.

14. T. Pownall, *A Topographical Description of the Dominion of the United States*, ed. Lois Mulkean (Pittsburgh: University of Pittsburgh Press, 1949), p. 24.

15. Both the quotations about the mountains and the oceans are from Nicolson, *Mountain Gloom and Mountain Glory*, pp. 305–6.

16. The quote from E. Warren is from his poem, *Geologia*, quoted in Nicolson, *Mountain Gloom and Mountain Glory*, p. 267; the quote from R. Bentley is also from Nicolson, p. 262. Bentley's book was originally published in London and the quotations are from pp. 35-38 of the 1693 edition.

17. The quote from Andrew Marvell is from his poem, "Upon the Hill and Grove at Bill-borow," *Poems and Letters*, ed. by H. M. Margoliouth (Oxford: Clarendon Press, 1927) I, p. 56. The quote from John Dennis is from Nicolson, *Mountain Gloom and Mountain Glory*, p. 277, while the quote from James Thomson is also from Nicolson, p. 335.

18. Quoted in ibid., p. 388.

19. F. E. Clements, "Nature and Structure of the Climax," *Journal of Ecology* 24(1936): 257. See Chapter 4 for direct quotations from Clements's writings.

20. R. H. Whittaker, "Recent Evolution of Ecological Concepts in Relation to the Eastern Forests of North America," *American Journal of Botany* 44(1957): 197–206.

Chapter 7

1. Edward Alden Jewell, " 'Machines, Machines!' The Futurist's Cry," *New York Times*, December 11, 1927, Section V, p. 13. Jewell was an art critic for the New York Times.

2. David Foster, *Santa Barbara News-Press*, June 17, 1987, p. B5.

3. The rise of the mechanical paradigm led to a change in the perception of God, beginning with Descartes's argument that God created nature and the human mind according to the same rational laws; thus it is possible to know nature through reason. The philosopher J. B. Callicott has written to me that later scientists-- theologians described their activity as "thinking God's thoughts after Him." In such ways, the mechanical view of nature began to change the perception of God from the divine patriarch, which is a more organic image, to the cosmic engineer.

An interesting discussion of a major change in our ideas about machinery, mechanics, and technology, can be found in Frederick Turner, "Escape from Modernism," *Harper's*, November 1984, pp. 47–55. Turner refers to a present-day "crisis of materialism," analogous to the "crisis of Christianity" that occurred 400 years ago.

4. M. H. Nicolson, *Mountain Gloom and Mountain Glory: The Development of the Aesthetics of the Infinite* (Ithaca, N.Y.: Cornell University Press, 1959), p. 161.

5. Ibid., p. 161. In *Science and the Modern World*, Alfred North Whitehead provided one of the classic discussions of the transition of ideas from the pre-scientific to the scientific, and the impact of the new physics on philosophy; he wrote that "the nature-poetry of the romantic revival (in the nineteenth century) was a protest on behalf of the organic view of nature, and also a protest against the exclusion of value from the essence of matter of fact" ([1925; New York: Mentor Books, 1959], p. 90).

6. G. W. Wetherill and C. L. Drake, "The Earth and Planetary Sciences," *Science* 209(1980): 96–104.

7. M. Hale, *The Primitive Origination of Mankind Considered and Examined According to the Light of Nature* (London: W. Godbid, 1677), p. 211. Quoted in F. N. Egerton, "Changing Concepts of the Balance of Nature," *Quarterly Review of Biology* 48(1973): p. 331.

8. See, for example, the excellent historical analyses of the changes in the extent of Alpine glaciers in E. Le Roy Ladurie, *Times of Feast, Times of Famine: A History of Climate Since the Year 1000* (Garden City, N.Y.: Doubleday, 1971).

9. A. von Humboldt, *Cosmos* vol. 3, (New York: Harper & Brothers, 1851), pp. 9–10.

10. A. von Humboldt, *Views of Nature* (London: Bell, 1986), p. 288.

11. G. P. Marsh, *Man and Nature*, ed. D. Lowenthal (1864; Cambridge, Mass.: Harvard University Press, 1967), pp. 29–30.

12. Hale, *Primitive Origination of Mankind*, p. 211.

13. Quoted in Nicolson, *Mountain Gloom and Mountain Glory*, p. 153. As another example, she cites Joseph Blancanus, *Sphaera Mundi* (1620).

Chapter 8

1. "In the Outlaw Area," a profile of Buckminster Fuller by Calvin Tomkins, *The New Yorker*, January 8, 1966.

2. F. Turner, "Escape from Modernism," *Harper's*, November 1984, p. 48.

3. *The Columbia Viking Desk Encyclopedia*, S. V. "bacteria."

4. S. Sonea and M. Panisset, *A New Bacteriology* (Boston: Jones and Bartlett, 1983), pp. 8–9.

5. L. Margulis, Preface to ibid., p. viii.

6. Sonea and Panisset, *A New Bacteriology*, pp. 1–8.

7. Kalm, *Travels in North America*, pp. 369–70. I originally recounted this

story in D. B. Botkin "Life and Death in a Forest: The Computer as an Aid to Understanding," *Ecosystem Modeling in Theory and Practice*, ed. C. A. S. Hall and J. W. Day, Jr. (New York: Wiley, 1977).

8. R. Leemans and I. C. Prentice, "Description and Simulation of Tree-layer Composition and Size Distributions in a Primaeval *Picea-Pinus* Forest," *Vegetatio* 69(1987): 147–156; D. C. West, H. H. Shugart and D. B. Botkin, eds., *Forest Succession: Concepts and Applications* (New York: Springer-Verlag, 1981). The idea that computer simulation can be used to mimic nature in any realistic way is not well known to the public or necessarily accepted among scientists in ecology.

9. G. E. Yule, "The Wind Bloweth Where It Listeth," *Cambridge Review* 41(1920): 184.

10. P. Frank, *Einstein, His Life and Times*, G. Rosen, trans. (New York: Alfred A. Knopf, 1947) p. 208.

11. As an example, radioactive isotopes will decay, but when any particular atom will undergo such decay seems to be a matter of chance whose probability can be determined. Einstein could not accept this interpretation. An alternative is that there are beneath these observations some other, completely deterministic rules that govern events such as the decay of an atom of a radioactive isotope, and therefore such events only appear random because of the level at which we observe them.

The uncertainty discussed in quantum theory has to do not only with the small size and high speed of particles, but more fundamentally with the idea that observations require the exchange of energy between the observer and the observed, that this exchange of energy affects the system being observed, and that subatomic particles are small enough for this energy exchange to have a significant effect. Thus in an attempt to determine the position and velocity of a very small particle, the observer strikes the particle with a photon, which then changes either the position or the velocity or both. This now fundamental idea, the Heisenberg uncertainty principle, is today familiar to students of physics. The amount of uncertainty in quantum mechanics can be calculated. While this is an important idea in twentieth-century physics, it is not my intention to make an exact analogy with it.

I am not trying to claim that at the level at which we observe wolves and trees, the process of observation necessarily has a significant effect on the state of the system we are observing. The Heisenberg uncertainty effect is too small for these middle-scale systems and for our means of observation. The point I wish to make is that quantum theory opened up a different perception of nature, nature as fundamentally uncertain, and thus provides a metaphor that may make it easier for us to accept a change in our perception of biological nature.

Clearly, my discussion is not meant to be a definitive treatment of any of the philosophical issues raised by quantum physics. My purpose is merely to show some of the connections between twentieth-century physics and the life sciences in regard to the fundamental ideas about nature. Other scholarly books deal with these aspects of the philosophy of science. One of the more interesting and easy to read is Erwin Schrödinger, *Science and the Human Temperament* and *Science and Humanism* (London: Cambridge University Press, 1952).

12. There are recent attempts among philosophers to grapple with these difficult issues: for example, J. B. Callicott, "Intrinsic Value, Quantum Theory, and Environmental Ethics," *Environmental Ethics* 7(1985): 257–275. Again, I am not attempting in this book to make a definitive analysis of these philosophical issues, but more simply to suggest through examples the changes that are taking place in our ideas.

13. M. A. Kominz and N. G. Pisias, "Pleistocene Climate: Deterministic or Stochastic?" *Science* 204(1979): 171–72.

14. The information on the whooping crane (*Grus americana*), is from R. S. Miller and D. B. Botkin, "Endangered Species: Models and Predictions," *American Scientist* 62(1974): 172–81; and R. P. Allen, *The Whooping Crane: National Audubon Society Research Reports* no. 3 (New York: National Audubon Society, 1952).

15. Branches of mathematics that deal with stochastic processes have advanced rapidly in the twentieth century and have, to a limited but growing extent, begun to influence the science of ecology. Thus they are also supporting the shift away from a mechanical metaphor of nature. There is an extensive scientific literature on stochastic processes in ecology. It is not my purpose here to provide a definitive review of that literature, but merely to introduce the general concepts.

As mentioned briefly in the chapter, there are curious deterministic systems that appear random in the sense that future states cannot be predicted simply from present states. For example, there are some mathematical equations whose future values can be determined only by calculating them one at a time. The relevance of this to ecological phenomena was discussed in the early 1970s by the mathematician J. A. Yorke (S. A. Woodin and J.A. Yorke, "Disturbance, Fluctuating Rates of Resource Recruitment, and Increased Diversity," in *Ecosystem Analysis and Prediction*, ed. S. A. Levin [Philadelphia: Society for Industrial and Applied Mathematics, 1975] and by R. May ("Biological Populations with Nonoverlapping Generations," *Science* 186[1974]: 645–7). Some of the methods used to generate "random numbers" by computers make use of such equations.

16. This is the work of Dr. Mel Manalis of the University of California, Santa Barbara.

17. As an example, I worked with an expert mathematician in the field of stochastic processes; we developed a model of a single population of elephants that took into account in an explicit manner that births and deaths are matters of chance. The analytic mathematics (the pencil-and-paper math) gave quite interesting results. The pencil-and-paper mathematics led to the framework of a model of the elephant populations, but only when this framework was translated into a computer program could the approach be used for realistic situations with an environment that changes over time. The pencil-and-paper part of the work was published as L. S. Wu and D. B. Botkin, "Of Elephants and Men: A Discrete, Stochastic Model for Long-lived Species with Complex Life Histories," *American Naturalist* 116(1980):831–49.

Chapter 9

1. *Concerning the Face Which Appears in the Orb of the Moon*, quoted in Glacken, *Traces on the Rhodian Shore*, p. 74.
2. G. E. Hutchinson, "The Biochemistry of the Terrestrial Atmosphere," *The Earth as a Planet*, ed. G. P. Kuiper (Chicago: University of Chicago Press, 1954) p. 372.
3. M. S. Gordon, G. A. Bartholomew, A. D. Ginnell, G. B. Jorgensen, and F. M. White, *Animal Physiology* (New York: Macmillan, 1977).
4. S. A. Tyler, and E. S. Barghoorn, "Occurrence of Structurally Preserved Plants in Precambrian Rocks of the Canadian Shield," *Science* 119(1954): 606–8.
5. L. Margulis, and J. E. Lovelock, "Biological Modulation of the Earth's Atmosphere," *Icarus* 21(1974): 471–89. Additional interesting information about the time when only prokaryotes lived on the Earth can be found in L. Margulis, *Early Life* (Boston: Science Books International, 1982), *Symbiosis in Cell Evolution* (San Francisco: W. H. Freeman, 1981).
6. L. Margulis, and R. Guerrero, "From Planetary Atmospheres to Microbial Communities: A Stroll Through Space and Time," in *Changing The Global Environment: Perspectives on Human Involvement*, eds. D. B. Botkin, M. F. Caswell, J. E. Estes and A. A. Orio (Boston, Mass.: Academic Press, 1989).
7. For a history of the Earth's atmosphere, see J. C. G. Walker, *Evolution of the Atmosphere* (New York: Macmillan, 1977). The early concentration of oxygen and hydrogen is discussed by Walker in "Oxygen and Hydrogen in the Primitive Atmosphere," *Pure and Applied Geophysics*, 116(1977): 222–31. The preceding two paragraphs are from D. B. Botkin and E. A. Keller, *Environmental Studies: The Earth As A Living Planet* (Columbus: Merrill, 1982), p. 57.
8. D. M. Gates, *Biophysical Ecology* (New York: Springer-Verlag, 1980).
9. Ibid.
10. D. B. Botkin, ed., *Remote Sensing of the Biosphere* (Washington, D. C.: National Academy Press, 1986).
The term *biosphere* is used in this book to mean the planetary system that includes and sustains life. The term has had other meanings; it was coined in the late nineteenth century by Edward Suess to refer to the total amount of organic matter on the Earth—which we now refer to as "total biomass," and it has been used to mean simply the place where life is found on the Earth, that is, the extent of the distribution of life. The term *ecosphere* is synonymous with biosphere.
11. D. B. Botkin and E. A. Keller, *Environmental Studies: The Earth as a Living Planet* (Columbus, Ohio: Merrill, 1987).
12. Quoted in C. Lyell, *Principles of Geology; Being an Attempt to Explain the Former Changes of the Earth's Surface, by Reference to Causes Now in Operation*, Vol. II (London: John Murray, 1832), p. 190. Sir Charles Lyell lived from 1797 to 1875. His book is usually accepted as the first modern book on the science of geology.

13. Ibid., pp. 190–91.

14. Ibid., pp. 191–92. An excellent modern discussion of the factors that determine erosion and the situations when vegetation can play an important role and when it cannot, is R. C. Sidle, A. J. Pearce, and C. L. O'Loughlin, *Hillslope Stability and Land Use*, Water Resources Monograph Series, no. 11 (Washington, D. C.: American Geophysical Union, 1985).

15. Lyell, *Principles of Geology*, p. 192.

16. Ibid., p. 192.

17. The mass of the Earth is 6×10^{24} kg, or 6 billion trillion metric tons; the total living biomass is estimated to be on the order of 1.2×10^{15} kg or 1,000 billion metric tons. 1.2×10^{15} kg divided by 6×10^{24} kg is 0.2×10^{-9}. The mass of the atmosphere is 5×10^{18} kg. Dividing total biomass (1.2×10^{15} kg) by the mass of the atmosphere (5×10^{18} kg) gives 0.24×10^{-3}.

18. L. K. Nash, *Plants and the Atmosphere*, (Cambridge, Mass.: Harvard University Press, 1952). Joseph Priestly (1733–1804) was a theologian as well as a scientist; born in England, he immigrated to the United States in 1794.

19. P. Westbroek, "The Impact of Life on the Planet Earth," *Changing the Global Environment: Perspectives on Human Involvement*, eds. D. B. Botkin, M. F. Caswell, J. E. Estes and A. A. Orio, (Boston, Mass.: Academic Press, 1989), pp. 39–40.

20. As an example, see C. A. Ekdahl and C. D. Keeling, "Atmospheric Carbon Dioxide and Radiocarbon in the Natural Carbon Cycle. I. Quantitative Deductions from Records at Mauna Loa Observatory and at the South Pole," in *Carbon and the Biosphere*, eds. G. M. Woodwell and E. V. Pecan, Brookhaven National Laboratory Symposium, no. 24, (Springfield, Virginia: U.S. Technical Information Service, 1973).

21. J. E. Lovelock, *Gaia: A New Look at Life on Earth* (New York: Oxford University Press, 1979). The first quote is from p. xii; the second from p. 127.

Lovelock adds a third Gaian principle, which concerns a more technical matter: "Gaian responses to changes for the worse must obey the rules of cybernetics, where the time constant and the loop gain are important factors. Thus the regulation of oxygen has a time constant measured in thousands of years" (p. 127).

Lovelock's ideas are in one way a return to the use of the organic model for nature. His statement that "Gaia has vital organs at the core" is one example, but of even greater interest is his statement that salinity control "may be a key Gaian regulatory function," which he explains in terms of the human kidney (p. 57). However, his ideas are a blending of an organic and a mechanistic view, and they include a use of organic, mechanistic, and computer-based metaphors to explain the functionings of the biosphere. In his book, the homeostasis of the biosphere is explained in terms of the temperature regulation of an electric oven, of the functioning of a cybernetic system (that is, calculating device, a computer), and an analogy with the human body, as mentioned. In some places, there is a tendency to view the biosphere only mechanistically, as in "the only difference between non-living and living systems is in the scale of their intricacy, a distinction which fades all the time as the complexity and capacity of automated systems continue to evolve" (p. 62).

A problem in discussions of this kind is that it is difficult, if not impossible, to avoid presenting the ideas as though there were purposefulness on the part of life. This difficulty is a well-known flaw in scientific discussions, known as a "teleological argument"—giving a sense of intentionality to objects that cannot have consciousness, desire, and purpose. Lovelock writes that "occasionally it has been difficult, without excessive circumlocution, to avoid talking of Gaia as if she were known to be sentient. This is meant no more seriously than is the appellation "she" when given to a ship by those who sail in her, as a recognition that even pieces of wood and metal when specifically designed and assembled may achieve a composite identity with its own characteristic signature, as distinct from being the mere sum of its parts" (pp. ix-x). The book is sometimes metaphysical, going beyond the issue of scientific observations (is the biosphere biologically regulated?) to the question of whether this regulation is purposeful, as in Lovelock's discussion of the possibility that "the Earth's surface temperature is actively maintained at an optimum by and for the complex entity which is Gaia, and has been so maintained for most of her existence" (p. 53).

22. L. Thomas, *The Lives of a Cell: Notes of a Biology Watcher* (New York: Bantam Books, 1975), p. 4.

23. Lyell, *Principles of Geology*, p. 189.

24. The evolution of diatoms provides another example of a one-way process in the biosphere. Diatoms are single-celled algae that have a hard shell made of silicon. When diatoms evolved, they were the first major group of organisms to make use of the dissolved silicon in the oceans. Their hard silicon shells provided protection against enemies and in this way were a major evolutionary advance. The diatoms made use of a previously unused resource and gained an evolutionary advantage from it. There were two results: the local biological result was the evolution of many kinds of diatoms; the global (biospheric) result appears to have been a change in the cycling of carbon. Diatoms live at the surface of the ocean, where there is enough light for photosynthesis; but when they die, their shells sink to the ocean bottom. This transport of diatom shells from the ocean surface downward produced a new major storage of silicon and carbon on the ocean floor, creating diatomaceous earth, which we know as chalk.

The evolution that resulted in calcareous shells and internal skeletons containing calcium also resulted in major new opportunities for animals because the shells provide protection against predators, among other advantages. This biological use of calcium led to an increase in the production of limestone and in the storage of large quantities of carbon in limestone, which indirectly allowed an additional buildup in the atmosphere of a large amount of free oxygen. Just as in the case of the evolution of diatoms, the evolution of calcium-based shells and skeletons led to a new wave of biological evolution and to a major change in the biosphere.

Chapter 10

1. P. Kalm, *Travels in America: The America of 1750*, ed. A. B. Benson, English Version 1770 (New York: Dover, 1966), pp. 300 and 309.

2. The first recorded observation of the giant sequoia (*Sequoiadendron giganteum* (Lindl.) Buchholz) was made in 1839 by Zenas Leonard of Clearfield, Pennsylvania, but his obscure publication was little known (R. J. Hartesveldt, H. T. Harvey, H. S. Shellhammer, and R. E. Stecker, *The Giant Sequoia of the Sierra Nevada* [Washington, D. C.: Government Printing Office, 1975]). The report published in 1852 in the *Sonora Herald* brought attention to the tree. Too big to move and display in their entirety, sequoia trees were cut apart and parts of them were displayed. The bark of one sequoia 30 feet in diameter was removed completely to a height of 120 feet (thereby killing the tree) and reconstructed at the Crystal Palace in England in the 1850s (p. 7). The sequoia were also actively logged for timber, even though much of the fragile wood of the tree was destroyed when the huge trunks crashed to the ground.

3. That national parks were America's answer to the cultural trappings of Europe is the idea of Alfred Runte, a historian of American national parks, as discussed in *National Parks: The American Experience* (Lincoln: University of Nebraska Press, 1979). The quotations in this paragraph are from pp. 21–22.

4. Yosemite Valley became a California state park in 1864; a national park was established there in 1890 (Ibid., p. 16, plate 1).

5. Hartesveldt, Harvey, Shellhammer, and Stecker, *Giant Sequoia of the Sierra Nevada*; and R. J. Hartesveldt, "Fire Ecology of the Giant Sequoia: Controlled Fires May Be One Solution to Survival of the Species," *Natural History*, 73(1968): 12–19.

6. Jan Van Wagtendonk, Sequoia National Park scientist, personal communication.

7. Some people believe that doing nothing is the same as having no policy, but, on the contrary, a policy of intentional inaction is a definite policy, while the absence of any plan can lead to any action on the environment.

8. The modern discussions of the more specific aspects of these problems began at a symposium, the papers for which were published as W. L. Thomas, Jr., ed., *Man's Role in Changing the Face of the Earth* (Chicago: University of Chicago Press, 1956). They have continued with many reflective books and proceedings of conferences, including A. A. Orio and D. B. Botkin, eds., "Man's Role in Changing the Global Environment, Proceedings of an International Conference, Venice, Italy, 21–26 October, 1985," *The Science of the Total Environment*, 55(1986): 1–399, and 56(1986): 1–415.

9. D. Pearce, "Sustainable Futures: Some Economic Issues," in *Changing the Global Environment: Perspectives on Human Involvement*, eds., D. B. Botkin, M. F. Caswell, J. E. Estes, and A. A. Orio (Boston, Mass.: Academic Press, 1989).

10. This information about sea otters is from: J. A. Estes and J. F. Palmisano, "Sea Otters: Their Role in Structuring Nearshore Communities," *Science*

185(1974):1058–60; and D. O. Duggins, "Kelp Beds and Sea Otters: An Experimental Approach," *Ecology 61*(1980): 447–53.

11. K. W. Kenyon, *The Sea Otter in the Eastern Pacific Ocean*, North American Fauna, no.68, Bureau of Sport Fisheries and Wildlife, United States Department of the Interior (Washington, D. C.: Government Printing Office, 1969).

12. Public Law 92–522, H.R. 10420, 92nd Cong., October 21, 1972.

13. M. E. Soulé, "What is Conservation Biology?" *BioScience 35*(1985): 727–34.

14. R. L. Fredriksen, "Comparative Chemical Water Quality--Natural and Disturbed Streams Following Logging and Slash Burning," *Proceedings of a Symposium: Forest Land Use and Stream Environment Oct. 19–21, 1970* (Corvallis: Oregon State University, 1971). The research at Hubbard Brook was initiated by Eugene E. Likens and F. Herbert Bormann, then of Dartmouth University. For an introduction to this research, see G. E. Likens, F. H. Bormann, R. S. Pierce, J. S. Eaton, and N. M. Johnson, *Biogeochemistry of a Forested Ecosystem* (New York: Springer-Verlag, 1977).

15. The young pines growing under the old red oak tree near Pellston, Michigan, suggested that there is a considerable lag in the response of a mature forest to climatic change, which is another way that forests are different from the simpler ideas that were dominant during the first half of the twentieth century, when it was assumed that natural vegetation would respond rapidly to changes in climate.

16. One can read any of Lewis Mumford's many books for insights about the city and civilization within nature, from his earlier books, such as *Technics and Civilization* (New York: Harcourt Brace Jovanovich, 1934), to the more recent ones, including *The City in History* (New York: Harcourt Brace Jovanovich, 1961), and *The Pentagon of Power: The Myth of the Machine* (New York: Harcourt Brace Jovanovich, 1964). Of course, there is a large field that deals with the history of cities, cities as environment, and urban planning. Books on these topics include *The Papers of Frederick Law Olmsted*, eds. C. C. McLaughlin, C. E. Beveridge, D. Schuyler, and J.T. Censer, 4 vols. (Baltimore: Johns Hopkins University Press, 1977–86); J. A. Burton, *Worlds Apart: Nature in the City* (Garden City, N. Y.: Doubleday, 1977); and A. W. Spirn, *The Granite Garden: Urban Nature and Human Design* (New York: Basic Books, 1984).

Chapter 11

1. Isabella Bird visited the Hawaiian Islands in 1873 and her experiences were published originally as *Six Months Among the Palm Groves, Coral Reefs and Volcanoes of the Sandwich Islands* (London: John Murray, 1890) reprinted as *Six Months In the Sandwich Islands* (Rutland, Vt.: Tuttle, 1983), p. 37.

2. Ibid., p. 35.

3. Some of the first important discussions of these measurements took place at a conference in 1972 at the Brookhaven National Laboratory and were published as *Carbon and the Biosphere*, G. M. Woodwell and E. V. Pecan, eds., Brookhaven

National Laboratory Symposium, no. 24 (Oak Ridge, Tenn.: Technical Information Service, 1973).

4. C. J. Glacken, *Traces on the Rhodian Shore: Nature and Culture in Western Thought from Ancient Times to the End of the Eighteenth Century* (Berkeley: University of California Press, 1967) p. 74. Glacken points out that writers from Plutarch through those of the seventeenth century, including John Ray, John Keill, and Edmund Halley, did argue that uninhabited parts of the Earth were useful. (The argument by Plutarch is quoted at the beginning of Chapter 9.)

5. *Santa Barbara News-Press*, April 24, 1988, p. A25. The article describes an analysis done by Lori Heise of the Worldwatch Institute of Washington, D.C. A recent article made the same point, reporting an estimate that an area the size of Australia would be required to absorb the 5 billion metric tons of carbon added every year from the burning of fossil fuels (W. Booth, "Johnny Appleseed and the Greenhouse," *Science*, 242[1988]: 19–20).

6. See G. S. Callendar, "The Artificial Production of Carbon Dioxide and Its Influence on Temperature," *Quarterly Journal of the Royal Meteorological Society* 64(1938): 223–37; "Can Carbon Dioxide Influence Climate?" *Weather* 4(1949): 310–14; "On the Amount of Carbon Dioxide in the Atmosphere," *Tellus* 10(1958): 243.

7. M. A. K. Khalil and R. A. Rasmussan, "Causes of Increasing Atmospheric Methane: Depletion of Hydroxyl Radicals and the Rise of Emissions," *Atmospheric Environment* 19(1985): 397.

8. The projected effect depends on which climate model is used. The models that we used were from Goddard Space Flight Center, New York, Princeton University, and Oregon State University.

9. R. H. Whittaker and G. E. Likens, "Carbon in the Biota," in *Carbon and the Biosphere*, eds. G. M. Woodwell and E. V. Pecan, Brookhaven National Laboratory Symposium, no. 24 (Oak Ridge, Tenn.: Technical Information Service, 1973). These authors used information available to them at that time, which tended to be on the optimistic side, since most studies of the production of organic matter are done either by ecologists, who like to study old or mature vegetation or otherwise interesting vegetation, or by foresters, who tend to focus on highly productive areas. Newer information suggests that the values that Whittaker and Likens used might be twice the real average—as for example, in a study of mine whose purpose is to obtain the first statistically valid estimate of biomass for any large area of the Earth.

10. These estimates are merely for illustration, since the estimates of annual organic matter production by natural vegetation are crude, and because such production would vary from year to year with variations in climate, incidents of fire and pest and disease outbreaks. It has become popular to make this sort of estimate, and the estimates vary considerably depending on assumptions.

11. A brief summary in graphic form of the major global environmental problems can be found in "Endangered Earth," the supplement to the *National Geographic*, December 1988. Other summaries can befound in L. R. Brown, *State of*

the World (New York: Norton for the Worldwatch Institute, 1988); N. Myers, *Gaia: An Atlas of Planet Management* (New York: Doubleday, 1984) and D. B. Botkin, M. F. Caswell, J. E. Estes, A. A. Orio, eds., *Changing the Global Environment: Perspectives on Human Involvement*(Boston: Academic Press, 1989).

12. T. E. Lovejoy, "Deforestation and Extinction of Species" in *Changing the Global Environment: Perspectives on Human Involvement*, ed. D. B. Botkin, M. F. Caswell, J. E. Estes and A. A. Orio (Boston, Mass.: Academic Press, 1989), p. 97.

Chapter 12

1. Plotinus, *The Enneads*, trans. S. MacKenna, revised by B. S. Page, 3rd edition (London: Faber and Faber Ltd., 1956).

2. "Driven to Extremes," *Los Angeles Times Magazine* (1987). MacCready is the designer of the sunraycer car and the Gossamer Condor, the first human-powered aircraft.

3. This discussion is based on P. G. K. Kahn and S. M. Pompea, "Nautiloid Growth Rhythms and Dynamical Evolution of the Earth-Moon System," *Nature* 275(1978): 606–11.

4. This assumes that the Earth's day length has changed slowly and measurably, and that the masses of the Earth and moon have been constant.

5. Kahn and Pompea, "Nautiloid Growth Rhythms and Dynamical Evolution of the Earth-Moon System."

6. G. P. Marsh, *Man and Nature*, ed. D. Lowenthal (1864; Cambridge, Mass.: Harvard University Press, 1967) p. 36.

7. P. Kalm, *Travels in North America*, 2 vols., trans. A. B. Benson (New York: Dover Books, 1966), pp. 308–9.

8. J. Campbell, *The Masks of God: Primitive Mythology* (New York: Viking, 1959), p. 468.

9. Sears, *Deserts on the March* (Norman: University of Oklahoma Press, 1935), p. 3.

10. A. Leopold, *A Sand County Almanac and Sketches Here and There* (New York: Oxford University Press, 1949), p. 207.

Postscript

1. This point is made in L. B. Slobodkin, D. B. Botkin, B. Maguire, Jr., B. Moore III, and H. J. Morowitz, "On the Epistemology of Ecosystem Analysis," in *Estuarine Perspectives*, ed. V. S. Kennedy (New York: Academic Press, 1980).

2. P. Sears, *Deserts on the March* (Norman: University of Oklahoma Press, 1935), p. 1.

3. Ibid., p. 136.

4. A. J. Pearce, "Erosion and Sedimentation" (Paper presented at the East-West

Center workshop, "Ecological Principles for Watershed Management," Honolulu, April 9–11, 1986). An excellent summary of the state of knowledge about erosional processes can be found in R. C. Sidle, A. J. Pearce, and C. L. O'Loughlin, *Hillslope Stability and Land Use*, Water Resources Monograph, no. 11 (Washington, D.C.: American Geophysical Union, 1985).

   5. D. B. Botkin, "The Need for a Science of the Biosphere," *Interdisciplinary Science Reviews*, 10(1985):267–78.

Some Key Ideas and Concepts

Biosphere In this book, this term is used to mean the planetary system that includes and sustains life, but originally defined as the total amount of organic matter on Earth. The term is also in general use to mean the *place* where life exists on the Earth (i.e., from the depths of the oceans to the summits of mountains).

Balance of Nature Generally speaking, the balance of nature includes three ideas: nature undisturbed is constant; when disturbed but released from that disturbance nature returns to its original, constant condition; that constant condition of nature is good and desirable. It has also been used to refer to the idea of a great chain of being, that is, every creature having its place in the harmonious workings of nature and well adapted to its purpose.

Carrying Capacity The original idea was the maximum number of individuals of a species that can be maintained indefinitely without damage to the habitat that would lead to a decline in numbers of that species that could be sustained. The term has also been used to mean, very specifically, the final size of a population that grew according to the logistic growth curve. More recently, the term has been generalized to mean the maximum size of a population of a species that could be supported without damage to other species or to the functioning of the ecosystem of which it formed a constituent part. The last idea is sometimes referred to as an optimum sustainable population.

Conservation To conservationists, this means the wise use of natural resources and the conservation of the ecosystems and their constituent species on the Earth.

Divine Order As applied to nature, refers to the ideas that (1) nature is the creation of an omnipotent and omniscient God and is therefore perfect in its

229

order and structure; (2) every creature has a proper role and proper relationship to every other and, when nature is not disrupted by evil forces, these roles and relationships are maintained.

Ecology The science that is the study of the relationships among living things and their environment.

Ecological Climax The ending stage of a classically ecological succession, originally thought to be the stage of maximum biomass and biological diversity, and thought to have the attributes of classical static stability. Now no longer thought to have these qualities.

Ecological Community Either (1) a set of interacting populations of different species found in an area, meaning that the community is the living part of an ecosystem; or (2) all of the species found in a local area, whether or not they actually interact; or (3) all of the species of the same kind found in a local area, as in a "plant community" or an "animal community."

Ecosphere A synonym for the biosphere used in its first sense, that is, the planetary system that includes and sustains life.

Ecosystem A set of interacting species and their local, nonbiological environment, functioning together to sustain life.

Equilibrium A fixed rest point, a condition of constancy.

Environmentalism The social, political, and ethical movements that concern the use of the environment.

Exponential Growth A population that increases by a constant percentage during each time period is said to grow exponentially. Such a population increases in number exactly as does money in a fixed rate interest account.

Machine Age The age that began with the industrial revolution but which flowered between the two world wars, and which seems to be ending now.

Maximum Sustainable Yield: (1) The maximum harvest of a population that can be obtained indefinitely without affecting the capacity of that population to sustain that yield. (2) The point on the logistic growth curve at which the population grows most rapidly, which is when the population equals one-half the size it reaches at the carrying capacity.

Nature Has been used to mean (1) the natural world on the Earth as it exists without human beings or civilization, that is, the environment including mountains, plains, rivers, lakes, oceans, air, rocks along with all nonhuman, nondomesticated living things; and (2) the universe, with all its phenomena, including the objects and the forces in the universe. Throughout this book, unless otherwise noted, the word *nature* stands for the first definition.

Organic   (1) Made of organic compounds; (2) living; (3) like an organism, having a birth, growth, and death, and all of the other characteristics of individuals.

Optimum Sustainable Yield   (1) The maximum harvest of a population that can be obtained indefinitely without affecting the capacity of that population, its habitat, or the ecosystem of which it is a part to sustain that yield. (2) The same as (1), but in addition, without having undesirable effects on other species or on other attributes of the ecosystem.

Optimum Sustainable Population   The maximum size of a population of a species that could be supported without damage to other species or to the functioning of the ecosystem of which it formed a constituent part. More specifically, in the 1972 U. S. Marine Mammal Protection Act, this term is defined as "the number of animals which will result in the maximum productivity of the population of the species, keeping in mind the optimum carrying capacity of the habitat and the health of the ecosystem of which they form a constituent element."

Stability   Classic static stability means that two conditions are met for any entity: it has an equilibrium condition; and when disturbed, the entity returns to the original equilibrium.

Succession (ecological)   The process of development (or redevelopment) of an ecosystem over time.

Wilderness   Generally thought of as an area undisturbed by human influence, but also believed to have certain specific attributes. A common connotation, not so commonly expressed, is the condition of nature prior to the influence of modern technological civilization, or any civilization beyond the hunter-gatherer stage.

Index

abalone, 157–161
acid rain, 180, 183, 194
Addison, Joseph, 95, 96
Africa, 15, 19, 45, 62, 63, 64, 65, 81, 98, 212 n.22
  See also elephant; Tsavo National Park, Kenya
Agassiz, Louis, 107
age structure, 200
air pollution, 167
Alaska, 59, 157–60, 213 n.31
alder, 3, 59, 67
algae, 140, 158, 174, 223 n.24
  See also diatoms
Alps, 96, 106, 108, 192, 211 n.15
Alyeska Pipeline, Alaska, 102
Amchitka Island, Alaska, 158
ammonia, 75, 135, 136, 139, 213 n.2
anchovy, 20
Andrewartha, H. G., 44, 208 n.17, 214 n.4
Anthropic principle, 213 n.3
Appalachians, the, 97
aqua alta, 167
aquatic plants, 28, 85
Aransas National Wildlife Refuge, 125
arctic, 28, 45, 47, 174
Aristotle, 35, 84, 87, 114, 133, 207 n.10
aspen, 28, 97, 178
associations, vegetation, 55, 97
Atlantic herring, 20

Atlantic menhaden, 20
atmosphere, 4, 6, 76, 133, 135–39, 141, 144, 147–50, 170, 172, 174–77, 179, 180, 183, 192, 200, 221–23 (notes), 226 n.6
Australia, 44, 64–66, 81, 137, 138, 157, 195, 212 n.27, 213 n.28, 226 n.5

Bacillus thuringiensis, 47
bacteria, 7, 20, 67, 113, 114, 120, 129, 131, 135–38, 144, 145, 182, 193, 218 n.3
  nitrogen-fixing, 131, 136
  photosynthetic, 137, 138
  See also Bacillus thuringiensis; Paramecium caudatum
Bahamas, 68
Baja California, 159
balance of nature, 15, 19, 30, 42, 48, 57, 80, 81, 84, 94, 109, 121, 145–47, 206–7 n.8, 215 n.12, 218 n.7
  definition, 25
  and twentieth-century ecology, 32–35
  See also structural balance
Barghoorn, Elso, 137
Bay of Bengal, 142
beech, 60, 61, 64, 97, 116, 211–12 n.21
Bentley, Richard, 96, 217 n.16
Bernardin de Saint-Pierre, Jacques-Henri, 82
Biblical statements about nature, 84, 87

feedback, 146, 151
fir, 28, 55, 97, 154, 172, 178
fire in ecosystems, 29, 34, 53, 55, 78,
    179, 212 *n*.27
  biological adaptations to, 69–70
  human influence, 63–64, 69–70, 86,
    208 *n*.8, 209 *n*.9
  after logging, 165
  management, 69–70, 153–54, 157
  suppression, 70, 162
firewood, 165, 196
fisheries, 19–20, 22–24, 41, 199–200
  and Lotka-Volterra predator and prey,
    37
Fitness of the Environment, The, 6, 75,
    88
Fletcher, Phineas, 94
flies, 21, 25, 37, 39, 68, 192
  tsetse, 45
Flood, Biblical, 93, 107
Forbes, Stephan A., 33, 206 *n*.8
forest(s)
  boreal, 27–28, 58–62, 67–68, 78
  and the greenhouse effect 178–80
  history, 58–62
  temperate New Zealand, 67
  temperate North American, 51–56,
    115–19, 162–66
  tropical, 62–66, 212 *n*.27
  undisturbed, 118
  virgin, 51
  See also deforestation; Hutcheson Me-
    morial Forest; reforestation; succes-
    sion, ecological; timber; *names of
    specific trees*
fossil, 137, 138, 141, 174, 177, 179,
    187–88
Fuller, Buckminster, 113, 203 *n*.4

Gaia hypothesis, 146, 222 *n*.21
Galileo, 91, 103, 141
Garden of Eden, 93
Gause, Georgii Frantsevich, 37, 39–41
Geologia, 96, 217
Germany, 45
glaciation, 57, 58, 60, 61–62, 63, 65,
    67, 68, 106, 107, 116, 124, 150,
    165, 180, 182, 212 n.26
  moraine, 57

Glacken, Clarence J., 82, 84, 87, 174,
    215 *n*.12, 226 *n*.4
global warming, 175, 194, 196
Goodman, Godfrey, bishop of Glouces-
    ter, 110
Grand Canyon, 76
  See also Kaibab Plateau
grassland, 8, 139
Grayling sands, 68
grazing, 64, 78, 134
great chain of being, 82, 85, 215 *n*.12
Great Lakes, 78
Greeley, Horace, 153
greenhouse effect, 175, 176, 183
growth rings of trees, 53, 56
Gunflint Chert, 137

habitat, 54, 125, 160, 162, 163, 178, 195
  introduction of wildlife into new, 78
  kelp beds as, 158–59
  of the Kirtland's warbler, 69, 70
haddock, 20, 208 *n*.20
Haeckel, Ernst, 32, 206 *n*.5
Hale, Sir Matthew, 106, 109
harmony, 24, 25, 35, 75, 81, 82, 86, 93,
    96, 186
  role of people in, 85, 88, 188–89,
    191, 197, 198
Hartesveldt, Richard, 154
Hawaii, 7, 171, 173
hazel, 62
Heisenberg, Werner, 124, 219 *n*.11
  See also uncertainty, principle
hemlock, 61, 211 *n*.21
Herodotus, 82
hickories, 51–53, 60, 172
Henderson, L., 6–7, 75–76, 88, 140
Homo sapiens, 10, 28, 58, 148, 211
    n.17, 212 *n*.27
Hubbard Brook Experimental Forest, 163
Hudson Bay, 45, 208 *n*.20
Hudson's Bay Company, 43, 45, 46, 208
    n.20
Hutcheson Memorial Forest, 51, 195,
    209–10 *n*.8–9
Hutchinson, G. E., 133, 140, 205 *n*.11

Indians, 27, 45, 53
  and the use of forest fires, 208 *n*.8

methane, 135, 136, 139, 175–77
mice, 35, 144, 208
Michigan, 61, 68, 69, 152, 164, 165,
    178, 180
microbes, 39, 112, 113, 134–37, 174
microcosm, 33, 206
midges, 45
Migratory Bird Treaty, 125
mill, 101–3, 110, 151
minimum viable population, 127, 161–
    62
Minnesota, 27, 58, 59, 138, 178, 180
Mississippi, 45
model, 31, 118–21, 123, 129, 130, 178,
    192, 220 *n*.17, 222 *n*.21, 226 *n*.8
    See also computer; simulation
Mont Blanc, 97
montane, 64
moon, 132, 185, 187, 188, 227 *n*.4
moose, 27–32, 34, 36–38, 47, 58, 61–
    63, 78, 133–38, 141, 144, 146–47,
    151, 167, 174, 178, 196
Morro Hermoso Island, 159
mosquito fish, 47
moss, 28, 58, 67, 164
mother Earth, 107
    See also Gaia hypothesis
Mount Aetna, 91
Mountain Gloom and Mountain Glory,
    216 *n*.6–7
mountain lion, 77, 80, 89, 214 *n*.4
mountains, 110, 143, 217 *n*.6
    glaciers, 106–7
    as metaphors for nature, 93–97, 104
    vegetation, 63–66
    See also Mauna Loa; Mount Aetna; vol-
        cano; White Mountains
mule deer, 75–80, 89
Mumford, Lewis, 166, 225 *n*.16
Mundus Subterraneus, 90, 91
Murie, Adolf, 29

Nash, L. K., 222 *n*.18
Nash, R. F., 205 *n*.15
National Oceanographic and Atmo-
    spheric Administration, 172
national park, 29, 78, 153–55, 196, 224
    n.3
National Park Service, 29, 78, 154

natural history, 33, 51, 57, 80, 81, 83,
    153, 193, 204, 206, 216, 224 *n*.3
*Natural Regulation of Animal Numbers,
    The*, 47
Nature of the Gods, The, 75, 83
nature preserve, 129, 197
    See also Aransas National Wildlife Ref-
        uge; Lala Shan Nature Preserve
nature undisturbed, 16, 18, 22–24, 27,
    28, 30, 32, 43, 48, 61, 62, 66, 82,
    85, 110, 143, 155, 156, 171, 188,
    189, 191, 197
    See also wilderness
Nelson, George M., 102
New Bacteriology, A, 113, 218 *n*.4
New England, 51, 52, 97, 101, 116,
    118, 164
New Guinea, 64–66, 212 *n*.25
New Hampshire, 101, 110, 119, 163
New Jersey, 51, 70, 117, 209
New Zealand, 67, 68, 119, 157, 195
Newton, Sir Isaac, 103, 104, 109, 141
Nicolson, A. J., 15, 55
Nicolson, Marjorie H., 12, 91, 103,
    110, 204, *n*.12, 204 *n*.1, 216 *n*.2,
    216 *n*.6–9, 217 *n*.9, 217 *n*.13, 217
    n.15–18, 218 *n*.4–5, 218 *n*.13,
nitrogen, 67, 129, 131, 135–36, 139,
    141, 163, 176
Northwest Territories, 125
Norway maple, 53

oaks, 51–53, 172, 179, 209 *n*.9
ocean(s), 150, 213 *n*.2, 223 *n*.24
    as demonstration of divine power, 95–
        96, 104
    ecosystems, 159
    and iron ore, 138
    as metaphor for nature, 93, 95–96,
        104
    and plate tectonics, 145
    salt spray from, 67
Odum, Eugene, 54
'ohi'a trees, 171, 172
Ontario, 27, 58, 59
order, 8–9, 18, 33, 42, 75–76, 78–89,
    91, 97, 104–5, 107, 190
    and beauty, 96
    conceptual, 109–10